Europeanization and Domestic Policy Change

This book examines the impact of Europeanization on the domestic politics of EU member states, focusing on agricultural policy, cohesion policy and employment policy through a detailed comparative case study on Italy.

Though a founding member, Italy has often had an uneasy relationship with the EU and found it difficult to be influential in EU politics and to comply effectively with EU policies and institutional pressures. The main focus of this book is the analysis of the Italy–EU relationship from a policy-based perspective, adopting the conceptual lense developed by Europeanization research. By looking at the evolution of agricultural, regional cohesion and employment policies, the book shows how the politics of adaptation have brought Italy closer to Europe in the past 20 years and further highlights the impact of the Italy–EU relationship on domestic institutions and politics. The author explains that, even though Italy has increasingly learned to respect EU membership requirements, its influence on agenda setting within the EU remains limited.

Europeanization and Domestic Policy Change will be of interest to students and scholars of European politics, Europeanization, comparative politics and Italian politics.

Paolo Roberto Graziano is Associate Professor at Bocconi University, Italy.

Europe and the nation-state
Edited by Michael Burgess
Centre for Federal Studies, University of Kent
and
Lee Miles
Europe and the World Centre, University of Liverpool

This series explores the complex relationship between nation-states and European integration and the political, social, economic and policy implications of this interaction.
 The series examines issues such as:

- the impact of the EU on the politics and policy-making of the nation-state and vice versa
- the effects of expansion of the EU on individual nation-states in Europe
- the relationship between the EU and non-European nation-states

1 **Poland and the European Union**
 Edited by Karl Cordell

2 **Greece in the European Union**
 Edited by Dionyssis G. Dimitrakopoulos and Argyris G. Passas

3 **The European Union and Democratization**
 Edited by Paul J. Kubicek

4 **Iceland and European Integration**
 On the edge
 Edited by Baldur Thorhallsson

5 **Norway outside the European Union**
 Norway and European integration from 1994 to 2004
 Clive Archer

6 **Turkey and European Integration**
 Prospects and issues in the post-Helsinki era
 Edited by Mehmet Uğur and Nergis Canefe

7 **Perspectives on EU–Russia Relations**
 Edited by Debra Johnson and Paul Robinson

8 **French Relations with the European Union**
   Edited by Helen Drake

9 **The Geopolitics of Euro-Atlantic Integration**
   Edited by Hans Mouritzen and Anders Wivel

10 **State Territoriality and European Integration**
   Edited by Michael Burgess and Hans Vollaard

11 **Switzerland and the European Union**
   A close, contradictory and misunderstood relationship
   Edited by Clive Church

12 **Romania and the European Union**
   Dimitris Papadimitriou and David Phinnemore

13 **The European Union and the Baltic States**
   Changing forms of governance
   Edited by Bengt Jacobsson

14 **The Czech Republic and the European Union**
   Dan Marek and Michael Baun

15 **Europeanization and Domestic Policy Change**
   The case of Italy
   Paolo Roberto Graziano

Europeanization and Domestic Policy Change

The case of Italy

Paolo Roberto Graziano

LONDON AND NEW YORK

First published 2013
by Routledge
2 Park Square, Milton Park, Abingdon, Oxfordshire OX14 4RN

Simultaneously published in the USA and Canada
by Routledge
711 Third Avenue, New York, NY 10017

First issued in paperback 2014

Routledge is an imprint of the Taylor & Francis Group, an informa business

© 2013 Paolo Roberto Graziano

The right of Paolo Roberto Graziano to be identified as author of this work has been asserted in accordance with sections 77 and 78 of the Copyright, Designs and Patents Act 1988.

All rights reserved. No part of this book may be reprinted or reproduced or utilized in any form or by any electronic, mechanical, or other means, now known or hereafter invented, including photocopying and recording, or in any information storage or retrieval system, without permission in writing from the publishers.

Trademark notice: Product or corporate names may be trademarks or registered trademarks, and are used only for identification and explanation without intent to infringe.

British Library Cataloguing in Publication Data
A catalogue record for this book is available from the British Library

Library of Congress Cataloging-in-Publication Data
Graziano, Paolo.
Europeanization and domestic policy change : the case of Italy / Paolo Roberto Graziano.
  p. cm. – (Europe and the nation state ; 15)
  Includes bibliographical references and index.
  1. European Union countries–Economic integration. 2. Central-local government relations–European Union countries. 3. Central-local government relations–Italy. 4. European Union countries–Foreign relations–Italy. 5. Italy–Foreign relations–European Union countries.
  I. Title.
  HC241.G727 2012
  320.60945–dc23   2012024736

ISBN 13: 978-0-415-57491-4 (hbk)
ISBN 13: 978-1-138-83032-5 (pbk)

Typeset in Times New Roman
by Wearset Ltd, Boldon, Tyne and Wear

E. nonostante...
To Sugi, once again.

Contents

List of illustrations   x

1 Europeanization and domestic policy change: a framework for analysis   1

2 Italian politics and EU decision making   26

3 Europeanization and Italian agricultural policy   53

4 Europeanization and Italian regional cohesion policy   77

5 Europeanization and Italian employment policy   102

6 Europeanization and the politics of domestic adaptation   131

7 Conclusion   151

Appendices   155
Notes   160
Bibliography   161
Index   176

Illustrations

Figures

1.1	Europeanization and policy change	14
1.2	Europeanization and national public polices	15
2.1	Positive evaluation of membership to the EU (1973–2011)	37
4.1	EU structural funds expenditure, Italy, 1996–2001	94
5.1	Employment protection legislation index, Italy, 1990–2008	122

Tables

1.1	The operationalization of the 'goodness of fit' concept	17
2.1	Systemic EU agenda setting and policy-based EU agenda setting capacities: the executive power fragmentation configuration	29
2.2	Systemic EU agenda setting and policy-based EU agenda setting capacities: the executive power concentration configuration	29
2.3	The Italian systemic agenda setting capacities	35
2.4	Italian parliamentary involvement in EU decision-making	52
2.5	The Italian policy-based EU agenda setting capacities	52
3.1	EU agricultural policy structures	60
3.2	Italian agricultural policy structures	71
4.1	EU structural funds expenditure	92
4.2	Financial execution by member state, 1994–1999	94
4.3	Italian and EU regional cohesion policy structures	100
5.1	Major changes in employment policy regulation and unemployment benefits, 1990–2008	120
5.2	Italian passive and active employment policies expenditure, in percentage of GDP – 1993–2009	123
5.3	Beneficiaries of 'active' (excluding training) and 'passive' policies	123
5.4	Italian and EU employment policy structures	128

1 Europeanization and domestic policy change
A framework for analysis

1.1 The emergence and consolidation of European studies

Over the past 15 years Europeanization has been an increasingly investigated political phenomenon. As we will further discuss in the following sections, Europeanization entered the scene after a long period of neofunctionalist versus intergovernmentalist struggle, which by the end of the 1990s seemed to have lost part of its analytical appeal (Risse-Kappen 1996). In fact, prior to Europeanization debates, the European political organization (today's European Union) had attracted rising interest among political science scholars. Surely, since the late 1950s European studies as a somewhat specialized discipline has become increasingly relevant in both international relations and in comparative politics (Jupille and Caporaso 1999). For almost 40 years, the main theoretical and empirical debates concerned the formation and consolidation of the new European polity, and the main focus regarded the ways through which the European political organization was set up. The 'ontological phase' of the scholarly analysis (ibid.) regarded primarily the nature of the beast (Risse-Kappen 1996): what kind of supranational political organization was the emerging European organization?[1] In Jupille and Caporaso's reading, the approaches used by US scholars of the EU have been substantially different from the analytical lenses developed by European scholars:

> American students of the EU have predominantly used the toolkit of IR. They have focused on the ways in which sovereign states have come together and (...) created a set of rules permitting them collectively to achieve outcomes unavailable to them individually. (...) Europeans, by contrast, have tended to use analytical tools drawn from policy analysis or public administration, more reminiscent of comparative politics.
> (1999: 430)

More specifically, since the late 1950s a predominantly IR debate resided at the heart of political science understanding of the functioning of the EU.[2] On the one hand, the 'neofunctionalist' reading of Europe provided initially by Haas (1958) focused on the societal driving forces of European political integration. Haas defined political integration as a 'process whereby political actors in several distinct national settings are persuaded to shift their loyalties, expectations and political activities toward a new centre, whose institutions possess or demand jurisdiction over the pre-existing national states' (ibid.: 16). In the original analysis provided by Haas, European integration was fuelled by the 'loyalty shift' expressed by non-state elites – such as the new 'regional' or supranational bureaucracy and interest associations formed at the level of the 'new' region – who considered a new (European) supra-national setting to be in line with their pre-defined social and economic preferences. The key motors of European integration, in this view, were non-state actors seeking a new centre that could be beneficial to their selected interests and their ultimate goal would be to 'regionalize' interests: 'As the process of integration proceeds, it is assumed that values will undergo change, that interests will be redefined in terms of regional rather than purely national orientations' (ibid.: 13). In the words of a 'proud' neo-functionalist:

> [R]egional integration is an intrinsically sporadic and conflictual process, but one in which, under conditions of democracy and pluralistic representation, national governments will find themselves increasingly entangled in regional pressures and end up resolving their conflicts by conceding a wider scope and devolving more authority to the regional organizations they have created.
>
> (Schmitter 2004: 47)

Put another way, in the neo-functionalist reading, European integration followed an 'expansive logic of sector integration' in the form of inevitable 'spillovers' from one economic sector to another (functional spillover), which eventually also leads to (European) political integration (political spillover).

On the other hand, the 'intergovernmentalists' – such as Stanley Hoffmann (1966, 1982) – or the 'liberal' pioneers of intergovernmentalism (Moravcsik, 1993, 1998) challenged both the empirical and theoretical strengths of neofunctionalism since, for the former, it increasingly appeared that neofunctionalism 'mispredicted both the trajectory and the process of EC evolution' (Moravcsik 1993: 476) and, for the latter, neofunctionalism 'lacked a theoretical core clearly enough specified to provide a sound basis for precise empirical testing and improvement' (ibid.). In fact, the main claim of intergovernmentalists was that, after years of European integration, the state was still 'alive and kicking' and capable of shaping further the process of supranational integration. As Hoffmann notes in his 1982 contribution: 'the most striking reality is not the frequent and well-noted impotence of the so-called sovereign state. It is its survival' (21).

More specifically, according to the intergovernmentalist reading of the process of regional integration, the main motors of European integration traditionally were not non-state actors that 'by-passed' the state but rather national governments, which remained at the heart of a new international regime. 'The best way of analysing the EEC is not in the traditional terms of integration theory, which assumes that the members are engaged in the formation of a new, supranational political entity superseding the old nations (...) and that there is a zero-sum game between the nation-states on the one hand, the EEC on the other (...). It is to look at the EEC as an international regime' (ibid.: 33). Therefore, intergovernmentalism clearly focused on the enduring presence of governments that domestically formed their preferences and subsequently negotiated at the regional (e.g. European) level, searching to obtain the preferred political outcomes.

We will not dwell further on a discussion of the two main contrasting theoretical approaches to European integration, but we sustain that such a background is relevant for a better understanding of the 'Europeanization turn' in EU studies, which was connected to the loss of attractiveness of other approaches, mainstream for decades. In fact, until the end of the 1990s – with few exceptions (Bulmer 1983; Ladrech 1994) – the main focus of European studies scholars remained the description and explanation of the European integration process, whereas very limited space was left for a systematic analysis of the ongoing relationship between European and domestic political institutions and policies. And this is where Europeanization comes in as a new phase in European integration studies or a 'third step' in a European-based regional integration theory because, 'with progress in European integration (...) it became clear that traditional theories of integration were not adequate to describe, let alone explain, developments at the European level' (Caporaso 2007: 25).

1.2 The Europeanization turn in European studies

From a historical perspective, the Europeanization turn was clearly connected to the ratification of the Maastricht Treaty, which – as is well known – provided new impetus to European integration by widening the scope of the European political organization. To be sure, prior to the 1992 Treaty within the scholarly debate, Bulmer was one of the first researchers to try to go beyond the 'supranationalim versus intergovernmentalism' debate. In his path-breaking 1983 contribution, Bulmer called for a 'domestic politics' approach to EU studies by advocating the use of more conventional analytical tools in order to better understand European integration since 'the supranationalism-versus-intergovernmentalist debate overshadowed some of the equally important findings concerning policy-making in the member states' (1983: 349).

In 1993, Anderssen and Eliassen devoted an edited volume to the analysis of 'Making Policy in Europe: The Europeification of National Policy-making', wherein 'Europeification' was considered to be an effect of the emergence of the European Union, defined as 'a system of transnational authority and policy-making' (ibid.: 255–256).

Notwithstanding Anderssen and Eliassen's important contribution, until the end of the 1990s the Europeanization turn in European studies was poorly visible. This was probably due to the often evocative use of the term prior to the analytical work provided by Radaelli (2000, 2003a). In fact, as Radaelli noted in his pioneering contributions on Europeanization, in order to be a particularly fruitful concept its conceptual limitation has to be clearly established. In several accounts, Europeanization had been used as a synonym for convergence and/ or European integration or as synonymous with mere effects determined by the European Union (Anderssen and Eliassen 1993). But this was particularly unsatisfactory if the concept was to 'travel' (Sartori 1970) and innovate with respect to the existing literature and not to simply introduce greater analytical confusion. Definitions are not the only concern for the development of new research challenges, as Olsen noted:

> [w]hile conceptual clarity is of great importance also in the European context (...), the research challenge is not primarily one of inventing definitions (...). The challenge is to model the dynamics of change in ways that make the simplifying assumptions behind various definitions accessible to empirical tests.
>
> (2002: 944)

Nevertheless, as we will further argue in the following section, clearly defining the object of study is the first step that has to be taken in order to then proceed rigorously towards empirical testing. As Caporaso rightly states:

> The research challenge involves both inventing definitions and model building. Indeed, the two are related. Among the criteria for assessing definitions, there is the standard that says we ought to use words in such a way as to strengthen the connections between our terms and other interesting phenomena.
>
> (2007: 24)

But prior to 'diving' into the analysis of the various facets of Europeanization, we need to (a) investigate further the link between Europeanization and the above-mentioned research strands of European studies, and (b) discuss the various empirical implications of the Europeanization turn in European studies.

At least implicitly, Europeanization research builds on the classic integration perspectives briefly discussed in the previous section. First, with respect to neofunctionalism, and its more recent variants – supranational governance (Sandholtz and Stone Sweet 1998) and multi-level governance (Hooghe and Marks 2001; Piattoni 2009) – the Europeanization literature is inspired by the notion of 'uploading' domestic societal preferences at the EU level and their interplay with domestic governments and European institutions. Second, with respect to the intergovernmentalist approach, Europeanization is inspired by the focus on the domestic state-related sources of European decision making and their consequences on the nature of EU institutions and policies. Nevertheless, the Europeanization approach clearly goes beyond this European-centred orientation of 'classic' integration theories by focusing primarily on a different target: the domestic level. To be sure, since the mid-1990s the domestic 'shift' was inbuilt in the public administration and public policy-orientated analysis of domestic patterns of adaptation to EU membership (Rometsch and Wessels 1996; Mény et al. 1996; Hank and Soetendorp 1998; Boerzel 1999; Kassim Menon et al. 2000, 2001; Heritier et al. 2001; Zeff and Pirro 2001). As already noted by Caporaso (2007), this reorientation was clearly connected to the expansion of EU powers that followed the adoption (and ratification) of the Maastricht Treaty, which reinvigorated the EU political arena as a provider of new political opportunities for both domestic governments and societal actors involved in national decision making.

The above-mentioned contributions, together with the first more explicit Europeanization studies (Olsen 1996; Harmsen 1999), were characterized by a clear change of focus since they were primarily centred on domestic administrative and policy adaptation, whereas other scholars have considered also the changes in the 'organizational logic of national politics and policy-making' induced by EU membership (Ladrech 1994: 69) or more broad changes connected to European integration that had occurred within 'national political systems' (Goetz and Hix 2000). In the early stages of the development of Europeanization research, the main analytical core of the studies was domestic implementation of EU policies that also shared several substantive – but not methodological – features with the 'EU directive transposition' research agenda (Boerzel 2001; Mastenbroek 2005; Kaeding 2006). The implementation studies originated from the idea that European integration remained an incomplete political project as long as European rules were not implemented according to their intentions (Sverdrup 2007). In fact, the first main empirical focus of Europeanization research was in the most developed European policy domains such as environmental policy (Knill and Lenschow 1998), transport policy (Héritier et al. 2001) and cohesion policy (Conzelmann 1998; Benz and Eberlein 1999). Among the 'classic' European policies, only agricultural policy has been relatively absent from early Europeanization research, arguably because it was the policy domain that had *par excellence* completely turned 'European' as a result of the integrated character of the Common Agricultural Policy. Yet, as Roederer-Rynning (2007) convincingly argued, even in the field of agricultural policy the domestic impact of European policies – for example, with regard to state–farmer relations – is far from self-evident. In the early 2000s, other policy domains in which the involvement of the EU was less important were also investigated, such as social policy (Graziano 2003), refugee policy (Lavenex 2001) or even citizenship policy (Checkel 2001; Vink 2001). These studies contain mainly qualitative case studies or focused policy-based comparisons of a limited number of countries, whereas another set of contributions were more country-based analyses that went beyond a mere sectoral analysis (Falkner 2001; Grabbe 2001).

Furthermore, Europeanization research has also provided more focused 'European' analytical lenses for the study of domestic politics and policy-making. Both political scientists and political sociologists have increasingly realized that the EU, as an advanced instance of regional integration, has become a significant part of national politics. Especially with regards to policy-making, it is currently very rare to find domestic policies that are not somehow connected to European

6 *Europeanization and domestic policy change*

ones. Without considering the European sources of domestic policies, today any domestic-centred policy analysis would neglect important international constraints and opportunities for political actors. This observation holds true beyond policy analysis and applies to changing domestic opportunity structures and political environments more generally. First, the study of the domestic executives could not be carried out without a clear understanding of how the governments developed and coordinated domestic preferences in EU negotiations and increasingly tried to oversee domestic implementation of EU policies (Zeff and Pirro 2001). Second, other aspects of national politics have also been increasingly investigated adopting – more or less explicitly – Europeanization analytical lenses: domestic Parliaments (Holzhacker 2002), political parties (Ladrech 2002), party systems (Mair 2007), interest groups (Grote and Lang 2003) and sub-national governments (Pasquier 2005). Without incorporating a Europeanization analytical angle, several aspects of the recent transformation of the above-mentioned features of domestic politics would not have been fully understood.

Taking a closer look at the development of the Europeanization literature, important publications peaked at the end of the 1990s and early 2000s (see Featherstone (2003: 5) for a bibliometric analysis of the period 1981–2001; see also Exadaktylos and Radaelli (2009) for a similar exercise, although more focused on research design in Europeanization studies). Why did the Europeanization turn in European integration studies emerge during the second half of the 1990s? Mainly because of two fundamental reasons: the first is endogenous to EU studies, and the second is exogenous. The first motivation is connected to the loss of analytical appeal of the almost four decade-long debate between 'neofunctionalists' and 'intergovernmentalists' and the intellectual saturation of a long-lasting scholarly debate. A 'new analytical space' (Caporaso 2007) in EU studies could be opened in order to provide new tools for the understanding of the overall functioning of the EU multi-level governance setting. As the authors of the path-breaking contribution on Europeanization (*Transforming Europe: Europeanization and Domestic Change*) point out in the introduction to their book, their publication was the result of a 'joint research project [that wanted to] examine the 'next phase' of European integration studies: the impact of the European Union on the members states' (Cowles *et al.* 2001: ix). In other words, by the end of the 1990s it clearly emerged – at least to some inspired scholars – that European integration studies needed to enter into a new phase that would predominantly focus on different topics with respect to the more consolidated European integration literature. The somewhat sterile contraposition between the two leading interpretations of the EU needed to be overcome by shifting the object of investigation from the construction of a new supranational level of government to its impact. The second reason is connected to the emerging relevance of EU policies and institutions after the ratification of the Maastricht Treaty: as in the case of national Parliaments, during the second half of the 1990s domestic institutional and political actors were discovering the new domestic obligations connected to the expansion of EU powers and therefore needed to adapt to a new multi-level political game. Also domestic political actors had increasingly to cope with the consolidation of, or new competencies emerging in, numerous policy fields such as social policy (Graziano 2003), immigration policy (Vink 2001) and foreign policy (Wong 2007). To be sure, the importance of European integration for domestic affairs has been a long-lasting phenomenon because domestic courts have applied and interpreted European law for over 30 years (Stone Sweet 2004) and, more recently, rulings have also had an increasing impact on poorly regulated EU policies (for example, social policy; see Ferrera 2005). The judicial construction of Europe may be well-acknowledged now, but until very recent times empirical evidence had been lacking on how national judges had made (and are still making) use of EU law both in 'old' EU countries and 'new' ones (Nyikos 2007; Piana 2009). As a result of Europeanization research, today a much more detailed and analytically grounded picture of the impact of Europe on domestic institutions is available to EU students.

In sum, Europeanization as a research agenda has managed to end the exhausted debate between neofunctionalists and intergovernmentalists by widening the research spectrum to previously under-researched topics such as the impact of EU institutions and policies on domestic political systems and by making selective use of international relations and comparative politics analytical tools. Of course, although highly fashionable, this new research agenda has been striving to gain a well-reputed scientific standing because over the years some scholars started to question its analytical validity or, more precisely, its theoretical value (Olsen 2002: 27) or innovativeness (Radaelli 2004). As we shall argue in the following sections, the Europeanization research agenda has primarily reframed old questions regarding the mechanisms of European integration, focused on the emerging relevance of the EU for national political systems and the increasingly dense set of interplays among the various levels of government involved in the EU multi-level governance game.

Prior to taking stock of the promises and pitfalls of Europeanization, let us turn to the main definitional and theoretical issues that have been raised by Europeanization research.

1.3 Definitional and methodological challenges

The path-breaking contributions by Radaelli (2000, 2003a) started a long-lasting debate on the definitory 'nature of the beast', which in this case is not the European political organization as in Puchala's (1972) or Risse-Kappen's (1996) analyses, but the analytical and semantic devices used in order to study Europeanization. From this standpoint, we are still in the middle of the 'ontological' phase in Europeanization studies 'since even now there are many different definitions in' the literature. But before the definitional debate fully developed (in the late 1990s), within the European integration literature some attempts to define the notion of Europeanization had already been made. The first acknowledged definition of Europeanization is the one provided by Ladrech: an 'incremental process re-orienting the direction and shape of politics to the degree that EC political and economic dynamics become part of the organizational logic of national politics and policy-making' (1994: 69). By 'organizational logic', the author means the 'adaptive processes of organizations to a changed or changing environment' (ibid.: 71). A few years later, when the Europeanization literature was just about to 'take off', in the first systematic and comparative attempt to look at Europeanization processes, the definition of Europeanization became:

> the emergence and development at the European level of distinct structures of governance, that is, of political, legal, and social institutions associated with political problem solving that formalize interactions among the actors, and of policy networks specializing in the creation of authoritative European rules.
>
> (Risse *et al.* 2001: 3)

In 2003 – in the final version of Radaelli's above-mentioned contribution – Europeanization was defined as a set of:

> processes of (a) construction (b) diffusion and (c) institutionalization of formal and informal rules, procedures, policy paradigms, styles, 'ways of doing things' and shared beliefs and norms which are first defined and consolidated in the making of EU decisions and then incorporated in the logic of domestic discourse, identities, political structures and public policies.
>
> (Radaelli 2003a: 30)

Finally, in a 'state of the art' contribution, Vink and Graziano provided a broad definition of Europeanization as a process of 'domestic adaptation to European regional integration' (2007: 7).

The first definition captures the most innovative feature of Europeanization: the domestic 'adaptive processes' connected to the 'changed or changing [European] environment'. In his study on France, Ladrech (1994) focuses on politics and institutions in a broad sense and carries out an empirical investigation of how the French institutional setting has been affected by the increasing role of EU institutions. Nevertheless, the definition seems to be particularly useful for institutional analysis rather than decision-making studies because of its privileged focus on the notion of 'organizational logic' rather than, more broadly, the behaviour of political actors. The second definition (by Risse *et al.* 2001) is strikingly similar to the (European) political integration definition provided by Haas, which is focused on the 'loyalty shift' to the European level. But, as noticed by Radaelli (2000), we should not confuse Europeanization with European integration since there would, in fact, be no need to invent new concepts with old meanings. To be sure, the various chapters that are inspired by the definition given in the introduction to Ladrech's (1994) book do treat Europeanization in a 'top-down' rather than 'bottom-up' fashion, as generally advocated, generating some analytical confusion notwithstanding the overall empirical richness of the study. The last two definitions try to combine both sets of processes ('bottom-up' and 'top-down') in order to provide a more detailed (albeit complex) characterization of Europeanization. In this respect, Radaelli's definition is quite explicit since it embodies both the construction and diffusion of a set of EU-related phenomena. In the Vink–Graziano definition, the notion of 'domestic adaptation' draws heavily on the 'adaptive processes' researched by Ladrech. As stated by the authors in the discussion of the concept:

> in order to study Europeanization we need to start at the domestic level, analyse how policies or institutions [or other political phenomena] are formed at the EU level, and subsequently determine the effects of political challenges and pressures exerted by the diffusion of European integration at the domestic level.
>
> (Vink and Graziano 2007: 7–8)

To avoid the danger of conceptual stretching, as Radaelli (2003a) rightly notes, we need to specify not only what Europeanization is but also what it is *not*. Europeanization should not be confused with convergence, harmonization or political integration. This specific point can be further clarified as follows. *Convergence* can be a consequence of European integration, but it must not be used synonymously with Europeanization because there is a difference between a process and its consequences (ibid.: 33). There may have been convergence in monetary policies towards monetarist policy and away from Keynesianism in the member states that joined the EMU (Sbragia 2001). Yet European regimes may be converging, as in the case of citizenship policies; not as a result of initiatives emanating from Brussels, however, but as a response to domestic considerations (Freeman and Ögelman 1998). *Harmonization* of national policies is often seen as an important goal of European integration, but empirical research suggests that Europeanization is often manifest in a 'differential' impact of European requirements on domestic policies (Héritier *et al.* 2001; Graziano 2011). European directives aimed at harmonization in, for example, gender equality policy, in effect often leave much room for continued national diversity (Caporaso and Jupille 2001). Understanding, finally, why countries pool and delegate sovereignty (Milward 1994; Moravcsik 1998) is not equal to understanding the specific dynamics, or even the unexpected consequences, this process of *political integration* brings about at the domestic level.

In recent years, Europeanization research has moved beyond these conceptual debates to a phase where '[m]ost scholars de facto favour a definition of Europeanization either as the domestic impact *of* the EU, and/or the domestic impact *on* the EU' (Flockhart 2010: 790). This does not mean that there is a universally shared acceptance of such definitions, but clearly much of the empirical work that has been carried out over the past years departs from an understanding of Europeanization as a process of either construction or diffusion of discourses, political strategies, institutions and public policies. In one of the few studies that empirically looked at Europeanization through both the 'bottom up' (construction) and 'top down' (diffusion) perspectives is the Quaglia and Radaelli (2007) analysis of the Italian case. Nevertheless, the authors argue that 'two research designs' can be followed in order to combine the two dimensions of Europeanization. Our study will try to show that, in order to fully capture the interconnections between the construction and diffusion dimensions of Europeanization, one and only one research design is needed to coherently match definitional concerns and empirical analysis: if the definition of Europeanization contains two dimensions, the empirical studies orientated by such a definition *must* combine the investigation of both construction and diffusion dimensions in one research design. A coherent link between the 'inventing definitions', 'model building' and operationalization may, however, be missing.

Moving beyond these conceptual discussions has also allowed the research agenda of Europeanization to 'enter into' a phase in which more explicit attention is paid to methodological concerns. These concerns relate in particular to the question of causality: for example, adopting a 'top down' definition of Europeanization, how can we show that European integration actually *causes* domestic changes? Haverland (2005) has been investigating the methodological problems connected to causality in Europeanization research, and more recently Exadaktylos and Radaelli (2009) have taken stock of its (limited) research design capacities. This book will try also to address these issues but for the purpose of this brief literature review it suffices to say that, at least with respect to the conceptual dimension, Europeanization has come of age – although from a methodological standpoint much work is to be done.

1.4 The theoretical challenge

According to one of the most prominent scholars in European studies, Europeanization represents a new step in European integration theory (Caporaso 2007). Surprisingly, however, more conventional studies of European integration and Europeanization studies have not often been clearly linked. And this relates not only to Europeanization scholars but also to those of European integration. It is, for example, quite telling that a recent article devoted to the development of a 'postfunctionalist theory of European integration' does not even mention Europeanization as a theoretical advancement in European integration research (Hooghe and Marks 2009). Although theoretically there may be a striking continuity within European integration and Europeanization studies, many authors seem to not address the issue and consider Europeanization as a mere phenomenon that needs to be (domestically) explained. In fact, as Bulmer argues, 'Europeanization is not itself a theory (…). Rather, Europeanization is the phenomenon which a range of theoretical approaches have sought to explain' (2007: 47).

The theoretical added value of Europeanization lies primarily in the opportunity to generalize on the causal mechanisms through which European political discourses, strategies, institutions and policies affect domestic political systems – that is, have led to political change. In Europeanization analysis, political institutions are one of the main objects of study, and this fits very well with the increasing relevance of institutionalism in the European studies research agenda (Jupille and Caporaso 1999).

More specifically, it is well known that institutional approaches put at the centre of their object of enquiry the role of institutions in decision-making processes and, more generally, in the functioning of political systems. And institutions are classically understood as formal rules, standard operating procedures and governmental structures. From this standpoint, Europeanization studies have mobilized all strands of the 'new institutionalist approaches' – historical, rational choice and sociological (Hall and Taylor 1996) and also the emerging 'discursive institutionalist approach' (Schmidt 2008, 2010). Historical institutionalist analysis in Europeanization research has been at the heart of several studies (Bulmer and Burch 1998; Bulmer 2009) – in line with the other historical institutionalist studies beyond Europeanization (Hall and Taylor 1996: 938). The main focus of this strand of research was – and still is – the analysis of the sequences of domestic adaptations in connection to the evolution of European political discourses, strategies, institutions and policies. Domestic political change – limited or greater – is explained in connection with concepts derived from historical institutionalism such as 'path dependency', 'increasing returns' and 'positive feedbacks'. The rational choice orientation, strongly connected with more traditional studies of European integration (Moravcsik 1993, 1998), emphasizes the increasing political opportunities provided by European integration. Several studies have shown the strategic organizational adaptation displayed by interest groups which since the early 1990s have tried to profit from the new multi-level European power structure (Eising 2007). Political change occurs primarily when domestic political actors 'rationally' use European resources in order to support pre-defined preferences. Finally, sociological institutionalism has been particularly used in connection with the analysis of 'cognitive' Europeanization, that is, changes occurred in the mental frameworks of domestic political actors. The construction and diffusion of EU ideas, the socialization provided by EU institutions and policies have constituted a motor of change in their own right. Political change may be less visible than in the other cases, but several authors have argued that – especially in those fields where the competences of the EU remain limited – this form of Europeanization may be as powerful as more conventional forms of Europeanization in more 'classic' institutional and policy domains of the EU (Checkel 2001). The new 'discursive institutionalist' approach introduced by Schmidt (2008, 2010) differs from the other three institutionalist approaches because: (a) unlike historical institutionalism, it endogenizes agency; (b) unlike rational choice institutionalism, it treats preferences not as fixed but as a product of how they are framed in terms of ideas and discourses; and (c) unlike sociological institutionalism, it does not consider preference formation in the light of macro-structural norms and frames but focuses predominantly on policy ideas expressed at the micro or meso political level (Schmidt 2008: 1–2). The specific added value of this analytical perspective with reference to Europeanization studies is that it provides greater space for two of the key resources used in EU policy-making (especially in non-binding policies such as social policies (Heidenreich and Bischoff 2008; Heidenreich and Zeitlin 2009): ideas and discourses.

But if we turn to the overall theoretical relevance of Europeanization, what can be said after over a decade of empirical research? Europeanization has by no means yet obtained a strong theoretical status probably because it is more concerned with *domestic political change* rather than *EU political development*. Therefore, Europeanization has been used as an analytical approach to understand domestic changes, being more relevant for country specialists and comparative politics scholars. In fact, from this standpoint, some theoretical elements can be found in the Europeanization literature that specifically concerns the mechanisms of domestic political change. Probably the most interesting (and best investigated) theoretical contributions of the Europeanization literature concern, on the one hand, the 'goodness of fit' and, on the other, the 'mediating factors' concepts (Risse *et al.* 2001). The goodness of fit hypothesis establishes a clear link between the development of EU 'institutional settings, rules and practices' and the possible 'adaptational pressure' exerted on the domestic levels when the domestic 'institutional settings, rules and practices' differ. More specifically, 'the degree of adaptational pressure generated by Europeanization depends on the 'fit' or 'misfit' between European institutions and the domestic structures. The lower the compatibility (fit) between European institutions, on the one hand, and national institutions, on the other, the higher the adaptational pressures' (ibid.: 7). We will thus expect domestic change particularly in those cases where the 'misfit' is high and the adaptational pressures are therefore strong.

Even relevant adaptational pressures, though, do not trigger domestic change automatically. The above-mentioned authors continue in their theoretical analysis and suggest that, 'in cases of high adaptational pressures, the presence or absence of mediating factors is crucial for the degree to which domestic change adjusting to Europeanization should be expected' (ibid.: 9). The authors then continue by identifying five mediating factors (three 'structural' and two related to 'agency'): multiple veto points, mediating formal institutions, political and organizational cultures, differential empowerment of actors and learning.

If we try to place these analytical tools – which can easily generate specific hypotheses – in a broader theoretical framework, we can read Europeanization as a possible element of a more general *multi-level governing* theory (Scharpf 2000) and not only a new step in *regional integration theory*. In fact, the above-mentioned analytical framework may 'travel' beyond Europe if we consider the European Union as a *species* of a broader *genus* that is regional integration. To be sure, the EU as a regional institution has very specific features, such as a high degree of supranational authority, which cannot easily be found in other parts of the world. Yet if we consider that adaptational pressures may differ significantly as a function of the institutionalization of a supranational entity, we could successfully study Europeanization as a variant of a broader, extra-EU trend of *regionalization* and apply similar analytical tools for the study of other supranational political organizations, albeit less developed than the European one.

1.5 Europeanization and its mechanisms

As noted previously, Europeanization is not a full theory – yet – but possibly a moving target that needs explanations and solid analytical tools for its understanding. With respect to the more consolidated regional integration approaches, it enables researchers to focus more on the *consequences* of European integration and not only on its *dynamics*. If we adopt a simplified version of Radaelli's definition of Europeanization as 'domestic adaptation to European integration' (Vink and Graziano 2007: 7), then we can start building our analytical framework that will guide us into the understanding of Italian patterns of policy adaptation in the fields of agriculture, regional cohesion policy and employment. More specifically, a solid and clear research design is required in order to study the dynamics and consequences of Europeanization (Exadaktylos and Radaelli 2009). If we take into consideration both the construction and the diffusion phases of Europeanization, we can most clearly disentangle the process from its effects – the *process* being domestic adaptation to European integration and the *effects* being more or less lasting changes in domestic institutional and political relationships.

Defining Europeanization as a dual process of construction and diffusion of EU policies and institutions enables us to limit the scope of the analysis by focusing on specific institutions and/or policy areas starting from the domestic level but also investigating carefully the multi-level game that can be found at the heart of contemporary EU policy-making. The advantage of such an approach is that it avoids taking for granted that the European level is somewhat predefined. That is certainly not the case within the EU: as Sharpf (2000) noted, the 'uploading' mechanisms – modes in Scharpf's terms – of Europeanization vary. Therefore, the outcome of the construction phase depends on the specific strength of the member state governments in terms of making their voices effectively heard at the EU level. During this phase – which was at the heart of classic EU integration studies – the various governments may be capable of striking good or bad deals at the EU level, which may then have specific (positive or negative) consequences during the diffusion phase. Put another way, depending on the relative strength of the member state governments in negotiating their preferences (however fixed), the institutional or policy outcomes at the EU level will reflect the governmental 'uploading' capacities. Here is where the governments may substantially differ: the more capable the governments are at uploading their preferences, the less problematic the diffusion phase will be. Member states may be characterized by greater or poorer EU policy-shaping capacities (Boerzel 2003), depending on their domestic preference formation and EU bargaining capacities. Furthermore, since policy-making at the EU level may follow either intergovernmental negotiations or joint decision Europeanization mechanisms (see Sharpf 2000[3]), policy-shaping capacities will also vary in relation to the complexity of the specific decision making involved. Whatever the 'uploading' Europeanization mechanisms may be, the 'fit' or 'misfit' emerges in the initial phase of EU decision making, and if the governments are weak in preference formation, have no well-defined preference and/or 'lose' in the negotiation at the EU level, then they will be under more pressure in the diffusion phase. Pressures may vary significantly in relation to the degree of coercion inherent in the EU outcome: the more legally binding the EU decision-making outcome, the more probable it is that 'unfit' countries will struggle and face high adaptational pressures in the diffusion phase.

But what are the possible Europeanization mechanisms in such a phase? Using as a guiding criterion the above-mentioned binding nature of EU decisions, in principle we may distinguish between four types of Europeanization during the diffusion phase: *imposition, direction, coordination and non-formalized pressure*. The imposition mechanism is linked to the most binding type of EU decision: the *regulation*. This is the case, for example, of agricultural and regional cohesion policies that have historically been regulated via *regulations* (Hooghe 1996; Rieger 2000). A less binding mechanism of Europeanization can be labelled *direction* since it is connected to the directives approved at the EU level. As is well known, unlike regulations, directives are not immediately applicable laws but they must be transposed at the domestic level. To be sure, the overall objectives of the directive may not change at the domestic level, but the means are typically selected by national authorities. Examples of such Europeanization mechanisms can be found in some environmental

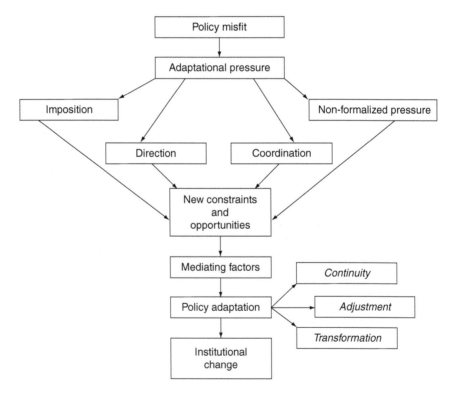

Figure 1.1 Europeanization and policy change: a conceptual diagram.

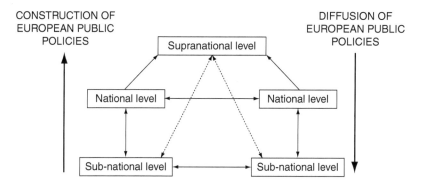

Figure 1.2 Europeanization and national public policies: stages of the process

policies (Boerzel 2007) or in biotechnology policies (Patterson 2000). The third, 'softer' mechanism is linked to other sources of EU legislation such as recommendations, communications and the like. In this case, the binding nature of EU decisions is substantially limited in comparison to the other Europeanization mechanisms. Nevertheless, Europeanization may be quite relevant – as research on the genesis and development of the European Employment Strategy and the Open Method of Coordination has suggested (Goetschy 1999, 2001; Mosher and Trubek 2003; Radaelli 2003b; Zeitlin and Pochet 2005; Heidenreich and Zeitlin 2009). The fourth, less intuitive mechanism of Europeanization regards those non-regulated EU policies that may 'spill over' other domestic policies; for example, the macroeconomic policies (connected to the Growth and Stability Pact) that may have specific effects on other non-EU regulated policies such as pension policies, constrained by cost-containment imperatives linked to the above-mentioned policy (Jessoula 2009). Why is such distinction among various Europeanization mechanisms relevant? Analytically, it is of great relevance since the intensity of possible pressures exerted by European decisions will vary in relation to the degree of coercion inbuilt in the policy: if a policy is regulated by binding EU decisions, and the analysed country is characterized by misfit, then we may assume that the adaptational pressures will be greater. Figures 1.1 and 1.2 summarize how Europeanization and its mechanisms may operate with specific reference to policy analysis.

1.6 Europeanization and domestic policy change: analytical framework, research design and main hypotheses

This book intends to contribute to both the Europeanization and policy change literature by adopting a two-step research strategy. Especially in relation to the latter, taking 'policy change' seriously is explicitly pursued because too often in the policy change literature there is a great variance in defining what change is and how it can be measured, and it seems particularly useful to be as rigorous as possible in defining and measuring policy change.

Thus, the first step of our overall research strategy is aimed at operationalizing policy change by adopting a specific analytical tool: the *policy structure* approach. The policy structure approach in greatly indebted to Peter Hall's (1993) analysis of social learning and policy change. Generally, literature on policy change (and how to analyse it) is considerable, and for the purposes of this section an in-depth literature review is unnecessary. Nevertheless, it is important to recall the notion of the policy paradigm and the related notion of 'orders' of policy change presented by Hall in his path-breaking contribution. A 'first order' change occurs when 'instrument settings are changed in the light of experience and new knowledge, while the overall goals and instruments of the policy remain the same' (ibid.: 278). Furthermore, 'when the instruments of policy as well as their settings are altered in response to past experience even though the overall goals of policy remain the same' (ibid.), this may be defined as a second order change type. A final, more radical (paradigmatic) type of change may occur in those cases where the change involves 'all three components of policy: the instrument setting, the instruments themselves, and the hierarchy of goals behind policy' (ibid.). The three components (or variables) are connected to the definition of policy-making: 'we can think of policymaking as a process that usually involves three central variables: the overarching goals that guide policy in a particular field, the techniques or policy instruments used to attain those goals, and the precise settings of these instruments' (ibid.).

This approach is very useful since it clearly 'unpacks' any given policy into specific analytical dimensions that can be easily operationalized. Nevertheless, it may be particularly useful to further distinguish the *policy-making process* from the *policy structure*, the former involving different phases from the agenda setting to policy evaluation via policy formulation, adoption and implementation (Howlett *et al.* 2009), and the latter being more closely related to the *content* of the policy. More specifically, the basic underlying assumption of this book is that any policy can be divided into four key dimensions: objectives, principles, procedures and financial instruments. The *policy objectives* – similar to Hall's 'overarching goals' – are the main goals of a policy; *policy principles* are the key normative assumptions supporting the policy; *policy procedures* – similar to Hall's 'techniques' – are the administrative mechanisms that are used in order to implement the policy; and the *financial instruments* are the funding sources of the policy. The basic advantage of the policy approach analytical tool is that – in line with Hall's analysis – it simplifies policy details that otherwise may be difficult to capture in both case studies and comparative analyses. As regards Hall's tripartition, the policy structure approach focuses more on the *mechanisms* of policy implementation (primarily by specifying the procedural dimension) and on the availability of specific financial instruments that may be allocated in order to support a given policy. Third, the policy structure approach further distinguishes between policy objectives (Hall's policy goals) and policy principles: the same objectives may also be met by framing the policy in accordance with different normative overarching assumptions. Finally, unlike Hall's analysis, we do not posit that change is not directly connected only to 'experience' but rather to the political games played by real political actors (Scharpf 1997).

Building on Hall (1993), it is suggested here that change can be detected when the above-mentioned specific dimensions of the policy structure (objectives, principles, procedures and financial instruments) differ from the same elements over time and the intensity of change varies according to the dimension involved – that is, more dimensions involved equals greater change. More specifically, we will call *policy transformation* those cases in which all four policy structure dimensions show relevant change, *policy adjustment* when two or three policy structure dimensions change significantly, and *policy continuity* when one dimension significantly changes or no policy structure change is detected. *Policy continuity* may also be registered in cases where minor changes involve more than one policy dimension, but the overall policy structure is substantially the same.

Moreover, the policy structure approach enables us not only to better 'analyse the evolution and possible change of domestic policies but also' to better operationalize the degree of fit/misfit between the European policy structure and the national one. In fact, one of the limitations of the existing Europeanization literature (Harmsen 1999; Cowles *et al.* 2001; Olsen 2002; Featherstone and Radaelli 2003; Graziano and Vink 2007; Trampusch 2009) is that it provides an interesting analytical tool (the 'fit/misfit' concept), but its operationalization is often inadequate, in line with the overall limited research design in Europeanization studies (Exadaktylos and Radaelli 2009: 526). Our assumption is that, at least with specific reference to agriculture, cohesion and employment policies but possibly also for other policy areas, it is possible to capture the key dimensions of both the European policy structure and the national policy structure, and therefore assess the existing degree of misfit. More specifically, if all four dimensions of policy structure (objectives, principles, procedures and financial instruments) at both levels are identical or very similar, then the relationship between the two policy structures denotes 'goodness of fit' (or no policy misfit); if three or four dimensions are significantly different, then the relationship between the European and the national policy structure is characterized by a high policy misfit; finally, if only one or two dimensions are significantly different, then the relationship is characterized by a low policy misfit. Table 1.1 summarizes the operationalization of the 'goodness of fit' concept.

Table 1.1 The operationalization of the 'goodness of fit' concept

Relationship European Union/National Policy Structures	Fit	Midfit	Misfit
No differences in the policy structure dimensions	X	–	–
One/two dimensions in the policy structure substantially differ(s)	–	X	–
Three/four dimensions in the policy structure substantially differ	–	–	X

18 *Europeanization and domestic policy change*

The second step in the research design is to develop a specific hypothesis derived from both the Europeanization and the policy change literature. Our general assumption, in line with policy analysis studies, is that 'policies determine politics' (Lowi 1972) and therefore in order to better understand the changes that have occurred in Italian politics over recent years, an in-depth policy analysis will simplify the endeavour. Furthermore, comparative policy change analysis regarding Italy is particularly lacking in the international literature and the gap needs to be closed. Consequently, the Europeanization hypotheses are going to be tested with explicit reference to policy change, although in the next section specific attention will be paid to the overall context of Italy's political relationship with the EU.

More specifically, in the early stages of Europeanization research, it was claimed that significant policy misfit between the EU and the national level would determine strong adaptational pressures, and the domestic change would be caused by 'mediating factors' such as multiple veto points, mediating formal institutions and political and organizational cultures (Cowles *et al.* 2001: 8–10). However, the most recent literature focused on Europeanization and policy change (for example, in the field of welfare state policies) has strongly questioned the hypothesis: '[H]igh levels of misfit are neither a necessary nor a sufficient condition for (…) domestic influence' (Zeitlin 2009: 233) and it has pointed out that 'questions remain open of how institutional changes in domestic welfare and employment regimes may be possible' (Heidenreich and Zeitlin 2009: 13). Still, other authors have showed that the 'fit/misfit hypothesis' holds (Mailand 2008: 362; López-Santana 2009: 147). Therefore, further policy-based comparative research aimed at testing the 'goodness of fit' hypothesis is still needed and the ambition of this book is to contribute to it.

In order to adapt – and simplify – the 'goodness of fit' hypothesis to the policy change analysis provided in this book, the first hypothesis could be the following: the greater the domestic policy-shaping capacities, the lower the degree of misfit. The underlying assumption is that, if preference formation and bargaining is successful, the EU policy structure will be identical or very similar to the domestic 'traditional' policy in order to avoid future, non-requested adaptational pressures from the EU. More specifically, we will focus on (a) the domestic preference formation and (b) negotiation at the EU level in order to further trace the role played by Italian governments in shaping the EU policies that interest us. This is particularly relevant for our study since we assume that, if the 'uploading capacity' is limited, then it is more probable that a policy misfit may arise and policy adjustment will be more difficult. Put another way, the less influent the domestic governments have been in EU policy adoption, the greater policy misfit we expect.

The second research hypothesis is that the greater the misfit between EU and national policy structures, the more we expect policy change to occur. This, however, would imply that adaptational pressures are *automatically* translated into policy change – which would reflect a too simplistic understanding of the EU multi-level system whereby member state governments, although sharing sovereignty at the EU level, are still the main actors in the EU policy adoption and implementation games. This specification is in line with the 'classic' literature on Europeanization (Cowles *et al.* 2001) and is needed in order to fully grasp the mechanisms of policy change. Once the 'fit/misfit' analysis has been conducted, we need to theoretically unveil the mechanisms of policy change by answering the following question: in case of misfit, will the adaptational pressures automatically determine policy change? The path-breaking contribution by Cowles *et al.* (ibid.), together with several other Europeanization and policy change studies (for an overview, see the policy surveys conducted by various authors in Graziano and Vink 2007: 212–334), posits that this is not the case because adaptational pressures (greater in cases of high policy misfit, non-existent in cases of fit) need 'mediating factors' (Cowles *et al.* 2001) in order to trigger policy change. Moreover, this specification is particularly crucial because it enables us to better focus on the role played by domestic actors in facilitating or opposing Europeanization: the policy misfit will be a cause of change only when the 'creative appropriation' (Zeitlin 2009: 231) of domestic actors is in line with EU prescriptions. In other words, without specific domestic acceptance and use of European resources, it is very unlikely that Europeanization will generate policy change – and eventually institutional change – at the domestic level. More specifically, we hypothesize that in cases of similar degrees of policy misfit (as we will see in the case of the various Italian policies analysed in this book), Europeanization will induce relevant policy change only if there is a shared preference among the key institutional and social actors (ministers and ministerial staff, top governmental officials and social partners) to fully adapt to the EU in the diffusion phase. However, even if the degree of misfit is relatively high, we will expect no or limited policy changes in those cases in which key institutional and social actors oppose the EU prescriptions. Taking stock of the available literature, and slightly modifying the mediating factors' definitions provided by Cowles *et al.* (2001), we identify three sets of mediating factors particularly relevant in the diffusion phase of Europeanization: *individual institutional and social actors* (such as top ministerial staff, ministerial bureaucrats, social partner representatives, etc.); *coalitions* (more or less formalized) between institutional and social actors such as those mentioned above; and *other formal institutions* not directly involved in decision making (such as the Central Bank and the like). Therefore, building on Cowles *et al.* (ibid.) and Zeitlin (2009), we further hypothesize that adaptational pressures determine policy change only if mediating factors are in place. More specifically, the second working hypothesis of the research documented in this book is the following: in cases of similar degrees of policy misfit, we expect Europeanization to induce relevant policy change only if there is an overall broad consensus among institutional and social actors with respect to EU guidelines, whereas we will expect limited or no policy change if there is overall limited consensus among institutional and social actors with respect to EU guidelines. We shall return to more specific hypotheses with respect to the Italian case in the next section.

1.7 Europeanization and political-institutional effects

Beyond policy change, the role played by European institutions and policies in reshaping domestic politics has increasingly become an object of study over the past two decades. In this book, we assume that policy-related institutional effects may be triggered by Europeanization. Following Morlino (1999), four political-institutional dimensions will be investigated with respect to the Italian case: *domestic executive-legislature relationships*, *centre-periphery relationships*, *political party–interest group power balance* and *bureaucratic functioning*. These dimensions have been investigated in several European countries (in particular, Southern European countries; Featherstone and Kazamias 2001; Costa Pinto and Teixera 2002), although systematic policy-centred analyses have been quite limited (for an exception, see Borras *et al.* 1998). With respect to the domestic executive–legislature relationship, what can be easily hypothesized is that Europeanization, because of its supranational decision-making features and increasing coverage of formerly domestic policies, has increased the decision-making power of the executives (especially the power of the prime minister) vis-à-vis the legislatures. For example, with respect to the French semi-presidential case, Cole and Drake (2000), Ambler and Reichert (2001) and – with a greater focus on agricultural policy – Montpetit (2000) have described the mechanisms of executive (and prime ministerial) empowerment in relation to the legislature. Balme and Woll (2005: 108) claim that over the years domestic legislatures have gained greater 'clout' with respect to European affairs, but only if 'clout' is interpreted as an opportunity to gain access to information. More generally, in a review of the comparative literature on the executives, Laffan states that: 'national governments are more embedded in the Union's policy and political networks than other national actors. They are a key nodal point in the interface between the national and the European because of their political and administrative resources, their underlying constitutional position and their legitimacy' (2007: 130). In another comparative survey, Kassim has stated that:

> [T]he dominant position of central government is a common feature. With few exceptions (...) national governments control the coordination process. They take the lead in defining policy and they operate in the diplomatic network that links the national capital with other member states and with Brussels. They possess the vital assets lacked by other member state institutions – information and access – but, crucially, are recognized at the EU level as *the* representative of their national populations.
>
> (2005: 296)

More specifically, European integration (which is, as discussed above, the construction phase of Europeanization)

> has weakened Parliaments in four ways. First, the transfer of competences from the national arena to EU level has removed decision making across

a wide range of activities from the purview of national legislatures. (…) Second, the Union's decisional processes disadvantage national Parliaments. (…) Third, the EU privileges executives over legislatures, offering them opportunities to bypass Parliamentary control. (…) Fourth, Parliaments lack the resources and the independence needed to scrutinize effectively the action and activity of their governments in Brussels.

(ibid.: 298)

In short, as a result of Europeanization it seems that Parliaments have lost significant ground with respect to central governments.

The second key dimension affected by Europeanization is the centre–periphery relationship. Here, because of the variation among European countries in federal and centralized countries, the findings are more mixed since 'domestic state structures in terms of central–regional relationships are affected by European integration, but in a differential way, due to the different pre-existing characteristics of the national polities' (Bursens 2007: 124). For example, in traditionally centralized states such as France and the United Kingdom, Europeanization has increased sub-national executive power vis-à-vis central governments (Ladrech 1994: 85), whereas in federal states such as Germany and Spain, Europeanization has provided an overall increase in central government powers vis-à-vis regions (Boerzel 2001: 156). Recent quantitative work has shown that there is evidence that sub-national authorities have increased their power, although this can be stated only with exclusive reference to the implementation of EU directives (Borghetto and Franchino 2010: 775–776).

The third dimension, the political party–interest group power balance, has also been investigated by several scholars, primarily in policy-centred case studies or in small-N comparisons. For example, Borras and others found in the analysis of environmental policy clear evidence that, as a result of Europeanization, Spanish decision making has become more inclusive (e.g. more pluralist) with respect to the past (Borras *et al.* 1998: 33); and in France new interests have been included in the implementation of water directives, opening up the traditional French corporatism that was associated with this policy area (Montpetit 2000: 588). More generally, the party–interest group relationship should consider two sub-dimensions: (a) the system of societal interest representation (the 'classic' contrast between pluralistic and corporatist models); and (b) the power balance between parties and interest groups in relation to decision making. With reference to the first sub-dimension, not much comparative research has been conducted; as Beyers *et al.*, introducing a *West European Politics* special issue devoted to 'Researching Interest Politics in Europe and Elsewhere', put it: 'the traditional pluralist versus corporatist debate that dominated the literature for many years is much less prevalent today' (2008: 1104). The main focus has been on interest groups (e.g. if and how the European dimension has been incorporated into national interest groups' activities; see Eising 2007) or on the impact of interest groups on EU decision making (Ladrech 2005). What we may hypothesize, in Ladrech's words, is that

> (i)n the longer run, however one may label a particular national system – pluralist, corporatist, statist – the expectations of convergence around one model, stimulated by adaptation to a single model of EU state–society relations, is unlikely, and instead 'moderate diversity' at the meso-level may be a more accurate description.
>
> (ibid.: 326)

Also with respect to the relationship between political parties and interest groups in decision making, apart from policy case studies that rarely take such a research question specifically into consideration, little research has been conducted because, once again, in the case of the analysis of Europeanization's impact on political parties, the main variables considered are opportunity, structure, organization and funding (Ladrech 2005). More generally, however, it has been proved that, because of prevailing decision-making features at the EU level and the limited accountability of the European Commission vis-à-vis the European Parliament, the overall power of political parties has diminished as a result of Europeanization. Put another way,

> Europeanization can be said (...) to have an effect on national parties in an indirect manner, that is, to the extent that national systems of governance have reduced their policy scope and have augmented the position of national executives vis-à-vis national Parliaments.
>
> (ibid.: 332)

Interest groups, instead, have clearly increased their opportunities as a result of both the European Commission's need for greater legitimacy and the availability of new decision-making and funding opportunities at the EU level (Ladrech 2005: 323–328; Eising 2007). Therefore, building on the existing research conducted in this area, we can assume that at least indirectly the power of the political parties has undergone increasing challenges as a result of Europeanization and that the overall balance of power with respect to interest groups may also have been challenged.

The fourth and final political-institutional dimension affected by Europeanization is bureaucratic behaviour. Although little specific research has been conducted in this area (with the noteworthy exception of Héritier et al. 2001), together with adaptational pressures connected to national institutions (especially with respect to their organization and power), bureaucratic bodies have also been severely challenged by Europeanization. More specifically, European bureaucratic governance is known to have become a mix between a Weberian and an 'entrepreneurial' (Kassim 2007; Gualmini 2008) type of bureaucracy, borrowing – among other things – from the former a specific attention paid to hierarchy, administrative procedures and rules, and from the latter management by objectives and result orientation. Domestic public administration systems have been significantly challenged by Europeanization because the management of policies has been increasingly shared within the emerging multi-level setting of the EU. Distribution policies, in particular, at the EU level have been managed following strict accountability criteria. This results primarily from the peculiar nature of the new European multi-level system and the need for coordination in the multi-level policy implementation process required by EU policies. The UK (in particular), French and German public administrations have been moderately challenged because their administrative systems are more in line with the European system, but Southern European administration systems have been significantly challenged in relation to their clientelistic and particularistic functioning (Gualmini 2008; Ongaro 2009). Once again, the administrative responses to Europeanization are strongly connected to the pre-existing administrative system and it has been proved that Europeanization has also determined differential forms of administrative adaptation (Gualmini 2008). In sum, the available research efforts have proven that – partially as the result of European policy-based adaptational pressures – throughout Europe accountability has increased, and policy experts (such as those incorporated into the European comitology system) have been increasingly incorporated into domestic decision making (Kassim 2005).

In this book, for each selected policy area the institutional effects of Europeanization will be explored with the specific aim of ascertaining whether the above-mentioned findings regarding political-institutional effects of Europeanization are also valid in the Italian case. Thus, it is useful to further clarify the overall assumption that guided the research presented here. As a result of its specific policy-based nature, we assume that Europeanization has primarily affected policies that may have then determined political-institutional adaptational pressures. Therefore, for analytical purposes we clearly distinguish between *domestic policy change* and *domestic political-institutional change*.

Finally, following the discussion on political-institutional effects, let us add a third hypothesis, which also takes into account the political-institutional effects of Europeanization: in the case of policy change, we expect subsequent institutional effects whose intensity will depend on the *intensity of change* (the greater the policy change, the more institutional effects we expect) and the *nature of the policy* (for example, in cohesion policy we expect relatively greater effects in centre–periphery relations, whereas in employment policy we expect relatively greater effects in the patterns of interest representation, and in agricultural policy we will expect relatively greater effects in administrative behaviour).

1.8 Europeanization and Italian domestic policy change: methods and case selection

This book focuses on three Italian-specific policies: agriculture, regional cohesion and employment. The rationale for this policy choice is connected to two strongly interconnected reasons: *historical* and *functional*. Historically speaking, agriculture was the first distributive policy to be regulated (also) at the EU level. Since 1958, the Common Agricultural Policy has been the most prominent policy in terms of funding (until the re-launch of regional cohesion policy, agricultural policy covered roughly 80 per cent of the EU's budget), and it has always been characterized by a high degree of coercion since the main decisional sources have always been regulations. Today, agricultural policy is still the most relevant EU policy in terms of EU expenditure because it accounts for almost 40 per cent of the EU's budget. Another minor reason for choosing agriculture is that the topic – with the noteworthy exception of Lizzi (2002, in Italian) and Settembri (2011, in Italian) – of such a relevant policy has been overlooked by EU studies focusing on the Italian case. Therefore, for both historical and functional reasons, agriculture has been selected as an object of study.

The second policy, regional cohesion, has been more analysed by Italian scholars (Piattoni and Giuliani 2001; Gualini 2003; Graziano 2004; Milio 2007, 2008; Brunazzo 2010) but still remains quite relevant – especially with respect to the Europeanization debate. Furthermore, regional cohesion policy is particularly crucial because it allows the analysis to broaden the perspective by also incorporating the 'multi-level' dimension of Europeanization, which is particularly relevant in current Europeanization and multi-level governance studies (Piattoni 2009). Moreover, regional cohesion policy is both *historically* and *functionally* interesting because it was already mentioned in the Preamble of the Treaty of Rome (1957), which stated that political representatives of the founding member states were 'anxious to strengthen the unity of their economies and to ensure their harmonious development by reducing the differences existing between the various regions and the backwardness of the less favoured regions'. This has become increasingly relevant over the past 25 years, becoming the second EU policy in terms of EU expenditure.

Finally, employment policy – also quite studied in Europeanization research, but in the Italian case primarily by the author of this book (Graziano 2007, 2011) – is historically speaking a relatively new policy, dating from the late 1990s. It has become functionally quite relevant, however, because of the enduring common EU and member state governments' concerns regarding how to create 'more and better jobs' within the EU. Another more general reason that justifies the case selection is linked to the different legal foundations of EU policies – from the most binding (agriculture) where regulations prevail, to the less binding (employment) where communication and recommendations predominate over other regulatory sources. Comparing these three policies will not only provide policy-based in-depth information not easily accessible to non-Italian reading scholars but it will also offer a unique opportunity to better understand the overall mechanisms and consequences of Europeanization through adopting a cross-sectoral research design.[4]

From a methodological standpoint, the research follows a predominantly historical neo-institutional perspective (Hall and Taylor 1993) – although the above-mentioned hypotheses are also valid for other neo-institutionalist perspectives – by focusing on in-depth process-tracing aimed at highlighting the trajectories and interconnections of Italian and EU policies. More specifically, triangulation (King *et al.* 1995) has been followed using semi-directed interviews, existing literature and primary and secondary evidence from EU and national official sources (documents, reports, evaluations and policy statements). Interviews have been conducted following the 'positional method' technique (Denzin and Lincoln 2005) and full coverage of the key actors involved in the policy formulation and implementation (ministerial, party, trade union and business association representatives) has been guaranteed. Interviews have been conducted (see Appendix 2 for full list) primarily in those policy fields where primary and secondary sources are particularly limited (e.g. regional cohesion and employment policy).

A final remark before we embark on the analysis of the Italian case. The investigation presented in this book refers to the 1945–2010 period in order to fully grasp both Europeanization and the previous domestic policy menus. As we shall see, most policy changes have a long-lasting nature and the role of Europeanization-induced policy changes occurred predominantly during the past 15 years. The same applies to political-institutional changes, which – as stated above – are directly linked to policy changes. Put another way, since policy evolution is by definition a dynamic process, we shall not see a final endpoint of Europeanization features and effects. Nevertheless, our research findings will unveil the mechanisms of Europeanization, particularly in cases of policy misfit, and will take stock of over 60 years of domestic adaptation to European policy-making. Therefore, building on the research evidence presented throughout this book, in the concluding section we will speculate on the conditions that have to be met for further policy change and its related institutional effects to occur and consolidate. In Europeanization research, as in other strands of European studies and political science, nothing is set 'once and for all', but predictions may follow a sound, analytically driven research design.

2 Italian politics and EU decision making

2.1 Italy in Europe: between high politics and low politics (1958–2010)

Italy, together with France, the Netherlands, Germany, Luxembourg and Belgium, was a founding member of the European Economic Community. From the late 1950s onwards, Europe became a stabilizing anchor for Italian democracy in systemic terms, but over the years also an opportunity with respect to the development of public policies. Nevertheless, for several years Italy has been mainly praised for its 'ceremonial' functions rather than for its capacity to perform actively in the EU decision-making process (see Sbragia 2001). To be sure, the Italian peculiarity that we will discuss in this section is not connected to a broader institutional feature. As Fabbrini and Piattoni rightly state, 'it is important to stress (...) that there is no ideal-typical political system that fits better than any other the EU political system' (2008: 3). In other words, the relationship between the Italian political system and the EU was not predefined by the presence of specific institutional factors such as the Parliamentary type of democracy or the multi-party system that are specific features of the Italian political system. What emerges quite clearly from the beginning of the European story is that Italy presents a quite peculiar, contrasting picture that does not overshadow the fact that in comparative terms the Italian political system has great difficulties in having its voice heard within the EU:

> the lack of political continuity in the leadership of the main ministries made the role of the Italian negotiators in Brussels inevitably difficult. The regular reshuffling of the ministers weakened the political input of the Italian Permanent Representation in Brussels (ITALRAP), obliging it to start anew each time a new minister entered into office.
>
> (ibid.: 3)

One the one hand, Italians have often been considered to be strongly in favour of European institutions (although overall support has been declining since the late 1980s); on the other hand, Italian governmental elites have often been considered ineffective because of the great 'traditional' governmental instability (see also Tallberg 2007: 8).

In general terms, this traditional weakness has historical roots because representing Italy within the EU has often been considered a burden and not an opportunity to properly serve the country – both for bureaucrats and for politicians. As for bureaucrats, the Italian public administrators very rarely made it to the top of the European Commission hierarchy (Olivi 2000). Furthermore, since the beginning of European integration, the nominated Italian political representatives within the European Commission were – unlike the representatives of other European governments such as Germany and France – not very prominent in Italian politics and therefore, as Varsori (1998: 135) convincingly argues, at the EU level the Italian governmental representatives were hardly capable of effectively connecting personal and governmental action. From a political party perspective, only for a decade (1947–1957) was Europe a truly contentious issue: the Christian Democratic (*Democrazia Cristiana*)-led government was particularly in favour and the main opposition party – the *Partito Comunista* – was fiercely opposed because Europe was considered to be a US-backed regional integration process and the main international alliances favoured by the party were connected to the geopolitical preferences of the Soviet Union (Putnam 1978; Conti and Verzichelli 2005; Varsori 2011). In short, Italy – just like other European countries – gradually became part of a new European political system, increased its presence in the newly established European institutions and was challenged by the developing policies adopted at the EU level, backed by a positive appreciation (until very recently) of the new European political organisation by the majority of the population.

In broad terms, although appreciation of the EU since the first Prodi government (1996–1998) has been unchallenged, with the noteworthy exception of the Berlusconi governments (2001–2006, 2008–2010) (see also Quaglia and Radaelli 2007), the capacity of the Italian bureaucratic and political actors to make a mark in EU politics because of action in Brussels has been considered to be extremely limited. Among other anecdotes, it is often remember that Malfatti, appointed to the European Commission in 1970, resigned in 1972 in order to stand as a candidate in the general Parliamentary elections in Italy – clearly a sign of limited attention to European affairs. Furthermore, more recently, although institutionally constrained, not even the Prodi EU Commission managed to significantly upgrade the Italian presence in the EU institutions, and the most recent missed appointment of D'Alema as High Representative shows how Italian politics is still seen as mainly domestically-centred since apparently the main reason D'Alema was not appointed was because of lack of Italian government support (*FT* Brussels blog, 16 November 2009; *Republica*, 23 November 2009). Put another way, at first glance even when the conditions seem to be favourable to an Italian upgrading in the EU decision-making system, the specific domestically-centred Italian political competition has not helped increase the Italian presence in European affairs.

Beyond the general (and anecdotal) picture, however, we need to disentangle the various components of the Italian political system and provide an account of the specificities that are not extensively covered in the literature. Once Italy joined the European Community, European institutions and policies became increasingly part of the Italian political system in three ways: first, with respect to the Italian executive, it provided a new political arena in which public policies could increasingl be discussed and negotiated with other European partners; second, although the political debate concerning Europe was limited prior to and after the Maastricht Treaty (1992), it entered firmly in party programmes and Parliamentary debates (Piermattei 2009); third, through the Eurobarometer survey it emerged from the beginning of the Italian participation in the European venture that the population was highly enthusiastic, thus making Italy since the early 1970s one of the most Euro-enthusiastic member states; fourth, and even more specifically, Italy has been increasingly challenged by the development of European public policies that bring new constraints and opportunities to the Italian decision-making system (Ferrera and Gualmini 2004).

As an overall introduction to the policy-based analysis that will be the core of this book, the next sections will be devoted to unveiling the various dimensions of the relationship between the most important features of the Italian political system and the European system in order to further understand how Italy 'mattered' in Europe and to assess the overall capacity of the key actors in representing effectively the national interests at stake.[1] The main objective of this investigation is to (a) provide background information on the (troubled) relationship between the EU and Italy, and (b) explore over time the overall governmental capacity to impose solid domestic preferences on European affairs and support them through effective negotiations at the EU level. In this respect, we need to further discuss the possible relationship between *systemic agenda setting* and *policy-based agenda setting*. As already mentioned in Chapter 1, member states may be differentiated with respect to their 'uploading' capacity to intervene in EU policy-making, especially as regards the agenda setting, formulation and adoption phases. But the relevance of the policy process may substantially vary in relation to the topic under discussion at the EU level because it may be regarded as a 'high politics' or 'low politics' issue. Within the EU, in cases of 'high politics' (for example, Treaty decisions or amendments) the key governmental actors are presumably the head of states or prime ministers (which since the mid-1970s meet regularly at the EU level in the European Councils). In the case of 'low politics' decisions, the key governmental actors will presumably be the competent ministers (who meet within the Council of European ministers). The consequence of this 'division of labour' is that – at least in theory – governments may be effective in systemic agenda setting ('high politics') and not effective in policy-based agenda setting ('low politics') or vice versa. This specification is particularly relevant for the Italian case, which has often been characterized as supportive in a 'ceremonial' rather than in a substantive way – as previously mentioned. What we may assume is that the differences between the two types of agenda setting may lead to different kinds of bargaining outcome (high/low misfit). More specifically, we may assume that the policy-based agenda setting capacities are more relevant than the systemic agenda setting

Table 2.1 Systemic EU agenda setting and policy-based EU agenda setting capacities: the executive power fragmentation configuration

Policy-based EU agenda setting capacities/Systemic EU agenda setting capacities	Low (policy agenda taker)	Medium (policy agenda adaptor)	High (policy agenda shaper)
Low, medium, high (Systemic agenda taker, adaptor, shaper)	Policy misfit	Policy midfit	Policy fit

capacities since policy subsystems may be autonomous and therefore our predictions will be the ones presented in Table 2.1 (*executive power fragmentation model*).

Alternatively, we may hypothesize that, as a result of the emergence of a core-executive model in Italian politics since the end of the 1980s (Cotta and Verzichelli 2007: 125), the two agenda setting capacities may overlap: in this case, predictions would be easier with respect to bargaining outcomes (*executive power concentration model*; Table 2.2).

If there is policy autonomy (*executive power fragmentation model*), we should expect policy misfit if policy-based agenda setting capacities are low (no preference formation and no bargaining capacities), mid-fit if policy-based agenda setting capacities are medium (preference formation but no bargaining capacities), and fit if policy agenda setting capacities are high (both preference and bargaining capacities are available). If there is full correspondence between systemic and policy-based agenda setting capacities (*executive power concentration model*), we should expect policy misfit if in both agenda setting dimensions the governmental capacities are low, mid-fit if in both agenda setting dimensions the governmental capacities are medium, and fit if in both dimensions the agenda setting capacities are high.

After an illustration of the government–EU relationship, the legislative and party relationship to Europe will be investigated. Furthermore, by analysing Eurobarometer data, the Italian citizens' relationship with Europe will be

Table 2.2 Systemic EU agenda setting and policy-based EU agenda setting capacities: the executive power concentration configuration

Systemic EU agenda setting capacities/policy-based EU agenda setting capacities	Low (policy agenda taker)	Medium (policy agenda adaptor)	High (policy agenda shaper)
Low *(Systemic agenda taker)*	Policy misfit		
Medium *(Systemic agenda adaptor)*		Policy midfit	
High *(Systemic agenda shaper)*			Policy fit

30 *Italian politics and EU decision making*

explored. Finally, the relationship of the EU to the three policies studied in this book (agriculture, regional cohesion and employment) will be more intensely scrutinized in order to assess the policy-based agenda setting capacities of Italian policy-makers, confronted with the systemic agenda setting capacities.

2.2 Italy–EU executive interaction: government leaders and government bureaucracies

As is well known, because of its peculiar institutional architecture in European affairs, the domestic executive plays a pivotal role as it performs the main interconnecting function between EU- and domestic-level policy. The prime minister and the various sectorial ministries (in particular, for several years, the foreign minister) carried out the main function of representing Italian interests in the European institutional setting and providing information to the domestic legislative. In the early days of European integration (1958–1968) both the prime minister and the foreign minister were crucial in shaping the national interest with respect to EU issues. Following Prime Minister De Gasperi's commitment to a federal Europe (1950–1954), several prime ministers and foreign ministers became advocates of the European idea: 'During the mid-1950s (...) [a] new generation of Christian Democratic politicians, such as Giovanni Gronchi and Amintore Fanfani, advocated the launching of bold initiatives in the international context'; furthermore, 'most Italian foreign policy makers did not forget the nation's Europeanist tradition and Italy joined the so-called "relaunching of Europe" to the Messina conference to the signature of the Rome treaties' (Varsori 2011: 50). Looking more specifically at the outcome of the Rome Treaties, the most recent historical research on the issue has re-evaluated Italy's capacity to promote and defend its national interest: 'Italy's policy on [EURATOM and EEC] issues was an effective and coherent one. If West Germany and France were obviously the major players in the diplomatic game, from the beginning the Italian authorities singled out relevant practical goals, which were coherent with Rome's major national interests' (ibid.). After the initial diplomatic successes, though, a period (1968–1980) characterized by fewer successful initiatives started, and 'by 1973/4 Italy was perceived by most member states more as a problem rather than an asset to the European Community' (Varsori 2011: 56), although the choice to enter into the EMS was a divisive one (the Christian Democratic government lost an external abstention by the Communist party on this decision). With respect to the previous period, between 1968 and 1983 the Italian government (which still meant primarily the prime minister and the foreign minister) lost the capacity to influence the European political agenda – which had also somewhat lost momentum in its own right – and started to act as a follower or 'policy taker', which meant losing its political capacity to (co-)shape the most relevant European decisions and to simply passively 'take' them – as in the case of the EMS. The following period (1983–1992) was characterized by greater capacities to influence the general European political agenda as a result of the strong leadership exerted by Craxi and his foreign minister, Giulio

Andreotti (ibid.: 59–62). Especially between January and June 1985, the Italian government managed to fruitfully promote and bargain for Italian preferences aimed at enlarging the European Community to Portugal and Spain and re-launch the European institutions through an Intergovernmental Conference that led to the adoption of the Single European Act (SEA), signed in 1986 (Cavatorto and Fois 2005: 305–325; Giuliani 2006: 57–59). Also during the 1990 presidency, Prime Minister Giulio Andreotti, Foreign Minister Gianni De Michelis and Treasury Minister Guido Carli managed to effectively (co-)shape the European political agenda by organizing two Intergovernmental Conferences (one on the European Economic and Monetary Union and one on the European Political Union, which then led to the Maastricht Treaty in 1992). According to Varsori: 'When the Maastricht Treaty was signed it seemed that (...) although Germany and France had played a major role in the negotiations, the Italian government had contributed to the successful outcome of a complex set of negotiations' (2011: 61–62).

The last period (1993–2011) was one of intense systemic change in relation to the Italian political system (Cotta and Isernia 1996; Fabbrini *et al.* 2000), which also had an impact on the overall capacities of Italian governments to influence the EU political agenda. More specifically, in a period of intense domestic political and institutional restructuring, the 'uploading' capacities were heavily affected. In fact, the only significant 'European' success of the Italian governments was under the Prodi I government (1996–1998), when Italy was formally accepted by the EU into the Eurozone. But such a 'success' was only linked to compliance capacity, not to the more systemic capacity of contributing to shaping, in a significant way, the European political agenda. In fact, the Prodi I government was more 'compliant' with European prescriptions but less capable of developing capacities to shape the European political agenda since the main concern of the government was to adopt EU-supported reforms in order to be in among the first wave of European Union member states. The other governments, even the Prodi II government (2006–2008), which lasted only 23 months and faced severe coalitional challenges, were not truly capable of shaping the European political agenda; on the contrary – especially during the Berlusconi governments (2001–2006, 2008–2011) – they created diplomatic problems, as in the case of the (in)famous speech delivered at the European Parliament at the beginning of the Italian presidency in July 2003. More specifically, the Berlusconi II and III governments were also largely ineffective with regard to the main political issue on the agenda in the early 2000s – macroeconomic policy – since the tactic of Prime Minister Berlusconi and Economy Minister Tremonti was to play *against* Europe rather than contribute to shaping the macroeconomic policy agenda. For example, in Della Sala's account: 'By April 2004, [the Commission] was ready to issue an early warning to Italy that it was in danger of running excessive deficits for 2004 and 2005. The Italian government's response was to attack on all fronts' (2008: 142). Clearly, the relationship was politically complicated by the fact that former prime minister Prodi was the president of the European Commission as well as being the former domestic political opponent; nevertheless the evidence that, during the Berlusconi administration, the governmental relationship with Europe was problematic (to say the least) and did not enhance the influence of Italian governments on the European political agenda is quite strong (Fabbrini and Piattoni 2008: 19). According to other accounts (Quaglia and Radaelli 2007), the Berlusconi administrations tried to change the traditional role of the Italian government by resisting the European political agenda but with disastrous results: 'The encounter with Europe was indirect, in the form of outrage and reputational losses in the quality press' (ibid.: 933). This new approach is analytically interesting, as Quaglia and Radaelli point out, but the overall 'shaping' capacity of the Italian government did not improve because the main governmental attitude was to react against or resist Europe as a whole rather than developing agenda shaping strategies or better adaptation performances. One of the reasons why it has been particularly difficult for Berlusconi's governments to engage effectively with EU politics is that one of the most important governmental coalition party members, the *Lega Nord*, was 'vehemently against the (...) widening and deepening of the integration process' (Albertazzi et al. 2007: 15). We shall discuss this issue in the section dedicated to the relationship between Italian parties and the EU, but it is relevant to also point out the governmental activities that resulted from the presence of such a hostile party actor within the Berlusconi governments.

In sum, between 1958 and 2010, a limited number of Italian governments were capable of acting as European political agenda (co)-setters. Solely for limited periods (1958–1968, 1985–1992) was the Italian government an agenda shaper, that is, capable of forming coherent domestic preferences and bargaining for them effectively at the EU level. During the other periods the Italian government can be labelled an 'agenda taker' (1968–1985, 1992–1996, 2001–2010) or an 'agenda adaptor' (1996–2001) since in the former period preference formation was either virtually nonexistent or less coherent and an overall bargaining capacity was similarly negligible, and in the latter period preference formation was coherent enough but bargaining aimed at 'shaping' the EU agenda was intrinsically limited by the previously adopted decisions at the EU level (such as the adoption of the euro) that were imposing adaptation rather than fostering agenda setting capacities.

The reasons for such an overall lack of political agenda shaping capacity do not constitute the primary focus of this book, but it is worthwhile mentioning some possible explanations presented in the literature and roughly test them in relation to the Italian case. In one of the few systematic studies covering the bargaining dynamics in the European Council, Tallberg (2007) convincingly puts forward three possible explanations: state sources of power (aggregated structural power and issue-specific power), institutional sources of power (power of veto, the power of the chair) and individual sources of power (personal authority and expertise). Italy can be characterized, like other relevant member states in the EU such as France, Germany and the UK, as being well-equipped with aggregated structural power, although such a power resource has been hindered by political instability. In the words of an interviewee: 'Italy has many of the general advantages – economy, demography, geography, founding state, etc –

but one important weakness in its political system: instability' (ibid.: 8). Also as regards issue-specific power, Italy does not stand out as it could. Tallberg (ibid.: 12) discusses the issue by mentioning 'Italy's loss of bargaining power on economic issues despite a sizeable GDP, because of long-running budget deficits and a growing government debt'. In other accounts and on other policy issues that will be further analysed in this book, the issue-specific source of power has been used but only to a limited extent and mainly in connection with other member states' initiatives, which were then 'followed' by the Italian government (as in the case of the inclusion of regional policy and social policy in the general aims of the European Community; Varsori 2011: 51).

If we turn to institutional sources of power, the power of the veto has not been used in general and the only country that was capable of using it in an effective way over the past 20 years was Spain – not Italy (Tallberg 2007: 16). Even if we go back to the early days of European integration, there is not much evidence of the capacity of Italian governments to use the power of veto (albeit informally) on EU political agenda making. Instead the Italian government has tried to play a broker function on a number of occasions, although generally perceived as a weak actor, as in the case of the support of the first UK candidature (1961–1963):

> Although the British cabinet appreciated the Italian delegation initiatives and they formed a positive opinion of Emilio Colombo, the head of the Italian delegation, the British government perceived the Italian government as a minor actor, unable to exert a vital influence on the political aspects of London's application to the Common Market.
>
> (Varsori 2011: 53)

The only institutional source of power that was effectively used on two occasions was 'the power of the chair': in 1985 and 1990 during the European presidencies, which were strategically used in order to boost European integration via the strong support of the Single European Act and the Maastricht Treaty. However, this may not be specifically attributed to Italian capacities because, as Tallberg notes (2007: 16–18), the presidency has traditionally been a moment when small (and weak) states have an opportunity to become somewhat influential in the bargaining processes. Therefore, what is striking is not the two successful cases, but the failure of the other four presidencies (see also Giuliani 2006: 53–66).

Finally, if we focus on the individual sources of power (personal authority and expertise), what is again striking is the quite variable capacities of the Italian actors called upon to perform top ministerial functions. One of the main features underlined by Tallberg's interviews is the relevance of seniority: in the development of European integration, people like Gronchi and Fanfani first, and then Andreotti and Craxi, were considered to be reliable and this had clearly to do with their seniority both in Italian politics and European affairs (especially in the case of Andreotti, one the most long-lasting political leaders in Europe). In particular, personal authority was used in the 1985 and 1990 presidencies, but in general personal authority was often weakened by the continuous change in Italian governments.

This short discussion leads to conclusions similar to those reached by Fabbrini and Piattoni (2008: 1): it would not be correct (or fair) to consider Italy an 'eternal loser' in shaping the European political agenda. A more nuanced picture has been drawn here, and the few periods of strong or medium overall agenda setting 'shaping' capacities (1958–1968, 1985–1992, 1996–2001) can be explained mainly by individual sources of power that were not replicated in other periods of time, whereas the overall political instability that has characterized Italian governments since 1958 – an average of more than one government per year – has lead to an overall limited capacity to shape the European political agenda.

If we go beyond the agenda setting phase and focus also on the formulation and adoption phase, although we have scant evidence, we can acknowledge that the influence exercised by Italy during the analysed period has also been quite limited. Political instability has been associated with poorly coordinated and ineffective administrative support. Even in the light of subsequent administrative reforms (the creation of a Ministry without Portfolio aimed at coordinating European policies in 1980, the upgrading of a Ministerial Committee for Economic Programming in 1987, the further upgrading of the Ministry without Portfolio with the creation of a dedicated Department in 1990, the most recent 2005 administrative reform introducing a European Affairs Interministerial Committee), overall administrative capacity to provide substantial support to European sectorial decision making – as performed by the Council of Ministers – remained very weak (Giuliani 2006). More specifically, the ongoing competition between the Ministry of Foreign Affairs and the Minister without Portfolio on European Affairs limited the capacity to form coherent governmental preferences even in the process of policy formulation and/or adoption (Kassim 2005). The recent appointment of a Foreign Ministry also responsible for European Affairs (November 2011) may contribute to reducing administrative competition, but it clearly is too early to issue an overall assessment of such recent change.

In sum, during four decades of European integration, the Italian executive has only very partially been an influential actor in EU decision making. Particularly in the agenda formation phase, a number of reasons (mainly ongoing political instability, limited political authority, lack of expertise and uncoordinated, limited administrative capacity) account for the Italian executive's ineffectiveness in relation to other member states such as Germany, France and the UK. Therefore, in general terms, the Italian executive has traditionally been much more of an 'agenda taker' than an 'agenda shaper' within the EU (Table 2.3).

2.3 Italy–EU party interaction: party attitudes and Parliamentary discourse and behaviour

As briefly illustrated in the introductory section of this chapter, initially Europe was a highly controversial issue. Geopolitical reasons made it quite difficult for

Table 2.3 The Italian systemic agenda setting capacities

Treaty/treaty amendment decisions	1958–1968	1968–1985	1985–1991	1991–1996; 2001–2010	1996–2001
Italian government systemic capacities	High (agenda shaper)	Low (agenda taker)	High (agenda shaper)	Low (agenda taker)	Medium (agenda adaptor)

the Italian Communist Party to accept the emerging European set of institutions since – in the context of the Cold War – they were considered to be too strongly supported by the US and not in line with other geopolitical interests connected to the Eastern bloc (Ramerà 1995). Nevertheless, during the 1970s (according to some observers, already in the 1960s; Barca 2004), the situation changed dramatically because – together with the long-lasting support of the Christian Democratic party – the Socialists increased their support of European institutions (in particular under the Craxi leadership that began in 1979) and the Communist Party (in particular under the Berlinguer leadership that began in 1972) followed suit (Ramerà 1995; Varsori 2011). Various reasons may account for such a realignment of partisan preferences (for example, increasing economic interdependence, or more strategic domestic political reasons connected to the Italian Communist Party and Eurocommunism; see Putnam 1978; Webb 1979) but the main novelty in the Italian competitive party configuration was that since the mid-1970s Europe was no longer a truly controversial issue and it even became, according to some scholars, an 'instrument for nation building' (Ramerà 1995).

To be sure, this change did not entail the main opposition party in Italy becoming an unreserved 'euro-enthusiast'. In fact, the Communist Party remained generally critical and was not in favour of the European Monetary System (EMS); therefore, in the second half of the 1970 there were also moments when EU decision making was controversial. More specifically, the decision to enter the EMS was so controversial at such a delicate moment in Italian political history that the Andreotti government actually encountered severe problems following the decision to call for a Parliamentary vote on the issue in 1978 (Barca 2004; Varsori 2011). Nevertheless, if we take a more general perspective, timidly since the 1960s and then more substantially during the following decades – with the limited above-mentioned exception – Europe was no longer a divisive issue: even if we look at Parliamentary decisions, an overall consensus over European issues is the rule (Giuliani 2006: 107). Only in the early 1990s and the so-called Second Republic (1992–; Cotta and Verzichelli 2007: 48–65) did a diversification among the political parties emerge because *Lega Nord*, *Rifondazione Comunista* (at least formally; see Conti 2010) and – to a reduced extent – *Forza Italia* and *Alleanza Nazionale* become more critical vis-à-vis European affairs (Piermattei 2009), whereas the main parties representing the Olive Tree coalition (*Partito Democratico di Sinistra* and *Partito Popolare*

Italiano), according to both experts and the analysis of party manifestos, have been increasingly pro-Europe (Conti 2010).

In fact, over the last 17 years the overall predominance of Parliamentary coalitions led by *Forza Italia* and including the fiercely anti-Europe *Lega Nord* have constituted an exception if we take a longer perspective and consider the overall perception of Europe among the Italian parties since the early 1960s. However, if we adopt a comparative perspective and use the data presented by Giuliani (2006: 104), we register that overall support for Europe expressed by Italian parties in electoral manifestos is limited. And the same applies to the role of the Italian Parliament in European decision making: it still remains to be seen whether the new Lisbon Treaty (2009) will enhance the power of national Parliaments. An examination of one of the few comparative analyses of the role of the national Parliament in European decision making reveals the striking weakness of the Italian institution. The European Centre for Parliamentary Research and Documentation (ECPRD) has carried out a very rigorous comparative analysis of the influence of national Parliaments on European policies by focusing on scope of action, frequency and overall impact (ECPRD 2002; see also Maurer 2002). A comparative table shows the overall poor performance of the Italian Parliament: with respect to scope of information, both in relation to EC and EU areas, there is limited available data, and there is a high dependency on the government for information transfer; as regards meeting frequency, the Italian Parliament is ranked 'low'; and finally, with respect to overall impact, Italy stands out as a weak country – unlike other countries more effective in EU policy-making, such as France and Germany. Future research analysing the aftermath of the Lisbon Treaty may present a different picture; for the moment, we observe that the overall Italian Parliamentary performance with respect to EU issues has not improved during a decade in which the governments (with the exception of the Prodi government, 2006–2008) and the Parliamentary majorities were composed of politicians from parties such as *Forza Italia – Popolo delle Libertà* and *Lega Nord*, which have often been very poorly lacking in terms of European decision making and policies (Piermattei 2009).

The succinct analysis conducted in this section has shown that: (a) the overall support of Italian parties and the Italian Parliament has been constant, though limited, but has decreased over the past decade in correspondence with a centre-right Parliamentary majority; (b) Europe however has not constituted a new cleavage because, in general, support has been universal between the different parties, with the exception of the most recent Parliamentary majorities up until the end of Berlusconi IV government (2011), and even when support changed over time preferences on EU issues were assimilated in the more consolidated Italian divisive issues (Conti and Memoli 2011); and (c) during the last two decades the centre-left parties have increasingly viewed Europe more favourably than have the centre-right parties. In sum, at least from a Parliamentary and political party perspective, support for the EU has been much stronger from centre-left political parties and Parliamentary majorities, although the overall role of both domestic parties and the Italian Parliament has been limited and strongly dependent on the government.

2.4 Italy–EU citizen interaction: the decline of eurosupport

Italians have often been labelled as the most euro-enthusiast citizens among the European Union population. According to the conventional Eurobarometer data used for this kind of analysis, such conventional wisdom seems only partially confirmed. Since the end of the 1980s there has been a constant decline in 'eurosupport', particularly accentuated after 2005 when the Italian figure became even lower than the EU average. As Figure 2.1 illustrates, since the first wave of Eurobarometer surveys (1973) Italy has constantly been above the European average in terms of positive support for Europe.

This overall positive appreciation has been connected to the hope that European institutions and policies could help the nation-state to surmount domestic problems: 'The EU is used as a proxy for symbolic protest against the present national political and economic situation. (...) [I]n Germany and Italy citizens show a weak commitment to the nation-state in political and economic issues' (Kritzinger 2003: 237). However, if we also take a closer look at the overall knowledge of Italians regarding the European Union, it is strikingly limited. In fact, following Bellucci and Conti (2012), we also observe the poor correlation between knowledge of European affairs and eurosupport and therefore we also interpret the strong support of the EU as 'blind support' because little is known about the EU and its functioning.

With respect to the most recent period (2005–2011), though, if we follow Kritzinger's (2003) hypothesis, we could claim that decline in support for the EU is connected to a greater appreciation of the performance of the 'Italian nation-state' (in Kritzinger's words). Nevertheless, if we consider the survey data available, in recent years Italian political institutions (especially political parties) have been increasingly considered negatively by Italians citizens (see the surveys at: www.sondaggipoliticoelelettorali.it). Therefore, at least in recent years and

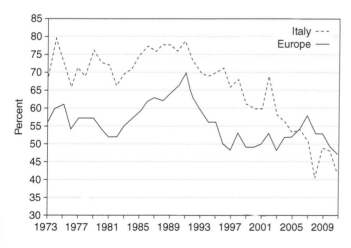

Figure 2.1 Positive evaluation of membership to the EU (1973–2011) (source: Eurobarometer).

38 Italian politics and EU decision making

within an overall European context of declining citizen support for the EU, it seems that the negative correlation between the evaluation of domestic political performance and EU support is no longer valid since negative political performance by the nation-state (as registered by the support of political and governmental institutions) has been increasingly matched with negative attitudes towards the EU. To be sure, it could be that Italians were influenced by the increasingly negative reading of European instituitions provided by the Italian government; during the troublesome relationship between Economy Minister Tremonti and the EU (2001–2004 and 2008–2011) and more generally the difficult relationship between the Berlusconi governments and European policy-making (Quaglia and Radaelli 2007; Della Sala, 2008), support thus significantly declined, whereas during the short Prodi II government (2006–2008) support for the EU increased. We do not have adequate data to fully support this claim, but for our purposes it suffices to note that – whatever the cause may be – Italian citizens' support for the EU has declined significantly since 1989.

2.5 Policy interaction: agriculture, cohesion, employment

In the following subsections we will briefly focus on the specific role played by the Italian government in the development of the policy areas that are the empirical core of this book. More specifically, using primary and secondary sources we will analyse the agenda and formulation-shaping capacities of the Italian government and the role it played in the negotiation that led to the adoption of EU policies and their main reforms.

2.5.1 The Common Agricultural Policy (CAP)

As is well known, together with the customs union and the common market, one of the first policy aims of the EU was agricultural policy. The Common Agricultural Policy (CAP) was introduced in 1960, at a time where farming was still a significant part of the EC member states' GDP and employment:

> In the late 1950s, primary agriculture accounted for one-third of employment and 20 per cent of GDP in the six founding countries. By the early 2000s, these proportions had fallen to 5 per cent and 2 per cent respectively.
> (Bureau and Matthews 2005: 3)

Agriculture was a key but conflictual concern among the EU member states because of its long state-based policy tradition (Friedman and McMichael 1989), and only the signing of the Treaty of Rome and the geopolitically strategic relevance of launching European integration made it possible for the German government to accept French (and Dutch) proposals (Webber 1998). As Lizzi states:

> [w]ith the signing of the Treaty of Rome in 1957 and the Stresa Conference of 1958 the general framework of the CAP was clearly outlined: it was

a policy of strong and indiscriminate support based on the maintenance of high prices set administratively in an internal market that was totally isolated from the world market.

(2008: 26)

In order to understand the member state power relationships and the specific role played by the Italian governments' representatives as regards the CAP, we will focus on the most important decisions that have been taken since the Treaty of Rome. Following – but slightly simplifying – the very accurate analysis provided by Webber (1998), we will explore three fundamental moments: the creation of the CAP, the first CAP reform (1992), Agenda 2000 and the milk quotas reform.

2.5.1.1 *The creation of the CAP: Italy as policy-taker*

As soon as the first agreement regarding the definition of the agricultural agenda (e.g. agriculture was fully included in the Treaty of Rome and therefore could not be easily dismissed in the subsequent years), the intergovernmental-supranational power struggle began. Following the French government's opposition to a strong role played by the new European Commission, agricultural policy was primarily designed in the early years (1958–1962) of the EU within the Council of Agricultural Ministers, with the European Commission and member states representatives (within the Special Committee for Agriculture) playing a key role in policy formulation (Webber 1998). Only after particularly acute moments of tension did the French representatives – supported by the Dutch and the Italians – manage to strike a somewhat balanced pact with the German government representatives, following a long-lasting relationship concerning agricultural issues that has been labelled 'French–German bilateralism' (Webber 1998; for further details on the creation of the CAP, see Lindberg 1963). The first fundamental decisions relating to the CAP – aimed at creating a Single Agricultural Market but also at supporting European agricultural prices and farmers' incomes – were substantially shaped by the French government, which was the most forceful supporter of a European agricultural policy (also due to the domestic pressures farmers were facing; Roederer-Rynning 2002), and after an overall agreement was reached with the German representatives, the decisions were adopted in mid-January 1961 (Webber 1998). Also, in the 'battle of the common cereal prices' (1964) and the dispute over the financing of the CAP, the game was played by the representatives of the French and German governments, leaving very limited room for manoeuvre of supranational organizations (such as the European Commission and the European Parliament), interest groups and other governmental representatives, including those of the Italians (Webber 1998; Kay 2000; Lizzi 2008).

2.5.1.2 The CAP reform 1992: Italy as policy-taker

By the second half of the 1980s, after over 20 years of CAP implementation, the view that policy needed to be thoroughly reformed was increasingly shared by member states and European institutions, for at least two reasons:

> First, the policy, with its tendency to produce growing produce surpluses, gradually grew so expensive that it threatened to 'break' the EU budget. Second, important trading partners of the EU began to exert pressure on the EU to change a policy which was held responsible for disturbing the world's agricultural markets – and enabling EU exporters to gain a growing share of them.
>
> (Webber 1998: 25)

With respect to their agricultural interests, French and German relationships had changed significantly over the previous 20 years since the enlargement processes had increased the diversity of agricultural interests in the EU. The main opponent of the long-lasting French support of the CAP was the UK, followed by the Netherlands and Denmark (Coleman and Chiasson 2002). Both in the Uruguay Round discussions and the MacSharry CAP reform (1992) the new EU decision-making game showed that the German and French governments were no longer the only key players in the field. The European Commission – which since the mid-1980s, under the Delors presidency, had increased its influence on EU decision making (Ross 1995; Sandholtz and Stone Sweet 1998) – became much more entrepreneurial than in the past: it is not by chance that the motor of the CAP reform was the Agricultural Commissioner, MacSharry, and the initial reactions of the French and German ministers were negative (Webber 1998: 29). As will be illustrated in greater detail in Chapter 3, the reform was aimed at reducing supporting prices, creating direct payments based on historical yields and introducing supply control measures and a 'set-aside' scheme aimed at reducing the overall agricultural production in the EU that was increasingly characterized by surpluses (Bureau and Matthews 2005: 9). Together with the stronger role of the Commission, the increasing relevance of the GATT Uruguay Round made it increasingly difficult for the French and German governments to vehemently oppose the CAP reform. In fact, after initial generic reluctance, 'no Franco-German front against the reform developed' (Webber 1998: 29) and the proposed reform – although partially amended – was passed, overcoming initial reluctance:

> There was a great debate at the time about [the reform] (...) and it took some time from being originally proposed to the end of the Council of Ministers when they unanimously rejected it at the beginning and unanimously accepted it in the end.
>
> (MacSharry 1998: 9)

Although voting for the reform, in defiance of the strong opposition of the most important Italian agricultural associations, Italy was considered to be the main loser from the reform (*Corriere della Sera*, 24 May 1992). In fact, the approval of the CAP reform and the Italian position is particularly emblematic of the more general agenda-shaping problems faced by the Italian government and the dynamics of preference formation and bargaining that have occurred since 1992. Seeing that unanimity was required in order to pass the CAP reform, Italy could have used the veto because its national interest was penalised (Italian agriculture being characterized by small agricultural firms that would not have benefited from the reform, the main beneficiaries being large Northern, internationally competitive agricultural firms). The Agricultural Minister, Goria, did not hide his criticism during the Council of Ministers, proving that – since the reform was so relevant – at least the domestic preference formation was clear, and also fully supported by agricultural associations (Serra Caracciolo 2006). But the negotiation capacities were very limited, since the only marginal success obtained by the Italian government was linked to the postponing of decisions relating to the dairy product quotas (*Corriere della Sera*, 24 May 1992). The later negotiation was however carried out by another minister – Fontana – appointed after the general elections of 5–6 April 1992. Although Goria was considered to be a knowledgeable politician and with some expertise in the agricultural field, at the time Italy was not considered to have sufficient credibility (because of overall low compliance with and fraud related to agricultural policy, especially with respect to dairy product quotas; *Corriere della Sera*, 5 July 1992) to stand up and try to truly shape the EU's agricultural policy agenda. The following minister – Fontana – could feel more satisfied because in December 1992 he obtained, after months of discussions and bargaining at the EU level – some (limited) concessions regarding the dairy product quotas. In sum, the best Italian representatives could do was to limit the negative consequences of decisions that were adopted primarily in opposition to Italian interests.

2.5.1.3 Agenda 2000, the reform of the milk quotas and beyond: Italy between policy adaptation and policy taking

Agenda 2000 is the most relevant overall policy reform proposal put forward by European institutions after the Treaty of Maastricht. Among other policy areas involved, the CAP was also substantially changed. In a nutshell:

> In a similar way to the first CAP reform, the Agenda 2000 arrangements used direct payments to compensate farmers for the loss from new support price cuts (…). This time, however, compensation was only partial. (…) Agenda 2000 also introduced a major change in the overall philosophy of the CAP by promoting the idea of a 'second pillar'. That is, instead of supporting agricultural production ('first pillar'), public policy would support more the provision of environmental and social services, or the promotion of quality products. While this 'second pillar' remained limited in terms of

budgetary outlays, it constituted a major change in the overall orientation of the CAP, paving the way for future reforms.

(Bureau and Mattews 2005: 10)

In the very accurate account of Agenda 2000 and the reform of the milk quotas, Lizzi (2008) shows very convincingly that – unlike in the past – the Italian representatives were capable of playing a pivotal role in the creation of the so-called 'band of four' (Italy, the UK, Denmark and Sweden) that effectively opposed the initial proposals of the European Commission. Especially with respect to the dairy product quotas – that had created numerous implementation problems in Italy over the years (Lizzi 1997, 2002) – for the first time the preference formation and negotiation of the Italian government was particularly successful because the 'band of four' managed to 'win when faced with the immobile stance of other member states, especially the Franco–German axis' (Lizzi 2008: 40). A particularly relevant role was played by the Italian agricultural minister (1998–2000, 2006–2008) who, together with the other members of the 'band of four' network, was capable of obtaining a 'satisfactory victory and Italy took home an overall increase of its quota of 600,000 tons, a result that ensured the Italian farmers would not exceed the quota and face further fines' (ibid.: 42). This result had been achieved thanks to the new ministerial entrepreneurial capacities in leading the preference formation process at home and co-leading the negotiation in Brussels. The Italian agricultural minister created further 'relationships with the Italian farming confederations, whose representatives were regularly consulted and who accompanied the minister to Brussels' and:

> promoted his interests among the ministers of the Italian government by keeping agriculture at the centre of their attention; at the European summits the prime minister (…), the foreign minister and the treasury minister all supported the line set out by the agricultural minister, thus strengthening Italy's negotiating power and credibility.
>
> (ibid.: 41)

Nevertheless, if we take a broader perspective and focus on overall agricultural policy agenda setting in the Agenda 2000 case, it is very evident that Italian representatives were only capable of adapting to an overall agenda framework that was set by other more powerful governments – such as those of France and the UK. Although some advancements in preference formation and bargaining capacities had occurred since the late 1980s (especially with respect to centre-left governments), policy agenda setting capacities remained limited in comparative perspective. Therefore, looking at its preference formation and bargaining capacities, it seems appropriate to label the Italian government during the most recent period as a case of *policy adaptor* and – after the Agenda 2000 reform – *policy taker* rather than *policy shaper*.

2.5.1.4 The CAP and Italy (1958–2010): from policy-taker to policy-adaptor ... and back

If we take a longer-term perspective, what has been the overall role played by Italian actors in shaping the CAP? For about 40 years (1958–1998), the preference formation and negotiating capacities of the Italian governments were very limited and 'scholars generally agree that the Italian difficulties at the negotiations were above all due to the lack of a clear vision for the future of Italian agriculture, or rather, to the absence of a real domestic agricultural policy as such' (Lizzi 2008: 27). To a certain extent, the early European policy initiatives could not be adequately fed by Italian governmental initiatives not – as on other occasions – because of its limited state or institutional sources of power but rather because of a lack of strategy regarding what agricultural policy should look like at the EU level – which we could, using Tallberg's (2007) words, label as an overall lack of expertise and political authority (e.g. a lack of individual sources of power). To be sure, the Italian governmental representatives during the creation of the CAP did take a position (in favour of the French proposals) but they were mainly observers of the 'French–German bilateralism'. During the first major CAP reform the Italian representatives were also more effective in shaping a national preference, but clearly not in shaping EU decision making by effectively influencing the final decision-making outcome – as previously discussed.

Put another way, since the creation of the CAP, the Italian capacity to form specific national preferences and to negotiate for them effectively has been particularly limited. Why has this been the case? Until the early 1990s, with the limited exception of the Marcora ministry (1974–1980) when EU agenda setting was rather meagre, overall capability at the ministerial level to form solid preferences and negotiate for them effectively were rather weak (Fanfani 1998) as a result of the high ministerial turnover and the lack of capacity and technical expertise of the ministry's civil servants.

Only the late 1990s (1998–2001) were marked by a greater overall capacity of the Italian government to shape EU decision making and obtain favourable deals – as in the case of the reform of the milk quotas. Nevertheless, these 'successes' were only aimed at better *adapting* new EU policies to Italian needs rather than (co)-*shaping* the overall agricultural policy agenda. Furthermore, this shift towards 'policy-shaping' capacities seems to have been quite limited over time; subsequent governments, although better able to state Italian preferences, were not able to obtain any relevant success at the EU level – such as failure in the sugar industry sector reform (Lizzi 2008: 42–46).

More generally, with the exception of the Agenda 2000 reform, in the specific case of agricultural policy it emerges quite clearly that the Italian governmental representatives were not capable of being influential in EU decision making, making Italy a policy-taker rather than a policy-shaper. To be sure, under specific conditions, the Italian government has been capable of acting as an effective policy-shaper – as in the case of the successful reform of the milk quotas mentioned above. Within the overall situation whereby political instability remained a constant of Italian politics, the case of success can be explained primarily by the 'individual sources of power': personal authority and expertise, embodied in recent times only in the case of De Castro, who 'not only knew the job but had also been one of the most active policy makers and an expert on the subject of agriculture, as well as on decision making in the CAP' (ibid.: 40).

2.5.2 Regional cohesion policy

In order to fully grasp the strategic relevance of the policy, it is worth mentioning the words of a former Regional Policy and Institutional Reform Commissioner, Barnier:

> It is not by chance that Community regional policy was introduced in the late eighties and now has the second largest budget in the Union. It was in the name of a certain idea of Europe which sees it as something more than just a big market.
>
> (Barnier 2001: 4)

In fact, regional cohesion policy – which is aimed at reducing socio-economic territorial disparities throughout the EU – was one of the first policies to be mentioned in the Preamble to the Treaty of Rome, which established that one of the main goals of the new European organization was to guarantee a harmonious development by reducing regional disparities; furthermore, Article 2 of the Treaty of Rome (1957) stated that: 'the Community shall have as its task, by establishing a common market and progressively approximating the economic policies of Member States, to promote throughout the Community a harmonious development of economic activities, a continuous and balanced expansion, an increase in stability, an accelerated raising of the standard of living and closer relations between the States belonging to it.' To a certain extent, it is precisely through the development of a solidarity-based territorial cohesion effort that the EU was created in order to enhance the distinguished European 'social market economy' (Predieri 1996). To be sure, it took almost 30 years for the principles to be translated into a fully-fledged policy. In fact, only since the mid-1980s has a proper socio-economic cohesion policy been adopted and implemented within the ECC/EC/EU. Only after the adoption and ratification of the Single European Act (1986–1987) did the European cohesion policy become a central policy in the overall European policy menu (Hooghe 1996).

Following a series of incremental reforms strongly supported by the European Commission (in particular, the 1975 creation of the European Regional Development Fund – ERDF), in 1988 an overall reform was approved. In the following subsection, we will briefly investigate the three most important moments in the development of cohesion policy by focusing on the specific role played by Italian governmental representatives: the establishment of the European Regional Development Fund (1975), the first comprehensive reform (1988) and the Agenda 2000 reform.

2.5.2.1 The creation of the ERDF (1975): Italy as policy-taker

Unlike agricultural policy, since the early 1970s one of the most powerful players in cohesion policy has been the Commission. Notwithstanding the constant pressures exerted by the Commission (such as the memoranda presented in 1962 and 1969 that called for greater European action on the matter, the first Communication on European regional policy (1965) and the creation of a specific Directorate General between 1967 and 1968; Wallace 1983), the member states remained quite reluctant to support the views expressed by the Commission. It was only at the beginning of the 1970s, when the first enlargement took place (taking in the UK, Ireland and Denmark in 1973), that the efforts of the European Commission started to become more successful.

One of the issues at the heart of the first enlargement negotiations was the creation of a fully-fledged regional cohesion policy, which would have been beneficial to the UK, Ireland and Italy. In fact, similar to the case of the creation of the CAP, in the creation of the ERDF Italy also engaged in the negotiation but did not have a firm preference and was not able to lead the negotiations. Taking advantage of the new preferences put forward by the new member states, and from the pivotal role played by the Commission and its UK Commissioner, Thompson, the Italian governmental representatives managed to have their voice heard within EC institutions and obtained over 40 per cent of the overall available budget – even though the overall funding of the ERDF remained quite limited (Armstrong 1995). Although the Italian government appeared to be a 'winner' in the negotiations over the ERDF (Varsori 2011), if we take a more comprehensive look at the role played by other, more influential member states it does not seem appropriate to label the governmental action as policy-shaping since the main triggers of the reform were the UK government and the (UK) Commissioner (Wallace 1983; Armstrong 1995). The Italian executive was particularly weak during the period when the first enlargement took place (between 1972 and 1976 Italy changed government five times and the political agenda was heavily centred on domestic social and economic issues; Lanaro 1992) and the overall timid Italian preferences regarding the launch of a regional cohesion policy would not have been considered seriously if not supported by more powerful member states (Olivi 2000: 151). In sum, the Italian government benefited from a concerted action put forward by the UK government and the Commission, but was very marginal in 'shaping' the policy agenda.

2.5.2.2 The 1988 cohesion policy reform: Italy as policy-taker

The most important cohesion policy reform is the one adopted in 1988, following the enlargement of the EU to include Greece (1981), Spain and Portugal (1986). The reform doubled the available resources for the various structural funds (together with the ERDF, the European Social Fund (ESF) – which had been established in 1960 but became particularly relevant for cohesion policy purposes with the 1988 reform – and the European Agricultural Orientation and Guarantee Fund – Orientation section (FEOGA-O)) and provided significantly more programming and allocation power to the Commission (for further details on the content of the reform, see Chapter 4). The key player in the 1988 reform was the Commission, which managed to take advantage of the inclusion of new member states – such as Greece, Spain and, to a limited extent, Portugal – and showed a strong preference with respect to the enhancement of the European cohesion policy and managed to consolidate it successfully during the other various rounds of accessions that led to EU-15 in 1995, EU-25 in 2004 and EU-27 in 2007. More specifically, with respect to the member state governments, Greece – also by virtue of the support of the Commission – managed to obtain the establishment of a new programme (the Mediterranean Integrated Programmes – MIP), which constituted an overall test for the subsequent cohesion policy reform. Spain strongly supported the reform of the cohesion reform because several Spanish regions were 'underdeveloped' in economic terms and would have profited significantly from the greater availability of EU structural funds (Bindi and Cisci 2005). The Italian government was largely supportive of the Commission's initiative but was mainly reactive and not capable of co-shaping the policy reform because of its limited regional cohesion administrative capacities (Hooghe and Keating 1994; Groete 1996).

Similar to what had occurred in the creation of the ERDF, Italy profited from the greater availability of funds, but was ill-prepared to manage the complex implementation of the new cohesion measures funded by the structural funds and did not play a relevant role in the negotiation of the reform since technical expertise was missing in Brussels (Groete 1996; Graziano 2004). In the words of Brunazzo and Piattoni:

> It was only in the mid-1990s that the Italian Permanent Representation in Brussels (…) was endowed with the technical support that subsequently allowed it to participate actively in the negotiations over the regulation of the structural funds. Because structural policy is discussed at the preparatory meetings held by the national permanent representatives in the EU within the General Affairs section of the Council of the EU, the negotiations for the programming periods 1989–1993 and 1994–1999 had been followed by career diplomats.
>
> (2008: 54)

Therefore, both with respect to preference formation and negotiation capacities, Italy in the 1988 reform was clearly not in a policy-shaping position.

2.5.2.3 The 2000–2006 and 2006–2013 programming periods: Italy as policy-adaptor

After a decade of cohesion policy implementation that had provided a clear picture of implementation successes and failures (Borras *et al*. 1998; Tondl 1998; Graziano 2004; Bindi and Cisci 2005), and in the light of the probable – at the time – future enlargements, at the end of the 1990s the negotiations over the allocation of structural funds became a crucial feature of the political agenda of all the member states significantly benefitting (at least in principle) from cohesion policies. Furthermore, the termination (1992) of an almost five-decade long period of domestic structural policy in Italy increased the political salience of EU funds: under increasing budgetary constraints, the fact that several EU resources remained unspent paved the way for an intense domestic public and Parliamentary debate. Within the Treasury ministry, in 1993 an observatory on regional cohesion policies (*Osservatorio delle politiche regionali*) was created, which then became a fully-fledged structure of interministerial coordination, the control room (*Cabina di Regia*). Also, between 1994 and 1996 a Parliamentary committee was created in order to understand the reasons why the implementation of cohesion policy in Italy had been so poor in the previous years, especially with respect to the low expenditure capacity (*Camera dei Deputati* 1996). Finally, within an overall context of major reforms in cohesion policy regarding the future inclusion of new countries as a result of the enlargement process, during the negotiations that led to the 2000–2006 and 2006–2013 programming periods, Italian policy-shaping capacities increased substantially because of the relevant institutional innovations: between 1997 and 1998 the Treasury Minister – Ciampi – created a ministerial department (*Dipartimento delle Politiche di Sviluppo e di Coesione*) in order to explicitly cope with EU cohesion policy. From early 1998 this department – led by a newly recruited top bureaucrat from the research department of the Italian central bank, Barca – was very active in the formation of domestic interest relating to cohesion policy and negotiating for it at the EU level (for further details, see Bull and Baudner 2004; Graziano 2004; Brunazzo and Piattoni 2008; Brunazzo 2010). The new department played a pivotal role in developing a shared domestic interest by involving sectoral ministerial actors (such as representatives of the Ministry of Employment and Social Affairs, Ministry of Infrastructure, Ministry of Agriculture, etc.), social actors (such as trade unions and business associations) and regional governments. Furthermore, the department took the lead with respect to both informal and formal negotiations with the European Commission and supported the Italian Permanent Representation in Brussels. Nevertheless, similar to the agricultural policy case, the new 'uploading' capacities were aimed primarily at better *programming* the overall EU intervention, not *shaping* substantive policy reforms – which after 1988 did not occur. Negotiating with the Commission for the 2000–2006 programming period also appeared to be quite complicated and, ultimately, not very successful (Bachtler and Mendez 2007: 552).

Therefore, although significant changes occurred in Italy regarding the regional cohesion policy and institutional changes were adopted, such as the creation of the DPS, it seems more appropriate to consider Italy as moving from a *policy-taking* to a *policy-adapting* position rather than to a full *policy-shaping* position.

2.5.2.4 Cohesion policy and Italy (1975–2010): from policy-taker to policy-adaptor

The analysis of the preference formation and negotiation capacities of the Italian governmental representative in the cohesion policy field conducted so far show that relevant changes have occurred over the past four decades. After years of 'policy-taking' (1975–1997), as a result of the greater salience of the problem and the progress of European integration that followed the Maastricht Treaty, the Italian governmental representatives managed to play a much stronger role within EU decision making. The overall change that occurred in the late 1990s can be explained by examining the changes in the individual sources of power: as in the case of the CAP, personal authority and expertise were the drivers of such change. As regards personal authority, the new treasury minister, Ciampi, was a former Italian central bank governor and as such had been previously appreciated within the EU during the definition of the EMU rules and the implementation of the single currency policy (Dyson and Featherstone 1996). Furthermore, the personal authority exerted by Ciampi was accompanied by the recruitment of new staff at the top ranks of the ministry – of which Fabrizio Barca was one of the most prominent representatives – who were experts on regional development and therefore could master the complexity of the cohesion policy issue. Finally, expertise further supported personal authority when Fabrizio Barca was individually appointed at the EU level as the leader of a task force created in order to contribute to discussion on the reform of European regional cohesion policy (Barca 2009).

2.5.3 Employment policy

Employment policy, and social policy more generally, is a relatively recent policy area when compared to the other two policy field objects of this study. Although employment and social affairs have been European concerns since the late 1960s and early 1970s (Falkner 1999), it was only in the aftermath of the Maastricht Treaty that the European institutions created an overall strategy aimed at increasing employment opportunities within the EU through the European Employment Strategy – EES (1997), the launch of the Open Method of Coordination (OMC) at the Lisbon Summit (2000) and the first mid-term review of the EES (2002–2003). In this subsection we will focus on the role played by Italian governmental representatives during the two most relevant moments in the development of the European employment strategy: the creation of the EES and the first mid-term review (2003).

2.5.3.1 The creation of the EES (1997): Italy as policy-taker

During the second half of the 1990s, and after the third wave of enlargement to countries characterized by high employment rates (Sweden, Finland and Austria), the European institutions – and the European Commission in particular

– decided to launch an overarching initiative aimed at enhancing the social dimension of the EU (Goetschy 1999, 2001). Unlike the other policies covered by this study, the EES was based on 'soft law' and on coordination mechanisms – the same that will be at the heart of the subsequent OMC (Mosher and Trubek 2003). Similar to the case of the reform of European regional cohesion, in the case of employment it was also the combination of pressure from new member states (mostly Sweden) and pressure from the Commission (Directorate General Employment and Social Affairs) that gave birth to the European Employment Strategy – EES (Casula Vifell 2011). The Italian governmental representatives were virtually absent in both the informal and formal debates that took place prior to the launch of the EES (interviews). Beyond being generically 'pro-European', the main concern of the Prodi government at the time was to adopt domestic policies that would make it possible for Italy to enter the eurozone, whereas other policy concerns were – although connected to Europe, as will be illustrated in Chapter 5 – mainly of a domestic nature, such as the employment policy reforms adopted by the Prodi government under the Treu ministry in 1997 (Graziano 2004, 2007). Furthermore, prior to the launch of the Lisbon Jobs Summit and the adoption of the Treaty of Amsterdam, which included a Title devoted to employment issues, at the domestic level no relevant discussion regarding specific domestic interests was carried out (interview) and the overall organizational infrastructure of the Italian government devoted to employment issues was virtually non-existent (Sacchi 2008) or not adequately used by the top governmental representatives in preference formation and negotiation (interview). Trade unions and business associations, the most relevant social actors in domestic employment policy decision making, were primarily concerned with domestic employment regulation reform (labour contracts and employment protection legislation, respectively) and no initiatives similar to those launched under the Ciampi ministry regarding European regional cohesion policy were organized. Such overall weakness in domestic preference formation was also mirrored by limited negotiation capacities within the Italian Permanent Representation offices in Brussels, which had no employment policy experts (interview). In sum, during the founding moment of the European Employment Strategy Italy was not able to perform as a policy-shaper but rather as a partially compliant (as we shall illustrate in Chapter 5) policy-taker.

2.5.3.2 The mid-term review (2001–2003) and beyond: Italy as policy-adaptor ... and back to policy-taker

Between 2002 and 2003 an impact evaluation of the EES was implemented throughout the European Union member states. Unlike during the original design and adoption of the EES, Italy was much more capable of having its voice heard when trying to influence the revision of the overall strategy. In Sacchi's words:

> In 2002, a constellation of circumstances allowed Italy to forge, express, and further [develop] a clear policy preference as regarded what it perceived as

a necessary and beneficial change in the EES objectives, and see it accepted by its European partners and the Commission.

(2008: 158)

The evaluation exercise was coordinated by the Institute for Labour and Training (ISFOL) and the final evaluation report used mostly background papers produced internally but also by academics who were experts in the field of employment policy – or social policy in general. In other words, the midterm evaluation triggered an overall domestic assessment of how the EES was working (and not working) in Italy and selective amendments to the goals of the strategy were drafted and supported in subsequent negotiations at the EU level. Furthermore, since 2001 the annual drafting of the National Action Plan on employment issues – required by the EES and the Amsterdam Treaty – enabled public domestic debates among the most relevant institutional and social actors (governmental representatives, trade unions and business associations), creating an overall improved capacity to form a specific domestic preference over employment issues vis-à-vis European decision making (interview). With respect to the negotiation of domestic preferences, the overall situation also partially changed:

> the Italian authorities put forward some proposals. The most important (...) was that of the need for a much better consideration, within the EES, of two issues that were at the centre of governmental policy action at the time: those of undeclared work and regional economic disparities. (...) Such preference was then strongly upheld by the Italian officers within the Employment Committee.
>
> (Sacchi 2008: 159)

Following the launch of the EES, the Employment Committee – a consultative body made of governmental representatives – became a relevant source of employment policy proposals and therefore being effectively part of it meant becoming potentially more effective in the 'uploading' of Italian policy preferences within the EU decision-making system. Nevertheless, it must be noted that Italy's greater effectiveness in applying pressure was limited to the inclusion of two of the ten guidelines that were issued in the 2003 Council Decision regarding the employment policies of the member states. Therefore, Italy's overall change in its ability to shape employment policy should not be overestimated; also, after the 2003 Council Decision no further 'uploading' exploits were registered.

In sum, in the case of employment policy since the second half of the 1990s, the Italian governmental representatives also managed to improve their preference formation and negotiation capacities, becoming increasingly more capable of 'shaping' EU policies than in the past. The source of this increased power capacity seems to be related to the enhanced availability and use of expertise by post-1996 Italian governments rather than to increased personal authority, although the enhanced preference formation and bargaining capacities were not fully institutionalized (interview). From being a *policy-taker*, Italy inaugurated a short *policy-adaptor* season but then went back to being a *policy-taker*.

2.6 An overall evaluation

What do the findings presented in this section reveal with respect to our Europeanization research design? First, they show that there may be a great mismatch between overall party, Parliamentary and public opinion support for Europe and the governmental capacity to be effective in Europe – i.e. a European political agenda 'shaper'. Especially if we take a closer look at the first half of the 1990s, we see that in times of declining party and citizen support for the EU, in at least one policy area (regional cohesion policy) governmental capacity to 'upload' EU policies increased. Second, it shows that, notwithstanding decreasing overall governmental capacity to form overarching fixed preferences and negotiate for them at the EU level (as illustrated in Section 2.1), from a policy-based perspective a more nuanced story can be told: in all three policy areas analysed (although with variable degrees of intensity), since the last years of the 1990s, the Italian governmental representatives – especially at political and the top bureaucratic level – have been capable of building and negotiating for domestic preferences more effectively than in the past. Put another way, the analytical distinction between the systemic agenda shaping/taking from the policy agenda shaping/taking was particularly useful because the patterns may be different in relation to both personal authority and, in particular, expertise. In other words, at least in the Italian case *there is no automatic correspondence between systemic agenda setting capacities and policy-based agenda setting capacities*. The Italian case has been characterized by declining and systemic agenda setting capacities and increasing – albeit unevenly – policy-based agenda setting capacities. The source of this policy-based enhancement is primarily related to an increase in personal authority (agricultural and regional cohesion policies) and available expertise (all three policies). Even in cases of political instability (as is the case for the second half of the 2000s), which in theory could have been extremely detrimental to domestic interest formation and negotiation, increased policy-based capacities made it possible for the Italian voice to be more clearly heard within EU decision making. Third, with respect to further specifying our Europeanization hypotheses, by virtue of the discussion presented in this chapter we may expect (a) prior to 1992 high policy misfit for all the policies analysed; and (b) after 1992 higher policy misfits for agricultural policy and employment policy, and lower (e.g. medium) policy misfit for regional cohesion policy.

Tables 2.4 and 2.5 summarize the findings presented in this chapter as regards governmental capacity to influence EU decision making. Adopting a long-term perspective (1958–2011), the evidence discussed in this chapter shows that the Italian case is closer to the executive power fragmentation model than to the executive power concentration model since the systemic and policy-based agenda setting capacities have often been disjointed, confirming the idea that, with respect to Europe, in the Italian case 'high politics' may easily not coincide with 'low politics'.

Table 2.4 Italian parliamentary involvement in EU decision-making

Scope of information			Meeting frequency	Impact		
EC Area	EU Area	Information tranfer dependent on gevernment		Weak	Policy influencing	Policy making
Limited	Limited	High	Low	X		

Source: ECPRD [2002].

Table 2.5 The Italian policy-based EU agenda setting capacities

Italian government policy-based capacities	CAP	Regional cohesion	Employment
Low (policy-taker)	1958–1998; 2001–2011	1975–1998	1997–2001; 2003–2011
Medium (policy adaptor)	1998–2001	1998–2011	2001–2003
High (policy-shaper)			

3 Europeanization and Italian agricultural policy

3.1 The Common Agricultural Policy

As already mentioned in the previous chapter, agricultural policy was one of the first policies to be shared between the European and domestic levels of government and, together with trade policy, agricultural policy belongs 'to the policy areas where the national governments have forfeited the most decision-making competences to the EU' (Webber 1998: 5). The relevance of the policy is also connected to the fairly high number of employees in the primary sector at the end of the 1940s, which was over 30 per cent of the employed population in the six founding members (Bureau and Matthews 2005: 3). In the following subsections we will provide a summarized description of the main features of the European agricultural policy evolution.

3.1.1 Guaranteeing agricultural self-sufficiency and managing agricultural surpluses: 1960–1992

The role of the state (e.g. governments) in supporting agriculture has been a common feature in developed countries since the end of the fourteenth century and governmental programmes have in both Europe and the US helped consolidate and expand agricultural production first for national self-sufficiency goals and then for export objectives. The long-lasting European statist tradition was challenged by the development of a European food regime (on the notion of 'food regime', see Friedmann and McMichael 1989), which was based on the member states' delegation of competencies to European institutions. The acceptance that powers could be allocated to the newly built European institutions was not to be taken for granted: as Webber noted,

> unsurprisingly, given the multiplicity of interventionist agricultural policies in the members states, the idea of including agriculture in the Common Market was controversial from the outset. No other international organisation had hitherto been able to subordinate agriculture or agricultural trade to international disciplines and previous schemes for liberalising or expanding agricultural trade in Europe had come to nothing.
>
> (1998: 7)

The main conflictual issues resulted from the member states being characterized by differing competitive agricultural sectors. By the end of the 1950s, France, Luxembourg and the Netherlands had the most competitive agriculture sectors, whereas Germany and Italy presented a particularly weak agricultural sector that had only very recently recovered from the consequences of the Second World War. These differences gave birth to differentiated positions as regards development of a common market in the agricultural sector: 'In general, the member states with competitive agricultural sectors – notably France and Holland – supported a common agricultural market and policy, while those with weak agricultural sectors, first and foremost Germany, opposed them' (ibid.). Once included in the Treaty of Rome, agriculture continued to be a controversial issue between France and Germany, which were the most active member states in terms of EU decision making (see also Milward 1994; Moravcsik 1998). The main concern of the newly established policy-makers (namely, members of the Commission) and member state representatives in the early years of European integration was to re-balance the import–export of agricultural goods in order to provide greater production capacities for the member states' agricultural sectors. The first decisions to be made regarded the overall organization and fundamental objectives and principles of the CAP, which were a peculiar mix of price support for the agricultural sector and liberalization; this meant primarily guaranteeing free movement of food products but at the same time – in continuity with the statist 'food regime' tradition – supporting domestic agricultural sectors via programming of targeted intervention (Grant 1997). In a nutshell, the main general objective set out by the Treaty was the creation of a common agricultural market, but more specifically the objectives were to 'increase agricultural productivity, ensure a fair standard of living for farmers, guarantee regular food supplies, and ensure reasonable prices to consumers' (Bureau and Matthews 2005: 7). The overarching principles were a compromise between liberalization and protectionism through price supports provided by the European institutions. More specifically, the key principles were:

> a unified market in which there is a free flow of agricultural commodities within the EU; (...) product preference in the internal market over foreign imports through common customs tariffs; (...) financial solidarity through common financing of agricultural programmes through the EU budget.
>
> (ibid.)

The main procedures – which became fully functioning in the late 1960s after the agreement over the common cereal prices in 1964 was reached – were standardized and automatic since the European Commission was in charge of transferring the funds to the member states with reference to specific national quotas decided within the European Council (Grant 1997). Nevertheless, the agreement that preceded the Commission's fund allocation was not uncontroversial since the member states' agricultural representatives tried to bargain over their specific preferences within the Council of Ministers on a regular basis. For example, price-setting routines were highly standardized from the initiation of policy implementation:

> Price-setting negotiations followed a yearly routine unfolding in three stages. During the first stage (September to November), the Commission examined agricultural prices and elaborated proposals for increases product by product on the basis of the 'objective method'. Policy precedents played an important role in this method: the decisions on intervention prices were influenced by past decisions on market regime prices, irrespective of the income trends of other economic sectors. The proposals were transmitted for consideration by the Council of Ministers, the EP [European Parliament], the Economic and Social Committee, and European Farm Organisations in the *Comité des Organisations Professionnelles Agricoles* (COPA). During the second stage (December to February), consultation took place at the national and European levels. (...) During the last stage (March to June) intense bargaining took place among governments of member-states. Final decisions where reached in the marathon session of the Agriculture Council.
> (Roederer-Rynning 2002: 111–112)

Once the annual agreement was reached, the Commission was in charge of policy implementation by following the agreed distribution allocation of funds to the member states.

The main financial instrument was – and still is – represented by the European Agricultural Guarantee and Guidance Fund (FEOGA is the French acronym, mostly used also at the EU level), divided into two sections 'Guarantee' and 'Guidance'. The FEOGA-Guarantee was and remains the most relevant fund used for market interventions, public storage, border protection and export subsidies so as to guarantee minimum prices to producers (Bureau and Matthews 2005). The FEOGA-Guarantee has been from the early days of the European integration process the most relevant distributive policy source within the EU budget, covering up to 90 per cent in 1970 and 70 per cent in 1985, prior to the introduction of the regional cohesion policy reform (Roederer-Rynning 2002: 210; for regional cohesion policy reform, see Chapter 4). The FEOGA-Guidance, instead, has been used for structural and rural development programmes and therefore it funded primarily the improvement of farm and processing structures, although it had always represented a residual source of funding with respect to the FEOGA-Guarantee because only a very limited percentage of the EU budget went into that fund. All agricultural sectors were involved, with the exception of potatoes and spirits.

For several years, the overall policy structure did not change. Although increasing tensions emerged in the international arena – especially in connection with the 'empty chair crisis' that resulted from the fierce criticism and fear of the French presidency (at the time, the president was de Gaulle) regarding any further delegation of powers to supranational institutions, primarily the Commission and the European Parliament. The controversy was triggered by the Commission's

> proposal (...) giving the EU direct control over revenues from import duties and thus increasing its financial autononomy vis-à-vis the member states and by expanding the budgetary powers of the EP, [which] would have substantially strengthened the EU's supranational character and so were bound to antagonise the French government.
>
> (Webber 1998: 15)

The crisis – solved by the Luxembourg compromise in 1966 – ended the French boycott but did not provide further funding powers to the European supranational institutions:

> On the financing of the CAP, the agreement reached corresponded fairly closely to the French government's aspirations (...). There were no changes in the Treaty of the kind that de Gaulle wanted to secure at the outset of the conflict. However, in practice, to the extent that unanimous voting on fundamental issues remained the norm in the EU during the following two decades, the French government also won the struggle over the constitution of the EU.
>
> (ibid.: 17)

In fact, the conflict went beyond the agricultural concerns of the French government and presidency, but it is quite telling that the crisis was triggered by agricultural policy – clearly the most important EU policy at the time, especially in terms of its distributive properties. To a certain extent, the CAP allocation of powers represented a first policy result of the overall functioning of the new European political organization and since a deal had been reached, no member state representative wanted to renegotiate because of the remaining domestic fears of losing sovereignty without acquiring adequate compensation in terms of supranational control over the emerging EU institutions. Not even the enlargement processes – which would be of crucial importance in regional cohesion policy, as we shall discuss in Chapter 4 – changed to the overall policy continuity that characterized the EU until the mid-1980s.

To be sure, a few years after the general agreement of the CAP was reached and since the Commission was not particularly satisfied with the Luxembourg compromise, in 1968 the Agricultural Commissioner – Mansholt – presented *Agriculture 80*, a plan aimed at introducing substantive changes in the CAP by supporting farm modernization by reducing the number of small European farms and increasing the number of bigger farms. The Commission noted that:

> agriculture has been a problem for very many years. A great deal of money has already been spent, considerable improvements have been achieved and labour productivity has gone up more in farming than in the economy as a whole, but no clear solution has been found to major problems. (...) It is impossible in the Commission's view to ensure, through price policy alone, that the farming population shall have a reasonable income and that the market shall be balanced. Market and price policies can help to increase

prosperity, but only if the pattern of production is adapted at the same time. The Commission therefore wishes to remove the economic and legislative barriers which are making it difficult to increase the scale of farms and improve the mobility of land and labour.

(Commission 1968: 1)

The proposal was strongly opposed by the French and German governments (Grant 1997) and thus was watered down into harmless directives, approved in the early 1970s, which did not alter the overall policy structure. In fact, the reform of the CAP was not a serious item on the European agenda until the mid-1980s – although attempts had been made to raise it, in particular by the German Schmidt government (ibid.).

Even the dairy quotas reform, introduced in 1984, did not substantially modify the CAP. To be sure, the dairy quotas decision did put a limit on EU price support intervention by imposing production quotas on member states' dairy producers, and the decision was not painless with respect to EU farmers who would have faced penalties if not compliant with the new EU prescriptions. Nevertheless, 'this reform appeared little more than cosmetic change in light of the continuing budget and production imbalances' (Roederer-Rynning 2002: 114). Furthermore, in 1988 a package of stabilizing reforms was approved, aimed at avoiding an EU budget collapse resulting from the high costs of the PAC, and relevant reductions in support prices in cases of excessive agricultural production with respect to agreed limits was approved (Webber 1998: 28). In other words, the cosmetic changes experienced by the CAP until the second half of the 1980s were primarily aimed at maintaining the overall structure notwithstanding societal (such as the agricultural employment decline) and production (such as incremental technical innovations that made surpluses and not self-sufficiency a challenge for EU member states) changes.

By the end of the 1980s, however, the overall functioning of the CAP was questioned. In 1988 the new EU agriculture guidelines issued in connection to the structural funds' reform already 'symbolised the end of prices as the main instrument of intervention in market policy, and broadened the [scope] of the CAP beyond the confines of market policy' (Roederer-Rynning 2002: 120). Commission reform proposals were put on the agenda for two main reasons:

First, the policy, with its tendency to produce growing produce surpluses, gradually grew so expensive that it threatened to 'break' the EU budget. Second, important trading partners of the EU began to exert pressure on the EU to change a policy which was held responsible for disturbing world agricultural markets – and enabling EU exporters to gain a growing share of them. With a view to curbing EU subsidation of its agricultural exports, the US and the agricultural product-exporting states that later coalesced in the 'Cairns group' insisted that agriculture be put on the agenda of the new GATT trade liberalisation negotiations.

(Webber 1998: 25–26)

Within the GATT trade liberalization package, agricultural issues were of upmost importance because of the external constraints mentioned above. More specifically, the US were requesting a cut of between 75–90 per cent, whereas the Commission – fully constrained by domestic preferences, especially coming from the French and German governments that wanted to limit the cuts as much as possible – proposed cuts not exceeding 15 per cent. As a result of the very distinct US and EU preferences, the 1990 GATT Summit was a total failure (ibid.: 28). But the time to reform the CAP was long overdue.

3.1.2 Reforming the CAP and changing the European agricultural policy structure: 1992–2010

Already in 1990, during the above-mentioned GATT Summit, Agricultural Commissioner MacSharry illustrated a comprehensive CAP reform proposal that transpired to be the starting point of the most relevant CAP reform until recent years (Daugbjerg 2009). The overall aim of the reform was to guarantee the survival of the EU agricultural policy in an overall context characterized by external (GATT and US) challenges that were endangering the overall existence of the policy. The 1992 reform reduced support prices and created direct payments that were based on historical yields. Furthermore, specific supply control measures were introduced. The reform affected several types of produce, adding some to the more traditional ones. The key element was a nominal cut of 30 per cent in cereal prices, together with (smaller) cuts in intervention prices for beef and butter. The impact on farmers' income of these reductions in support prices was compensated for by a generous per hectare payment in the case of cereals, and by premium payments. Furthermore,

> the 1992 reform introduced a set-aside scheme which allowed the Commission to curtail the area devoted to arable crops. The reform was accompanied by an early retirement scheme, an agri-environmental scheme and a scheme for afforestation, designed to reduce production capacity, to improve the structure of farming, and to address some growing environmental concerns about the effect of agricultural practices.
>
> (Bureau and Matthews 2005: 9)

After minor reforms whereby variable levies were converted into fixed tariffs – although with some exceptions (such as in the case of fruit and vegetables) – another significant reform took place at the end of the 1990s: the Agenda 2000 reform, proposed by the Commission in 1997 and approved in 1999:

> The Agenda 2000 programme, introduced in 1999, was the second major reform implemented in the preparation of EU enlargement to include the ten countries of central and eastern Europe. In a similar way to the first CAP reform, the Agenda 2000 arrangements used the direct payments to compensate farmers for the loss from new price support cuts (15 per cent for

cereals and 20 per cent in beef production). This time, however, compensation was only partial. Agenda 2000 introduced a major change in the overall philosophy of the CAP, by promoting the idea of a 'second pillar'. That is, instead of supporting agricultural production (the 'first pillar'), public policy would support more the provision of environmental and social services, or the promotion of quality products. While this 'second pillar' remained limited in terms of budgetary outlays, it constituted a major change in the overall orientation of the CAP, paving the way for future reforms. Following Agenda 2000, the various environmental and rural development measures were brought together into a single Rural Development Regulation.

(ibid.: 10)

In short, after the MacSharry reform, an overall reorientation in principles and goals took place within the CAP because, although the basic objective of protecting farmers by supporting their income was still at the heart of the policy, new environmental and social objectives were progressively added. From a mainly single-target policy, the CAP increasingly became a multi-target policy with broader concerns than farmers' income and support. The introduction of a 'second pillar' was aimed at going beyond the mere price-support policy to also address environmental concerns (Lenschow 1999).

The most recent CAP reform – which to a certain extent was a continuation of the Agenda 2000 reform – was adopted in 2003 and consolidated the new 'deal' of agricultural policy in the EU. In general, the 2003 reform was aimed at decoupling support from production by introducing the 'single farm payment'. Limited coupled elements could be maintained only to avoid abandonment of production. The 'single farm payment' was linked to complete observation of environmental, food safety, animal and plant health and animal welfare standards, as well as the obligation to keep farmland in good agricultural and environmental condition. Innovations also included the further 'greening' of the CAP by strengthening rural development policy, introducing new measures to promote the environment, quality and animal welfare and to help farmers meet EU production standards. Furthermore,

> a reduction in direct payments ['modulation'] for bigger farms to finance the new rural development policy. A mechanism for financial discipline to ensure that the farm budget fixed until 2013 is not overshot. Revisions to market policy of the CAP.
>
> (Bureau and Matthews 2005: 11)

Finally in 2004 a reform regarding hops and Mediterranean products (such as cotton, tobacco and olive oil) was introduced following the same 'decoupled' principles adopted in the 2003 reform. The 2003–2004 reforms set the targets for the 2007–2013 programming period and only very recently has the debate over the 2014–2020 period commensed – as such, the most recent developments will be discussed in the concluding chapter of this book, together with the most recent developments relating to the other policy field objects of this study).

In short, since 1992 the CAP has undergone considerable changes. Although the broad objectives have remained unaltered (farmers' income protection), the degree of protection has been limited and transformed over the years. For example, in the cereal sector intervention prices have been cut by over 45 per cent and today 'a large share of the support to the farmers, which was paid by consumers through high institutional prices, is now paid by taxpayers as direct payments to farmers with no direct link with the quantity the[y] produce' (Bureau and Matthews 2005: 11). Furthermore, a quota system was introduced for specific products (such as dairy products) and increasingly expanded to other sectors, thus partially changing the nature of the CAP objectives, which until then had remained anchored to general objectives such as farmers' income protection. The principles have not truly changed since the 1960s since still today a mix between internal and external liberalization and protectionism rules the CAP. What has significantly changed is the set of procedures that – although remaining highly standardized and automatic – have moved from price support to farm payments, which are now the main redistributive mechanisms used by the CAP. Also the financial instruments have changed, not with respect to fund names or functions but rather in relation to the total EU fund package devoted to the CAP: from 70 per cent in 1985 to about 41 per cent in 2011.

Summing up, by following the policy analysis lenses introduced in Chapter 1 – the policy structure approach – we may define the overall policy changes as an example of *policy adjustment* since only two of the four policy structure dimensions have significantly changed (the principles and the procedures), whereas the financial instruments have been unaltered, although the funds available have been significantly decreased (for a similar reading of the 1992 reform and its long-lasting consequences, see Daugbjerg 2003). This change is particularly interesting because, focusing on the domestic patterns of adaptation, our

Table 3.1 EU agricultural policy structures: 1962–1992 and 1992–2010. A case of policy adjustment

	EU (1962–1992)	*EU (1992–2010)*
Objectives	Farmers' income protection	Farmers' income protection Rural sustainable development
Principles	Mix between protectionism and intra-EU liberalization	Mix between protectionism and intra- and extra-EU liberalization
Procedures	Coupled direct payments (standardized and automatic)	Decoupled direct payments (standardized and automatic)
Financial instruments	FEOGA-Guarantee FEOGA-Guidance (70–80 per cent of EU budget)	FEOGA-Guarantee FEOGA-Guidance (40 per cent of EU budget)

analysis will have to take into consideration two policy structures: the first valid between 1960 and 1992 and the second between 1992 and 2010. In other words, the overall European adaptational pressures may have changed because of the changing nature of the policy structure. Nevertheless, since the early years of the European integration process, the domestic agricultural policies could not ignore the presence of a supranational policy that placed constraints on and offered opportunities to domestic political and social actors. In the following section we will see how the EU policy evolution has created subsequent adaptation patterns at the national level in the Italian case. Table 3.1 summarizes the two policy structures developed at the EU level between 1960 and 2010.

3.2 Italian agricultural policy

Similar to other European countries (Friedmann and McMichael 1989), in Italy also public support aimed at the promotion of agriculture has been one of the main tasks of the newly developed nation-states since the fourteenth century. Although these tasks have primarily been interpreted by governments not as interventionist policies but initially as protectionist policies aimed at indirectly supporting the development of the agricultural sector and then export-supporting governmental initiatives, by the end of the nineteenth century in Italy state intervention started to go beyond trade policies as the first draining – mainly concentrated in the northern part of the country – was co-funded by public resources (Lizzi 2002: 129). During the first half of the twentieth century, Italian governments consolidated an interventionist approach that would then be further developed after the end of the Second World War. The following subsection presents a succinct analysis of the evolution of Italian agriculture policy over the past 60 years.

3.2.1 The development of the Italian agricultural policy structure: 1944–1960

In the early years of the Italian republic, poverty in the rural part of the country was still very diffused and almost 50 per cent of the working population was still employed in agriculture (Ginsborg 1989). The main policy problems concerned land ownership and the extreme backwardness of Italian agricultural capacity, further aggravated by the devastating consequences of the war (Daneo 1980). Furthermore, land concentration was very high: 85 per cent of owners owned 28 per cent of the land and 0.19 per cent owned 16.4 per cent (ibid.). Beyond the intense public and social debate (Morlino 1991b) regarding land distribution reform, which was finally approved in 1950 (Ginsborg 1989), one of the first choices to be made regarded the protectionist nature of the overall agricultural policy.

As regards the policy objectives, the first period was not characterized by a clear choice of supporting farmers since the harsh contrasts between big land owners, on the one hand, and peasant and small land owners, on the other, did not facilitate a focus on a unitary category of farmer because the divisions were too marked. Nevertheless, several laws approved during the 1950s (Law 1208/1951, 1090/1952, 949/1952, 777/1957) were implicitly aimed at medium or large agricultural enterprises that could more easily benefit from the credit facilities provided by them (Lizzi 2002: 153). Another general objective was to support productivity and the modernization of agricultural practices since in comparative terms the backwardness of Italian agriculture did not facilitate easy (and cheap) access to food for the population. It should be noted, however, that from the early years of the development of Italian agricultural policy another – first implicit, then explicit – objective was present, e.g. a social objective of reducing poverty in the rural areas by adopting non-selective procedures in the allocation of available financial instruments (see below). Put another way, agricultural goals were associated with social goals that were unconnected to agricultural policy effectiveness. Through specific financial incentives and the use of the *Cassa per il Mezzogiorno* – which was a key actor in the development of Italian regional cohesion policy (see Chapter 4) – relevant irrigation and land amelioration initiatives were funded, especially in the Southern part of the Italian territory. Although somewhat reluctantly accepted (ibid.: 147) with respect to the guiding policy principle, the choice adopted was of full opening up of the agricultural market, with the limited exception of wheat protection that covered over 15 per cent of total agricultural enterprises (Fabiani 1986). The procedures regulating the distribution of incentives and loans, though, were very much in line with the categorical and clientelist model that would prevail in other policy sectors – such as in the second period of the Italian regional cohesion policy evolution. More specifically, a generous and non-selective distribution of resources in the form of subsidies and fiscal incentives developed the specific productivist and clientelist traits that characterized Italian agricultural policy from its launch and was consolidated over the following decade (Lizzi 2002: 159–160). The main financial instruments available during this first period of the Italian agriculture trajectory were numerous (agricultural rotation fund, special loans, etc.) but were all characterized by the above-mentioned discretionary procedures and primarily managed by the *Federconsorzi* (a private organization that also performed public functions such as allocating special funds), which was a 'paying authority' performing resource allocation functions. An indirect financial instrument was represented by the limited taxation level that characterized the Italian agricultural sector until very recently. In short, if we take an overall picture of the first period of Italian agricultural policy structure we detect the goal of generically supporting farmers, the principles followed were a mix between protectionism and trade openness (especially in comparison with other European countries), the procedures were discretionary and the various financial instruments used were primarily incentives and fiscal breaks.

From an institutional standpoint, the key player in the field with respect to the executive–legislature relationship was the government, since the main decisions were adopted following pressure from the agricultural ministers, especially in the De Gasperi government (1948–1953). The legislative was an important forum wherein agricultural interests were discussed and represented, but legislative activity was not very effective in relation to influencing the decision-making process. The policies were managed in a centralized manner, because regions had not yet been created, although the Federconsorzi were organized in a decentralized fashion and often implementation was differentiated territorially. With respect to the political parties–interest groups relationship, the first period of the Italian agricultural policy was characterized by full control of the leading governmental party (Christian Democratic party) over the two main agricultural associations – the *Coldiretti* and *Confagricoltura* – which only in the following periods became partially more autonomous and effective in policy-making terms (Lanza 1991; Morlino 1991b). Finally, the bureaucratic management of the available funds – with the exception of the infrastructural initiatives managed by the *Cassa per il Mezzogiorno* – was orientated toward the formal validation of administrative acts that were required in order to proceed with the allocation of incentives, but since no programming or specific evaluation activities were required, no specific performance-based orientation can be detected during this period.

3.2.2 Adapting to the CAP between 1960 and 1992: a case of mid-fit and policy continuity

From the early 1960s the Common Agricultural Policy had the potential to become a key element in the overall Italian policy menu. Instead, one of the striking features of these years is that, notwithstanding the expected influence that the new European policy would exert on domestic agricultural policy, very little public debate occurred during that period (Lizzi 2002: 162). The lack of public debate was, however, matched by alignment of Italian policy to the emerging European policies. The creation of the so-called 'Green Plans', approved by Law 454/1961, was clearly in line with the emerging programming guiding principles of the CAP because they were aimed at increasing productivity, facilitating agricultural activity by subsidizing the purchase of means of cultivation and supporting innovation in farming. Increasingly following the CAP requirements, the objectives of price stabilization and structural reforms were included in the overall policy structure, which also integrated with specific domestic funds for those products initially not subsidized by the emerging European agricultural policy, such as fruit and vegetables. From a procedural standpoint, the CAP funds required institutional adjustments in order to cope with the selective incentive provision supported by the EU. In 1966, Law 303 created a new institution, the Agency for Agricultural Support (AIMA – *Azienda per gli interventi sul mercato agricolo*), which was supposed to implement the CAP, substituting the *Federconsorzi*. As Lizzi notes: 'As a matter of fact, AIMA overlapped, without qualifying powers, with the existing institutions which continued more or less to function as in the previous period since Federconsorzi was the main contractor of AIMA' (Lizzi 2002: 165). The domestic financial instruments – those used to fund the 'Green Plans' and others that were created in the previous period – were increasingly accompanied by the FEOGA-Guidance, although the selective nature of CAP funds limited expenditure capacity, which was particularly low in comparative perspective: between 1965 and 1971, only 3.2 per cent of the funds were spent, in comparison to 28 per cent in the case of the Netherlands, 24.5 per cent in the case of Germany and 11 per cent in the case of France (Amato 1976: 70). Also the second Green Plan (1966–1971) was characterized by a mix of productivism and social assistance features that had already been revealed during the implementation of the first post-war agricultural policies. Furthermore, it emerged even more clearly that Italian agricultural policy had to face new challenges (and obligations) put forward by the CAP and was not adequately equipped to cope with them (Nomisma 1994).

To a certain extent, the most significant transformation witnessed by the Italian agricultural policy was that the problem was less pressing; during the 1960s there was a 50 per cent reduction in people employed in agriculture – more than 3 million workers had left the countryside and emigrated to urban areas in order to profit from the industrial economic boom that characterised Italy between 1958 and 1968 (Ginsborg 1989). Formally, the Italian agricultural policy structure started to change in order to accommodate the management of the new CAP resources. Nevertheless, in more substantive terms the overall difference of the Italian policy structure and the emerging European one was striking because Italian policy was not aimed at sectoral price stabilization and structural interventions to reduce costs but rather was supporting a non-selective distribution of resources that could be used more generally for clientelist purposes. In other words, the Italian policy structure was not well-equipped for substantive adaptation to the new EU agricultural policy.

From the mid-1970s onwards the delegation of functions to the regions (regionalization) occurred – although their competences still remained vague and great uncertainty existed regarding the allocation of resources. More specifically, Law 382 passed in 1975, which transferred agricultural policy functions to the regions, was already poorly designed with respect to the coordination of the various functions between central and regional levels of government, and furthermore was not effectively implemented (Lizzi 2002). The overall administrative situation therefore became increasingly chaotic and the procedures increasingly discretionary in various spheres of agricultural policy implementation. Furthermore, one of the consequences of the economic turbulence experienced by European countries during the 1970s and of the maintenance of high agricultural prices was the emergence of a negative balance of payments in the agricultural sector, which became the main policy concern of the period (ibid.: 175). The PAC was severely criticized for supporting high prices, which were considered to be the main factor responsible for the overall imbalance of payments. With the help of three programming national agricultural plans (Piano *Marcora*, 1979–1982; Piano *Pandolfi*, 1986–1990; and Piano *Mannino*, which was approved in 1989 and implemented until 1992), Italian agricultural policy tried to focus on the trade deficit by fostering productivity enhancement of the Italian agricultural sector. More specifically, the *Marcora* plan was aimed at a selective increase of overall Italian agricultural production, import substitutions and export support and a reorientation of the main targets of the policy – not only small and medium family-owned agricultural enterprises but also the agricultural industry as a whole. As Lizzi notes: 'In principle, the innovative design put forward by the minister *Marcora* was aimed at providing the Italian agriculture with an economic programming instrument focused on production and commercialization which considered the problems and opportunities offered by the CAP' (ibid.: 178). However, the overall policy design was relatively poor since it did not effectively provide tools for the coordination of the various levels of government involved (primarily regions and the central government) and the ambitious goals in terms of productivity increases were not met.

These are also years when it emerges quite clearly that the implementation of the CAP was not particularly effective because those production units that could have benefited the most from the CAP did not have the competences to do so and technical assistance tools were very limited throughout the country (Fabiani 1986: 316). Finally, one of the overarching goals of the various programming documents – an increase in agricultural employment – was never really met and the overall trade deficit remained until the early 1990s (Commission n.d.).

Also the following agricultural national action plan (the so-called Piano *Pandolfi*) remained anchored to price and employment support and – although better designed with respect to procedures – it did not further specify the overall principles that were implicitly a mix of productivism and clientelist protectionism. The key objectives of the policy – in line with the European guidelines – continued to be farmers' income support, agricultural employment protection and support and trade deficit reduction. Functions were shared between the central level (incentive management, services, research, commercial and marketing support), whereas other specific activities were delegated to the regions (interventions in selected sectors and of a structural nature). Finally, the new national action plan also included an institutional re-design of the ministry and more continuous relations with the Parliament through the annual production of a report on the state of Italian agriculture. The budget was approved on a multi-annual basis – which further reduced the discretionary power of the Parliament to intervene on a yearly basis – although the plan was supposed to be updated annually in order to better target the overall intervention. Also in this case the implementation of the plan was not successful as a result of both its complexity and the limited administrative ability of the regions to effectively manage the new competences (Daneo 1980).

More specifically, the main sources of poor implementation can be seen in the high procedural complexity of the overall policy design, the co-existence of contradictory goals and the lack of effective coordination between national and European goals. First, although on paper the allocation of competence between the two levels of government (regional and central government) was satisfactory, the overall implementation proved how complex the relationship could be, especially with regard to the programming capacities of the various administrative actors involved. The overall consequence of this specific configuration was that the programming goal remained primarily on paper since the implementation followed a 'programming without programmes' (Lizzi 2002: 184) principle that was clearly detrimental with respect to overall capacity to reach the set objectives. In the early 1990s, only a limited number of regional agricultural plans were approved and the overall content of the plans was often not coherent with the overall policy objectives set by the national action plan. This was made possible because of lack of monitoring and evaluation tools, which severely limited the foreseen targeting capacity of the adopted measures (ibid.: 185). Second, and most importantly for our analysis, the coordination mechanisms between European policies and domestic and regional policies were very limited, if existent (Daneo 1980). To a certain extent, the policies seemed to proceed along parallel lines that never merged. This was particularly striking during the mid-1980s, when public discussion at the EU level regarding reform of the PAC grew (see Chapter 2) and the future of domestic agricultural policy could not be seen as separate from European policy developments.

The final plan adopted in the 1980s (Piano *Mannino*, approved in 1989) tried to rebalance the policies by taking into greater account the European and international changes. The foreword to the plan takes into account the implementation of the previous plans and puts forward quite critical remarks with respect to past policies. For example, in occupational terms the decline continued and the overall trend relating to farmers' incomes was also negative, that is, not positive, as had been foreseen by the goals of the national action plans of the 1980s. Furthermore, the *Mannino* plan discussed the Italian policies in the European and international context by showing how challenging they had become over recent years and how even more challenging they would become in the near future: in the document, the reorientation towards the 'single farm payment' principle is seen as quite problematic with respect to the policy tradition developed over the years at the Italian level. Nevertheless, apart from generic criticism, the goals supported by the *Mannino* plan are not substantially different from those that were at the centre of the previous action plans: agricultural employment support, environmental protection and agricultural self-sufficiency. To be sure, the plan was extremely critical with respect to the most recent developments of the EEC/EC/EU agricultural policy, but it failed to elaborate a convincing alternative that could also be negotiated for effectively in European bargaining. The overall consequence of the adoption of this plan was to further 'decouple' Italian decisions from the emerging European decisions. An indicator of such divergence can be seen in terms of the expenditure capacity of European agricultural funds, which remained significantly lower than in other European countries – as it did in the mid-1960s (Daneo 1980). This divergence was, after the approval of the reform of the structural funds (1988, see Chapter 4) and the launch of CAP reform that was anticipated by the Green Paper on the reform of agriculture adopted by the Commission in 1985 (Commission 1985), deemed to be substantially reduced by the end of the decade.

In short, the 1960–1992 policy structure was not substantially altered with reference to the previous period, even though the CAP entered permanently into the agricultural policy design. The main reason for the limited change was that – unlike other policies analysed in this book – the overall degree of misfit was lower. In the terms presented in the first chapter of this book, the Italian policy structure was 'mid-fit' with the European one since the objectives and main principles developed prior to the EU intervention were already in line with the European ones. More specifically, the farmers' income protection orientation was already inbuilt in Italian agricultural policy as far back as the 1950s and continued to be at the heart of the policy during the following three decades. Associated with this broad objective, more domestic-specific objectives (self-sufficiency, agricultural employment promotion, etc.) were also pursued by mobilizing domestic funds that were largely available – in comparative terms – until the end of the 1980s. The principles during this period were also marked by continuity with respect to the past, since a mix of protectionism and openness (especially with respect to other EU partners) remained the guiding principle. All the subsequent plans approved by the Italian government did not challenge the protectionist principle and often criticized the excessive openness supported by European institutions (as in the case of the Mannino plan described above), but never acted consistently at the EU level in order to shape the policy in a more favourable way. The policy procedures were also marked by continuity, although since the 1960s the availability of EU resources required some adjustment by introducing more selective and less discretionary allocation procedures. Nevertheless, because of the continuous availability of domestic funds, the prevailing procedures remained the 'traditional' domestic ones since the European procedures concerned only a limited amount of funds from the overall available domestic package and the European resources – which became increasingly available – were not adequately spent, as mentioned previously. Finally, the financial instruments remained primarily domestic because the FEOGA-Guarantee funds available for Italy were still a limited percentage of the overall agricultural resources available (Daneo 1980). As a matter of fact, the total domestic resources devoted to agriculture until the end of the 1980s remained as high as 2 per cent of Italian GDP, whereas the EEC/EC/EU resources – although significant with respect to the European budget – never exceeded 0.5 per cent of domestic GDP. Therefore, the Italian governments managed to pursue European objectives (although with a poor implementation record) and continue with the previous agricultural policy that was characterized by social assistance aims and not only agricultural development ones (Amato 1976; Lizzi 2002).

From an institutional standpoint, prior to 1992 the government further accentuated its decision-making role thanks to the approval of the 'Green Plans' and subsequent national action plans that granted resources on a five-year basis and therefore reduced the legislature's budgetary allocation power. Furthermore, often the agricultural plan formulation – as in the case of the Marcora plan – was done autonomously by the governmental officials, without prior consultation of Parliament (Lizzi 2002: 178). By the end of the decade, the centrality of the agricultural ministry was reduced because – in order to comply with the 1988 European regional cohesion policy reform that also dealt with agricultural fund management – the spending decisions were allocated to the Interministerial Committee for Economic Programming (*Comitato Interministeriale per la Programmazione Economica* – CIPE), which became the pivotal player also as regards agricultural expenditure. The centralized nature of policy formulation and implementation changed increasingly over the years following the introduction of the regions and the overall reallocation of agricultural competences provided more power to the periphery – although regional implementation varied quite substantially and overall centre–periphery coordination remained rather poor – whereas further autonomy was granted by the availability of greater resources in the hands of the *Federconsorzi*, which was politically controlled by the Coldiretti leader, Bonomi (Lanza 1991). Finally, even with the creation of the AIME the formalistic orientation of the bureaucracy did not change; on the contrary, its limitations became particularly visible through the limited administrative capacities shown in the expenditure of the new European funds, which, as stated above, were not spent as in other European countries such as Netherlands, Germany and France. In other words, the adaptational pressures induced by Europeanization were not only limited because of the mid-fit nature of the relationships between the EU and domestic policy structures, but also by the fact that domestic policies continued to prevail. This combination of mid-fit and domestic policy continuity allowed the pre-existing institutional configuration to remain virtually unchanged and the limited changes registered during the period are connected to endogenous factors (such as governmental changes) rather than to exogenous (e.g. European) determinants.

3.2.3 Adapting to the CAP between 1992 and 2010: high policy misfit and policy transformation

Similar to the other policies investigated in this book, the early 1990s are marked by a series of relevant policy structure changes with respect to agricultural policies. The main subsidy provider associated with the policy (*Federconsorzi*) was investigated and virtually eliminated, the new policy principles and procedures introduced by the CAP (especially as regards dairy product quotas) constituted a further challenge for Italian agricultural policy functioning and the 1993–1997 reform of the ministry that followed a referendum initiative supported by 11 regional administrations are the key policy events that characterized the 1990s. First, in 1993 the main institution that for almost four decades had been the main fund provider was investigated because of its accumulated debt that was unsustainable in the post-Maastricht era. Also, following a Parliamentary investigation aimed at understanding the increasing fund mismanagement of the *Federconsorzi*, in 1999 Law 410 reformed agrarian consortia and allocated specific functions to the reformed provincial agrarian consortia that had already emerged after the end of *Federconsorzi*. Furthermore, the non-compliance with emerging EU rules such as the dairy quotas, already in place during the 1980s but never fully implemented by Italian producers, became a source of controversy with European institutions, which repeatedly asked the Italian government to comply.

The quite complicated controversy (see Lizzi 1997) was partially solved over the course of the decade when the Italian government managed to find a temporary compromise with the European institutions and the increasing 'loud' domestic agricultural associations. To a certain extent, it is only during the 1990s that the changing European rules with respect to specific targets (for example, fixing dairy product quotas) had a strong impact on domestic policies because until then, also as a result of the 'relaxation' in the application of the rules by both European and Italian institutions, the adaptational pressures exerted by the new CAP were still very limited. Finally, the 1992–1993 referendum – launched by the regions in order to fully obtain recognition of the powers related to policy allocated by the Italian Constitution – led to a structural reform of the national ministry. The referendum was initiated by the regions, but it was also made possible by the reform of the CAP, which gave increasing powers to sub-national authorities in agricultural decision making and therefore reduced central administration competences.

Only in 1997 was an overall reform of the ministry put forward by the new Prodi government that fully reorganized the functions of the ministry within the new multi-level setting of agricultural policy. The ministry maintained a coordination role and a representative role with respect to EU decision making, whereas the main implementation functions were fully delegated to regional authorities. Subsequently, an incremental adjustment to the new CAP procedures was implemented with respect to the rationalization of the funds used in order to allocate incentives and subsidies. Similar to European developments, income support became less central to the overall strategy of the Italian governments, which adopted a subsequent set of decisions that paved the way for new ministerial programming capacities such as those represented in the multi-annual agricultural and forest document (*Documento di programmazione per l'agricoltura e gestione delle foreste – DPAF*) that constituted one of the key innovations of the 1999 law. Within the first DPAF the key objectives were fully aligned to the European 'multi-functional' turn, and with respect to the principles less protectionism was guaranteed and more attention was devoted to rural development and environmental issues. Law 57, in 2001, further marked changes in the objectives of the Italian agricultural policy because not only did single farmers (and farms) become the target of the policies but – in line with EU policy developments aimed at broadening the policy objectives – the targets were also represented by other actors (for example, organizations active in the tourism sector, environmental associations, etc.) connected to the 'multi-functional' turn of the CAP. Therefore, the definition of 'agriculture' changed, broadening it in both scope and meaning.

If we analyse the latest ministerial programming document such differentiation with respect to the past emerges quite clearly: in 2010, the main domestic policies were centred on multi-functional objectives, whereas protection of farmers' income became residual. More specifically, beyond the generic objective of supporting (agricultural) development, the key objectives of the ministry for 2011 are the following: supporting Italy's role in the international environment (namely, within the formulation of the new CAP and WTO negotiations), enhancing competitiveness of Italian agriculture especially via support to rural youth and the female population, rural development and environmental protection, and promoting entrepreneurial activities (*Ministro delle politiche agricole alimentari e forestali* 2011: 5). In other words, the multi-functional targeting of agricultural public policy is now fully part of the national strategy, even beyond the mere implementation of European programmes and a clear shift in both policy objectives and principles has taken place during the past two decades. As a result of the increased role of the regions in the implementation of agricultural policies, the procedures have also been significantly changed in order to accommodate more targeted and selective forms of intervention that are now more territorially based. From purely distributive, resource allocation has become more selective, standardized and automatic since the requirements for the obtainment of (both domestic and European) funds has been substantially altered, creating a break with the past. To a certain extent, the policy focus is now at the regional level and no longer at the central level because of the full implementation of the constitutional provisions and subsequent reinforcement of federalist procedures that followed the adoption of the 2001 Constitutional Law (Fabbrini and Brunazzo 2003). The financial instruments – which were rationalized during the 1990s, as mentioned above – are now a mix of European and national funds, but unlike past periods European funds are currently as relevant as national funds. To be sure, the regionalization of the policy is now offering a differentiated picture of agricultural policy, since clearly today's agricultural policy is much more federal than it was 20 years ago and therefore the policy menus are different among the regions. For example, the introduction of genetically modified organisms (GMOs) – a highly controversial issue at both EEC/EC/EU and national level – has been differentiated in regional policy menus, some regions strongly supporting their use and others making them de facto illegal. Table 3.2 summarizes the changes experienced by the Italian agricultural policy structure over the past 60 years.

3.3 Mechanisms of Europeanization and political-institutional effects

If we turn to the mechanisms of Europeanization, the case of agricultural policy is quite different from the other two policies studied in this book. Since the early 1960s, when the PAC was launched, the main legislative instrument used at the EU level has been the regulation – which, as is well known, is the most binding form of legislation at the disposal of EU institutions. Therefore, the overall prevailing mechanisms have been those which have regulated the allocation of FEOGA-Guidance funds since 1962. Regulations were approved at the EU level and implementation had to follow accordingly because there was no room for domestic manoeuvre in adapting domestic legislation to the European prescriptions (as in the case of directives or 'soft laws', which will be investigated in the case of employment policy). Europeanization typically followed the route

Table 3.2 Italian agricultural policy structures: 1962–1992 and 1992–2010. Between policy continuity and policy transformation

	Italy (1945–1962)	Italy (1962–1992)	Italy (1992–2010)
Objectives	Farmers' income protection Rural social assistance	Farmers' income protection Rural social assistance	Farmers' income protection Rural sustainable development
Principles	Protectionism	Mix between protectionism (predominant) and intra-EU liberalization (residual)	Mix between protectionism and intra- and extra-EU liberalization
Procedures	Direct payments (discretionary)	Coupled direct payments (discretionary)	Decoupled direct payments (standardized and automatic)
Financial instruments	Domestic agricultural funds	Domestic agricultural funds (predominant) FEOGA-Guarantee FEOGA-Guidance (residual)	Domestic agricultural funds (residual) FEOGA-Guarantee FEOGA-Guidance (predominant)

of preference formation and negotiation among the representatives of the EU member states, and agricultural policies, once adopted, were implemented by the Commission, national governments and, increasingly, regional authorities. Unlike other imposition mechanisms used in the cases of regional cohesion policy, until the early 1990s domestic funds and policies were available and were even more relevant than those of the EU. Imposition mechanisms started to exert an impact in terms of policy change and institutional effects only very recently, e.g. when domestic funds were not as relevant as in the past. Therefore, the substitution of 'traditional' agricultural policy with the 'new' European policy was particularly slow: similar to the case of regional cohesion policy (discussed in Chapter 4), policy changes occurred only once the domestic national policies (and funds) were no longer available. Unlike regional cohesion policy, however, agricultural policy was also based on possible sanctions in cases of non-compliance with more severe EU regulation – as in the case of the implementation of the 1984 dairy product quotas. Only when the imposition mechanisms were fully implemented (in the early 1990s) was EU policy much more effective and truly binding with respect to domestic governmental behaviour. As we will discuss in the case of regional cohesion policy, penalizing, inbuilt policy elements were not relevant for the domestic government: if non-compliance occurred, no fund allocation would take place, the only penalization being not obtaining the funds allocated by the European institutions. In the case of the agricultural distributive policy, since the early 1990s both sanctions and allocation mechanisms were better targeted, and therefore – in comparison to regional cohesion and employment policy – the political costs of non-compliance were significantly higher within an overall context of domestic cuts aimed at respecting the Maastricht criteria. In other words, incremental adaptation was required not only in order to benefit from EU policies, but also to avoid being sanctioned and penalized by European institutions. More specifically, together with imposition, since 1992 non-formalised pressures also started to play a relevant role as a specific Europeanization mechanism: with the adoption of the Maastricht criteria and the overall, transversal EU-supported goal of cost containment and public budgets reductions, domestic agricultural policies were reformed and lost relevance in comparison with the CAP policies. In other words, after 1992 when CAP fund allocation bcame increasingly the prevailing 'game in town', fewer incentives related to 'showing the back' – or, in less metaphorical terms, not complying with European agricultural policies – were set out. The combined effects of such Europeanization mechanisms were particularly relevant for the policy-centred Italian institutional balance, to which we now turn.

From an institutional perspective, until the mid-1990s the impact of Europeanization on the institutional functioning or relationship patterns has been very weak: although the predominant Europeanization mechanism (imposition) was the strongest available to the EU, since other agricultural policy resources and policies were still operating and implementation was confined to member states' political and administrative action, the institutional changes witnessed prior to

1992 were mainly endogenously driven. After 1992, however, Europeanization started to have a role in relation to the recalibration of institutional activity or balances. Like other policies challenged by similar Europeanization mechanisms, although preference formation and negotiation were conducted by the executive and a decision adopted at the EU level had an immediate effect at the national level, because of the poor implementation of EU policies and the still prevailing availability of domestic policies, the Europeanization-induced empowerment of the executive had not been particularly relevant prior to 1992. After 1992, however, the picture started to change significantly. First, the executive – and especially the Prodi executive – became increasingly central because the importance of domestic policies was significantly reduced (as illustrated in the previous section). This occurred especially through the programming activity – which was a key goal in Agenda 2000 and heavily influenced the institutionalization of the Italian '*Tavolo verde*', which was promoted in 1998 by Agricultural Minister Pecoraro Scanio and 'contributed to the enhancement of the executive and the agricultural ministry especially' (Lizzi 2002: 203). Furthermore, the executive was increasingly pivotal in the interaction with the regions – which, especially after the 2003 referendum, gained significant power under the form of greater implementation autonomy from the central executive. Clearly, this empowerment did not mean that the Parliament lost entirely its powers since it maintained important legislative functions, but the overall institutional balance was increasingly favourable to the executive (interviews). From the early 1990s, the centre–periphery relationship has changed significantly in favour of the regions because agricultural policies – already partially regionalized over the previous decades – have continued to be regionalized and the impetus of the European prescriptions in that direction has been particularly significant since Agenda 2000 (interviews). As will be discussed in greater detail in Chapter 6, the role played by the European policies was not exclusive since domestic triggers also supported further regionalization. Our argument, nevertheless, is that European policies and institutions have substantially facilitated and supported such a process via increasing adaptational pressures.

The political parties, which had already been weakened by the 'political earthquake' of the early 1990s (Cotta and Isernia 1996), in the agricultural sector lost prominence with respect to the concertation activity launched by the Prodi government and never truly dismissed by the subsequent agricultural ministers. At the heart of the new policy style a concertation process developed, which was strongly in line with the partnership principle introduced in regional cohesion policy and also targeted by the Agenda 2000 reform (Commission 1997). The main agricultural interest groups (*Confederazione Italiana agricoltori* – COLDIRETTI, *Confederazione Italiana Agricoltura* – CIA, which was created in the late 1970s, and *Confederazione Generale dell'Agricoltura Italiana* – *Confagricoltura*) became increasingly pivotal both in the formulation and implementation phase since the government involved them extensively in the 'Green Tables' that became one of the main political forums for policy discussions (interviews). Furthermore, given the increased centrality of EU policy, the formation of Italian preferences included to a great degree not only agricultural associations, but also environmental associations such as Legambiente and the World Wide Fund for Nature (WWF), which played an increasing role in the new environmentally-friendly agricultural policies supported by the reformed CAP (interviews). Finally, political parties lost power because of the increasing impact of Europeanization on agricultural decision making (interviews; Lizzi, 2002: 268). Finally, also from a bureaucratic behaviour perspective, the overall situation has changed significantly over the past two decades: from the predominant orientation of mere validation of administrative acts (which were directly connected to the allocation of resources and, furthermore, were also characterized by discretional and non-selective features), the new interaction between national and regional bureaucracies is more focused on standardized procedures that follow selective allocation criteria. Such a reorientation is strongly connected to the new 'multi-functional' goals put forward by European policies. For example, since 2006 a specific new programme aimed at the training of young farmers has been implemented and the requirements in terms of administrative capacities go far beyond the mere formal validation of administrative acts that had been deployed in previous years (interview). The policy is implemented according to clear selection criteria and following a set of 'actions' aimed at improving the capacities of young agricultural entrepreneurs in launching new entrepreneurial activities, consolidating already established farms or increasing their managerial skills. Another example regards the support for wine (national programme for the support of the wine sector), which has been following rigid selection criteria over recent years and has required the enhancement of administrative capacities in order to cope with EU-related project management and evaluation functions. Finally, also with respect to direct transfers, several administrative changes have been implemented, such as the 1997 creation of a specialized agency (*Agenzia per le erogazioni in agricoltura* – AGEA), which is responsible for the implementation of the CAP. The agency was created after the inglorious end of the previous agency (AIMA) and has been characterized by a greater capacity to implement CAP policies and greater transparency (interviews). The agency is currently responsible for a limited package with respect to public agricultural expenditure (35 per cent), but apart from tax relief, which is not very demanding in terms of administrative capacity (30 per cent), the remaining domestic and regional policies (35 per cent) have been increasingly driven by a 'management by objectives' bureaucratic orientation in line with European prescriptions because the funds were allocated for research, services for development, processing and marketing, farm investment and infrastructure (INEA 2008: 106). In short, in all four relevant dimensions analysed, Europeanization has supported power concentration in the executive, regional and interest group empowerment, and administrative practices increasingly in line with performance-based and project-management principles both at the national and regional level.

3.4 Europeanization and agricultural policy change in Italy: an overall assessment

The CAP was one of the first policies to go 'European' and since 1962 – when the FEOGA-Guidance was introduced – it constituted an increasing point of reference for Italian agricultural policies. But did it also exert adaptational pressures on the Italian policy structure? In order to answer this question, in the previous sections of this chapter the main features of the European policy structure have been presented and discussed, followed by an illustration of the Italian agricultural trajectory. The main findings are that: (a) after the mid-1980s European agricultural policy changed (*policy adjustment*); (b) the Italian domestic policy structure was characterized by a 'mid-fit' during the first period of CAP (1960–1992), whereas since the CAP reform – consolidated after 1992 – the misfit has become more relevant; (c) the adaptational pressures have increased over the years because of the growing degree of misfit between the EU and the national policy structure; and (d) the pressure on 'traditional' Italian policy has given birth to domestic policy transformation over the past two decades and exerted institutional effects. Whereas in Chapter 2 we assessed more specifically the role European policies played in the overall policy structure change and the institutional balance change by focusing on the politics of adaptation, here it suffices to present the main findings regarding the interconnections between the EU policy structure and that of Italy.

First, unlike other EU policies covered in this book, one specifically interesting trait of EU agricultural policy is that it changed significantly over the years. Initially, it was primarily aimed at supporting farmers' income, following a primarily protectionist policy principle, via automatic, standard but not substantially selective procedures of direct payments to farmers with the help of one main financial instrument – the FEOGA-Guidance. Since the mid-1980s, primarily as the result of the overall budget reduction linked to expansion of regional cohesion policy, the CAP was increasingly aimed at supporting farms' multifunctionality, which meant more specific targeting of environmental and rural development concerns associated with farmers' income support; the overall principle thus shifted from mere protectionism to a more balanced protectionist and market-orientated principle as a result of WTO pressure; the procedures widened because coverage of the policy was not limited to direct payment and therefore, whereas still remaining automatic and standardized, the post-1992 procedures were increasingly selective; and, finally, the financial instruments became more complex because, together with the FEOGA-Guarantee, other structural funds (such as FEOGA-Guidance, and other sectoral funds) were also adopted in order to meet the new, ambitious policy goals. Furthermore, the Italian government had already developed an agricultural policy prior to the EU intervention that was only partially in line with the European one; for this reason, the first domestic policy structure relationship with the EU can be labelled a case of policy mid-fit, that is, a case of limited policy misfit and not of full 'fit'. Notwithstanding the consolidation of the CAP, the evolution of the Italian agricultural policy was not severely challenged until 1992 when – especially because of the increased imposition mechanisms of Europeanization discussed above and the CAP policy structure change – the Italian policy structure converged with that of the EU. Put another way, the adaptational pressures were not promptly transformed into domestic agricultural policy change. This was only partially the result of limited misfit since, as we shall discuss in the concluding chapter, prior to 1992 there was not enough domestic institutional and social support to translate adaptational pressures into full policy changes.

After 1992, because the policy misfit grew, in line with our research hypotheses, adaptational pressures also increased, becoming more demanding in terms of policy change. Finally, such pressures provided a specific impulse to change, which, as argued in the previous sections, can be labelled *policy transformation* since all the key dimensions of the policy structure have been fundamentally altered, together with the logics of institutional relationships. Similar to regional cohesion policy and employment policy, policy transformation occurred during a period of great systematic changes that affected the Italian political system during the 1990s (Cotta and Isernia 1996; Fabbrini 2000; Fabbrini et al. 2000). Such endogenous change makes it rather difficult to isolate the specific role played by European policies: the issue will be addressed more systematically in Chapter 6. It must be remembered that our working hypothesis does not predict any form of automatic change since the intergovernmental (or even neo-functionalist) nature of EU decision making would not allow such a prediction to be made. Particularly because of its implementation limitations, whatever policy structure is adopted at the European level and whatever degree of policy misfit could be registered, in the past and current functioning of the European multi-level political system domestic institutions and policy actors have the capacity to veto or accelerate EU-based pressures because of the adaptation required for EU policies to be effective domestically. In fact, as the agricultural case shows, the mere existence of policy mid-fit or misfit may not – although generating adaptational pressures – automatically trigger policy change if (a) specific domestic policies exist and are not marginalized by the emerging EU ones, and (b) domestic institutional, political and social actors do not find any specific convenience in supporting it. EU adaptational pressures may drive policy change only if the main institutional and non-institutional actors acknowledge the overall political advantage of 'complying', and no other relevant actor has a specific preference in stopping policy adaptation. In the case of agriculture, changes in the preference of key institutional actors (primarily, the government and its ministries) and the increasing salience of Europeanization mechanisms (both imposition and non-formalised pressures) paved the way for policy transformation. In short, the 'sequence' analysis provided in this chapter supports the claim that the *timing* and the *policy direction* of the changes have been strongly influenced by European institutions and policies. The political dynamics of policy adaptation will be discussed in greater detail in the concluding chapter.

4 Europeanization and Italian regional cohesion policy

4.1 European regional cohesion policy

Since the early days of European integration, together with the goal of creating a common market and a customs' union, other policies also were – at least on paper – considered of common concern by the founding members of the EEC. Regional disparities and a regional cohesion policy were already at the heart of the first policy discussions before and after the approval of the Treaty of Rome. This chapter is devoted to the analysis of the trajectory of the European regional policy and its interplay with the existing domestic regional cohesion policy.

4.1.1 Designing the European approach: 1958–1960

As already briefly discussed in the previous chapter, regional cohesion goals were already mentioned in the Preamble to the Treaty of Rome and in Article 2 of the 1957 Treaty. Although the key goals of the recently created European Community, at the end of the 1950s regional disparities within the founding six members (France, Germany, Italy, Belgium, the Netherlands and Luxembourg) were considered to be a political problem. Nevertheless, beyond such symbolic declarations, for several years the European institutions lacked any specific policy structure aimed at tackling the issue: as Helen Wallace pointed out, the declarations were symbolic rather than substantial (1983: 83). To be sure, some indirect financial instruments were used in order to reduce the overall impact of the common market on weaker, poorer regions. The European Investment Bank (EIB), established by Article 129 of the ECC Treaty, was explicitly aimed at 'contributing, via operations in the capital markets, to the harmonious and balanced development of the common market pursuing the overall interest of the Community'. More specifically, the EIB had the primary task of issuing individual or global loans via domestic financial institutions to small and medium enterprises that would otherwise probably have been excluded from traditional banking loans. Nevertheless, the EIB financial instruments were not part of a well-developed policy structure aimed at reduced territorial socio-economic disparities since

> the European Investment Bank (…) was designed as an intergovernmental body, owned and governed by the Member States. Its statute was clear in assigning to the Member States the final say concerning the admissibility of projects for loans, and the Bank had only functional links with the European Commission.
>
> (Manzella and Mendez 2009: 6)

The first direct financial instrument somehow linked to regional development adopted by the EU was the European Social Fund – ESF (1960). Although primarily aimed at 'increasing the employment opportunities of workers of the Community and therefore contributing to the [citizens'] life standards' (Article 123, Treaty of Rome), in the early 1960s its main territorial target was represented by less-developed territories. To be sure, its regional cohesion impact was limited – if not counterproductive – since the available resources were not directly aimed at supporting local development initiatives but rather to facilitate workers' migration from less-developed member states to developing members states because the available funds were primarily used in order to cover the migration expenses of workers, financial compensation in cases of temporary work loads reductions and vocational training initiatives for unemployed or underemployed people. Therefore, it is not a surprise that the country which benefited most from the first ten years of ESF was Germany – which had already substantially recovered from the Second World War – whereas Italy, characterized by the highest regional disparities and by the lowest GDP per capita in the EEC, came only second.

As Manzella and Mendez note, the reasons for such a limited policy structure are threefold:

> The first [reason] relates to the policy context of the time. While there were some important experiences in the field – the established British and North-American practices, as well as the emerging policy initiatives in France and Italy from the early 1950s – regional policy was still largely a nascent policy area. (…) A second factor was the prevailing economic orthodoxy, which was generally not supportive of the creation of a comprehensive regional policy at Community level. (…) Finally, it should not be overlooked that the World Bank was founded in this period and that, more generally, the early 1950s represented a period of great expectation about the capacity of Public Investment Banks to activate dynamics of growth in underdeveloped contexts.
>
> (2009: 5–6)

Put another way, in the early days of the EU there was no fully-fledged regional cohesion policy structure, since the only available policy dimension was the ESF financial instrument, whereas with respect to objectives, principles and procedures the policy was virtually non-existent. Each member state had to rely solely on the available domestic policies, which were quite differently organized, targeted and funded.

4.1.2 The hesitant take-off: 1960–1975

At the beginning of the decade following the adoption of the Treaty of Rome, the Commission decided to open a new policy front that explicitly targeted the territorial dimensions of European economic development. In 1961 the Commission organized a conference on regional economies, during the following year (1962) it prepared a memorandum presenting a framework for Community action with respect to regional development and in 1965 the Commission issued the first path-breaking communication that emphasized the role of the subnational dimensions of the Community and called for specific, targeted policies explicitly aimed at the reduction of regional disparities within the member states. In a famous speech to the European Parliament, the then-president of the Commission, Jean Rey, argued strongly in favour of the full adoption of a regional (cohesion) policy:

> Il est clair que trop de régions en difficulté attendant de la Communauté una action plus efficace et plus dynamique, et que les espoirs nés de la creation même du gran marché européen se sont réalisés géographiquement de façon trop inégale dans la Communauté. (…) La politique régionale doit être dans la Communauté ce que le cœur est dans l'organisme humain.
>
> (1968: 9)

Furthermore, between 1967 and 1968, a new Regional Policy Directorate General was created (DG XVI) with the aim of increasing the institutional capacities of the Commission in the regional policy field. As a consequence of the institutional innovation, in 1969 the Commission presented a second Communication (*A Regional Policy for the Community*) containing a memorandum and a proposal in which a specific supplementary fund that could support the EIB was advocated. In the Commission's view, 'the objective of regional policy is to establish, develop and operate the facilities needed for the location of economic activities and people, in the light of technical and economic requirements, human needs and aspirations and the characteristics of the areas in question (Commission 1969: 24).

During the late 1960s, however, the initiatives of the Commission did not find a fertile ground in the policy preferences of the key governments of the member states because: (a) the problem pressure was limited; (b) growth was still fairly solid; and (c) the governments of the member states did not want to share sovereignty over such an important policy. More specifically, the only member state to witness severe regional disparities was Italy, because the other countries with some territorial disparities (such as France and Belgium) were globally better off than Italy (since the national GDP per capita average was higher than the EC average) and therefore did not perceive the issue as highly problematic. Furthermore, the EC member states were still in the middle of the most impressive economic growth trend ever registered and therefore, implicitly, the member state governments did not consider having a dedicated policy covering regional development necessary because – it was believed – growth would have automatically adjusted over the years and also the underdeveloped regions would have profited from such solid and continuous growth rates during the 1960s. Finally, the member state governments were still quite reluctant to share competencies over a policy that was so relevant for the definition and consolidation of national sovereignty. States were created over centuries via centralization of competences and increasing the control over peripheries (Poggi 1978); giving up – at least partially – control over the allocation of funds for development, thus reducing the territorial integrity of the member states by allowing a supranational organization (the Commission) to enter into what was at the time seen essentially as a national issue.

In sum, notwithstanding the political pressures exerted by the Commission, until the end of the 1960s a fully-fledged European regional policy was still to come.

Since the beginning of the 1970s, the Commission emphasized that in order to pursue the goal of creating a common market domestic aid to regions also had to be regulated. Moreover, according to Manzella and Mendez, the 'catalyst for the creation of a Community regional policy was the deepening of the debate on Economic and Monetary Union, which had been launched in the late 1960's' (2009: 8). This strategy was shared among Commission and member states' representatives and such common vision institutionally strengthened the overall supranational preference for the creation of a European regional policy. The conclusion of the Paris Summit held in October 1972 put regional cohesion policy right at the top of the EU political agenda:

> The Heads of State and Government give top priority to correcting the structural and regional imbalances in the Community which could hinder the achievement of the Economic and Monetary Union. The Heads of State and Government invite the Commission to prepare as soon as possible a report analysing the regional problems of the enlarged Community and offering suitable proposals.
> (Meeting of Heads of State of Government 1972: 18)

Furthermore, the beginning of the 1970s was also characterized by an economic crisis 'which raised social issues to the fore within EC debates and drew attention to the close link between declining industries and specific territorial areas' (Manzella and Mendez 2009: 7). Finally, and most importantly, the early 1970s were also the years during which the first wave of enlargement took place; in 1973, the UK, Ireland and Denmark joined the ECC. As mentioned in the previous chapter, two of these countries were experiencing severe regional development disparities (the UK) or were particularly badly equipped for domestically coping with industrial reconversion (Ireland). With respect to the former, all the regions had lost out in terms of GDP per capita from 1950 to 1970 and the decline was particularly acute in the North, for example Yorkshire and Humberside, the East Midlands and Scotland (Graziano 2004: 39–40). Ireland also experienced an overall decline between 1950 and 1970, although it had already been an underdeveloped country in GDP per capita terms in 1950 (ibid.).

During the negotiations that led to the accession of the new member states, the regional issue became increasingly relevant also among the member state governments. The above-mentioned 1972 Paris Summit paved the way for the creation of a new, dedicated financial tool for a European regional cohesion policy that was established in 1975: the European Regional Development Fund (ERDF). Although the initial proposal by the Commission was much more ambitious in terms of allocated funds, the ERDF became the first financial instrument at the disposal of the Community for regional cohesion purposes. More specifically, the supranational dimension of the policy implementation was severely limited because the main powers remained allocated at the domestic level as the member state governments were entitled to select the regions that were considered to be 'underdeveloped' and no common, European criterion was adopted. The success of the intergovernmentalist approach, however, should not downplay the relevance of the overall policy innovation: since 1975, the European regional cohesion policy started (slowly) to come of age, although the policy structure was still limited to the availability of financial instruments and no fully-fledged common objectives, principles and procedures were agreed upon. The Commission (and the European Parliament) managed to at least play a decisive role in the adoption of the package devoted to regional policy, which then also became a European concern.

4.1.3 The road to the European regional policy structure: 1975–1988

The first years of the implementation of the European regional policy were not considered particularly satisfactory because of the lack of resources and the limited European added value in the domestic appropriation of the ERDF. First, ERDF covered only a limited share (around 5 per cent; Manzella and Mendez 2009: 10) of the already meagre European budget, and even taking into account all the other structural funds that were mobilized for regional purposes (ESF, FEOGA-Guidance Section funds), the overall available resources covered only 7.9 per cent of the EU budget (Commission 1999). Second, several member states did not follow the (weak) European co-funding prescription contained in the regulation establishing the ERDF (Regulation 724/1975) and therefore used the European resources as substitutes for domestic funds (Mény 1992).

Nevertheless, from the end of the 1970s the Commission steadily enhanced the overall regional policy package and became increasingly central in both policy formulation and adoption. First, in 1979 the Commission increased its implementation powers by introducing a 5 per cent 'non quota section': 5 per cent of the ERDF would be exclusively managed by the Commission in order to increase overall European added value to the regional policy. Furthermore, in the following years the European Parliament — directly elected since 1979 — continuously supported the Commission in its request for increasing the available structural funds that, in 1982, covered 22.2 per cent of the EU budget (Wallace 1983: 95). Finally, since regional disparities did not decline significantly, notwithstanding the increased financial efforts of the EU, in the academic community a call for a greater role for the Commission (and European institutions in general) was also made. In an article quite significantly entitled 'Should the Community Regional Policy be Scrapped?', Mény investigated the reasons why the European regional policy was so ineffective and identified the main factor as the limited role of European institutions. The implicit answer in the article, therefore, was that EU regional policy should not have been 'scrapped' and greater power allocation to European institutions was deemed necessary.

During the 1980s, the Commission insisted that specific European criteria be set with respect to domestic funds allocation, supported a programming approach connecting fund allocation to regional development plans and asked for further guarantees that the European funds would be additional with respect to domestic regional policy expenditure. The success of the Commission's strategy was clear when Regulation 1787/1984 was approved because it provided greater formulation and implementation powers with respect to the member state governments. More specifically, the regulation placed the Commission at the centre of European regional cohesion decision making by acknowledging its coordination role as regards other domestic regional policies (Article 1) and established the 'community programmes' formulated by the Commission and approved by the Council under the qualified majority rule (Article 7). Put another way, with respect to the past the European policy lost its feature of mere intergovernmental allocation and became increasingly supranational thanks to the new pivotal role played by the Commission (see also Manzella and Mendez 2009: 11–12).

Another sign of the new centrality of the Commission in the European regional policy framework is represented by the adoption of the Integrated Mediterrean Programmes (IMP) in 1985. In 1981, Greece had joined the EEC and called for greater, selective attention for rural regions (Buresti and Marciani 1991), which was then guaranteed by the adoption of the IMP regulation. The regulation that established the IMP provided further implementation and evaluation powers to the Commission and established the possibility of direct links between the Commission and the concerned regions (beyond Greece, in Southern France and Southern Italy), further supporting an enhanced strategic role played by the Commission – inaugurated by the adoption and implementation of a 5 per cent non-quota section.

Summing up, since 1975 the EU regional cohesion policy had gained momentum and by the mid-1980s it developed financial instruments and increasingly well-defined common objectives, whereas supranational procedures and principles were still underdeveloped. But the time had come for the adoption of a fully-fledged regional cohesion policy structure.

4.1.4 The European regional policy structure: 1988 and beyond

After the adoption of the Single European Act (1987) and the second wave of enlargement, orientated towards Southern Europe (Greece, 1981; Portugal and

Spain, 1986), the 1988 reform provided the EU with a fully developed policy structure with a pivotal role assured to the Commission. The 1988 reform better defined the specific goals of the European regional policy, which were not simply to 'reduce socioeconomic disparities' in the EU, but rather to facilitate regional convergence towards a similar level of GDP per capita. In fact, since the main targets of the policy were the regions that fell below 75 per cent of average EC GDP per capita, the implicit objective was to raise all the 'underdeveloped' regions above that threshold. Although the objectives were numerous (seven in the first programming round, 1989–1994; three in the following programming rounds), the main objective since 1988 has been convergence. With respect to the policy principles, the 1988 regulation and the subsequent (minor) reforms have fixed four overarching elements: programming, partnership, additionality and concentration.

The programming principle, which was strongly connected with the abovementioned experience of the IMP, innovated significantly with respect to the functioning of the previous European regional cohesion policy. Although it had not been made explicit, until the 1988 reform the funding principle was project-by-project (Marks 1992: 20), which limited the overall strategic programming role of the Commission. The programming activity – which initially covered a five-year timespan (1989–1994) and currently covers a seven year time span (2007–2013) – was a very powerful tool for the Commission since it enabled supranational control over medium-ranging regional cohesion policy expenditure. The articulation of programming (Community Support Frameworks – now Community Strategic Guidelines on Cohesion; National Programming Documents – now the National Strategic Reference Framework; and Operational Programmes) provided specific new tools for the Commission to oversee the entire policy process. It allowed the Commission to be particularly relevant in both formulation and implementation phases, by contributing to fixing the overall strategic goals of the policy at an EU level and by monitoring the implementation – which since 1988 has increasingly been delegated also to regional authorities.

Another major innovation regarded the introduction of the partnership principle, which provided greater overall support to the European regional policy by initially bringing in sub-national authorities and (with the 1993 reform) also social partners at the various levels of government. Furthermore, the 'involvement of the regional level of government in the planning, implementation and monitoring of programmes was an important innovation, one which contributed to the supranational "feel" of the new policy' (Cini and Mura 2010: 9). The partnership principles gave a further opportunity to the Commission to broaden its political reach by mobilizing sub-national (institutional and social) interests over the years, which often were highly supportive of the EU policy since it provided new political opportunities to play a greater role in regional cohesion policy implementation. Furthermore, the partnership principle enhanced the overall legitimation of the Commission since it became increasingly central in the multi-level governance setting that governed European regional cohesion policy (Bache and Olsson 2001; Bache 2007).

The third guiding principle – additionality – regarded the specific nature of European funding with respect to available domestic funds. Put another way, the European regional cohesion funds had to be complemented by domestic funds, and not substituted for them as had happened in the past (see previous sections). There was a call for greater incentives to make member state governments (and sub-national authorities) adopt and implement programmes that were also of strategic relevance at the domestic level since such programmes would have to be co-funded; 'free riding' (e.g. substituting domestic resources with EU resources) on EU funds was no longer allowed. This principle has generated considerable tensions between the Commission and member state governments because it was a clear sign of loss of sovereignty in regional policy issues and limited the autonomous implementation capacities of the governments. An exception to this principle was made for the fund that was introduced in 1993 (Cohesion Fund), since its main goal was to help 'underdeveloped' member states (e.g. with a Gross National Income (GNI) below 90 per cent of the European average) in performing structural adjustments needed to meet the EMU convergence obligations.

The fourth principle, concentration, was adopted in order to better target the European regional cohesion policy as regards those (regional or sub-regional) territories that were most in need. This innovation was particularly satisfactory for the Commission, which had previously tried several times to overcome the national quota system and had never succeeded – apart from the limited 'non-quota' policies. The concentration principle increased the Commission's capacity to map the areas where the policy was needed most by combining this principle with the above-mentioned convergence objective. In Cini and Mura's words:

> In practice it meant a focusing of funding to particular regions and countries, a strategy in line with the spirit of the new Cohesion Fund, and in addition, a focus on particular kinds of support, reflected in the 'Objectives' which grouped together the eligibility criteria for support.
>
> (2010: 10)

All the principles introduced in 1988 are still valid since, notwithstanding some minor adaptations and changes, the core principles are still part of the current (2007–2014) policy structure.

As regards procedures, the 1988 reform introduced quite a number of changes as it primarily allowed greater 'standardized' criteria in the implementation of the European regional cohesion policy. In fact, the reform introduced transparent and automatic procedures that governed the allocation of regional cohesion funds, reducing the discretionary power of the governments of the member states (Bouvet and Dall'Erba 2010). Following the fixed rules for the selection of the territories where the European cohesion policy would be implemented, the 1988 reform foresaw a three-step selection procedure: 'First, the Commission and the member states negotiated eligibility criteria and decided which regions were to get support. Second, regions and national governments developed plans. Finally, the Commission adopted those plans, which were then implemented' (Cini and Mura 2010: 11). Put another way, through the standardization of the procedures, the Commission managed to reduce the discretionary implementation powers upheld by the members state governments prior to the 1988 reform.

Finally, with respect to the financial instruments, the ESF, ERDF and the FEOGA-Guidance Section funds were substantially increased by the 1988 reform, and in 1993 a new fund – the Cohesion Fund – was introduced. Throughout the 1990s the overall financial package of structural funds and cohesion policy – the financial instruments of EU regional cohesion policy – covered over 30 per cent of the EU budget.

Since the 1988 reform, minor policy changes have been approved by EU institutions but the overall policy architecture has not substantially altered. This is particularly impressive since the third wave of enlargement (to Central and Eastern European countries, Cyprus and Malta, between 2004 and 2007) has significantly challenged the capacity of the EU to continue to deliver a sound cohesion policy without creating too many political problems among the member states, in particular as regards the old member states that had for several years benefited from the policy (especially Spain and Italy). In fact, according to some scholars the policy is no longer suited to coping with the new needs and challenges faced by the European Union in the 2000s (Bachtler and Méndez 2007). Nevertheless, over the past 20 years the European regional policy constituted a substantial challenge for all the members states that were particularly concerned by regional disparities – and Italy was one of the most concerned.

4.2 Italian regional cohesion policy

Before analysing the interaction between the European policy structure and the most recent Italian one, it is necessary to provide an analysis of the trajectory of Italian regional cohesion policy in order to understand how the key policy structure features have been created and changed over the years without the possible presence of European adaptational pressures. This analysis is particularly fruitful since it provides an opportunity to test the policy change hypothesis connected to Europeanization by questioning if European policies are the only triggers of change within an overall context of continuity. Against a simplified version of the evolution of the Italian regional cohesion policy evolution, this section will provide an illustration of the changes that have occurred over the past 40 years in Italian regional cohesion policy, and provide evidence of how the overall Italian policy structure became increasingly a 'misfit' with respect to the European regional cohesion policy. Put another way, this section will illustrate how policy change may clearly be determined by domestic factors (namely, prior to 1988 when the regional cohesion policy was fully crafted), but it will also provide evidence of the specific links between domestic changes and EU policy changes after the 1988 reform.

4.2.1 The trajectory of the Italian policy structure: 1950–2010

Since its unification (1861–1870), Italy has been characterized by increasing economic and social dualism, which created a quite evident differentiation between the more industrialized and rich North from the more rural and poorer South. The problem of Southern 'underdevelopment' and the investigation of its political and social determinants has been analysed from several disciplinary perspectives – ranging from history to sociology, and from political science to economics (Cazzola 1979; Graziano 1980; Zamagni 1990; D'Antone 1995; Cafiero 1996; La Spina 2003) – and several diagnoses and policy recommendations have been put forward since the late nineteenth century; nevertheless, prior to the Second World War the territorial divide was very striking. After the end of the war the situation was even more dramatic in comparative terms. To be sure, the Northern regions (especially the Northwestern regions) had quickly recovered from the tragedy of the war, whereas the Northeastern regions and especially the Southern regions were lagging behind (Zamagni 1990). Nevertheless, for the first time in Italian history, the foreseen systemic political stability was promising with respect to the creation of regional cohesion policies that could have reduced such a cumulative economic and social gap. The so-called *intervento per il Mezzogiorno* (policies for the South) was institutionally structured in a peculiar way since it was approved by the newly created democratic Parliament, following specific governmental policy proposals, but primarily managed by an external institution – the *Cassa per il Mezzogiorno* (the *Mezzogiorno* fund).

4.2.2 The early years: 1950–1965

Since the mid-1940s ideas concerning the creation of an autonomous entity responsible for the promotion of development in the South had emerged within the circles of the International Bank for the Reconstruction and Development (IBRD – then World Bank, WB) and strongly supported by the current president of the Italian central bank (*Banca d'Italia*) – Menichella. Within the IBRD/WB, a document entitled 'Financing of Economic Development of Southern Italy' provided an analysis of the specific traits of the Southern underdevelopment problem and suggested the formulation of a comprehensive plan of public intervention that was explicitly targeted at Southern Italian economic needs. Furthermore, the allocation of spending powers to an autonomous institution – such as the future *Cassa per il Mezzogiorno* – was particularly supported by the IBRD/WB, which preferred to establish future collaborations not with several ministries but rather with one dedicated institution that could more effectively monitor the fund's allocation and use, and effectively interact with the IBRD/WB (La Spina 2003).

Finance Minister Vanoni (1948–1954) was particularly supportive of the plan, and acted as a main sponsor by promoting it in discussion with Prime Minister De Gasperi. A governmental proposal was then drafted and its main content was the creation of a dedicated institution and fund (*Cassa per il Mezzogiorno*) that could financially support the promotion of development in Southern

Italy. The main foreseen advantage of such an institutional design enabling an autonomous institution to independently manage the fund was to avoid the discretionary allocation of resources that could have been triggered by governmental or Parliamentary interference (Cafiero 1996). It is not by chance that several representatives of the Christian Democratic governmental and Parliamentary majority were concerned by the excessive autonomy granted to the *Cassa* and the subsequent loss of political control over the allocation of funds for Southern economic development (Graziano 2004). In fact, with respect to the initial governmental proposal, an amendment was introduced that provided an opportunity for the ministries to control – at least to a limited extent – the allocation of funds. The modification introduced a ministerial committee for the *Mezzogiorno*, appointed by the Council of Ministers, which would have the task of approving any funding programme supported by the *Cassa per il Mezzogiorno*. This specific instrument gave some room for political control over the concrete allocation of the resources proposed by the representatives of the *Cassa*. This amendment was not enough for the Parliamentary majority, however, which was still concerned that the new institution would hold too many autonomous allocative powers and in the final legislative text approved by the Parliament less autonomy was granted to the *Cassa* and greater control over it was granted to the ministerial committee (Cafiero 1996; La Spina 2003). Nevertheless, in the following years, the overall autonomy of the new institution remained significant both in the formulation of the development programmes and their implementation – unlike what Italy experienced in the following regional cohesion policy implementation periods.

Therefore, in the early years when the Italian cohesion policy was set up, the policy structure was defined as follows. First, the overall *objectives* of the policy were very general since the law that introduced the *Cassa per il Mezzogiorno* stated that the key objective was to promote 'a harmonious economic and social development of Southern Italy' (Article 1, Law 646/1950) without further specifying the goals via quantified targets. Furthermore, no subsequent programming documents were produced specifying clearer economic and social development targets. Put another way, the objectives drawn in such a general fashion meant that any kind of monitoring or evaluation activity would have been very difficult to implement. Second, the main explicit *principle* guiding the policy was territorial concentration – the Italian *Mezzogiorno*, which meant eight Southern regions, Campania, Abruzzi, Molise, Basilicata, Calabria, Puglia, Sicilia and Sardegna, and two provinces, Latina and Frosinone – but no further specification regarding sub-regional targeting was introduced in the law. Third, the *procedures* of fund allocation were standardized and automatic since they were carried out independently by the representatives of the new institution, once the ministerial committee had approved the overall funding programme. Nevertheless, no specific monitoring and evaluation devices were foreseen for a more systematic assessment of the outcomes of policy implementation. Finally, with respect to *financial instruments*, these were represented by the national funds used for loans or contributions targeted at development programmes (especially infrastructural projects in the early years of the *Cassa*'s activities).

The institutional configuration supporting the policy can be characterized as follows: first, the government was the pivotal player since – through the ministerial committee – it was responsible for the approval of the development programmes implemented by the *Cassa*. Nevertheless, the Parliament had specific budget allocation powers since the funds used by the *Cassa* were mainly public funds and the Parliament – on a pluri-annual basis – had to vote on budget allocation laws. Through this legislative function, the legislative had a voice with respect to the overall package granted to domestic development programmes. No specific powers were granted to sub-national authorities since the regions had not yet been created and the provinces were not involved in any stage of decision making. With respect to the relative influence exerted by political parties and interest groups, political parties – and in particular the leading political party of the time, the Christian Democratic party – were not as capable as in other policy sectors to influence the allocation decisions adopted by the *Cassa*. To be sure, De Gasperi – the Christian Democratic leader and prime minister between 1945 and 1953) granted full support to the *Cassa* but also believed that allocation decisions were better adopted by an autonomous body rather than political institutions that could have limited the effectiveness of allocation decisions by exerting political discretionary power (Zoppi 2003). This is a very important feature, which differentiates regional cohesion policy from other policies whereby the strength of the main ruling party – also in discretionary terms – was much more relevant (Morlino 1991a; Cotta 1996). Once the decision regarding the creation of the *Cassa per il Mezzogiorno* was adopted, the limited party control over resource allocation was determined by the specific institutional design of the *Cassa*, which left very little power of interference to external actors. Interest groups – rapidly developing in other policy sectors (Feltrin 1991; Mattina 1991) – were absent from regional cohesion policy decision making due, possibly, to the technical nature of the policy and the overall support for it. In fact, the early years of the Italian regional cohesion policy were years of sustained economic growth and the development programmes supported by the fund were considered positively without significant interest group attempts to intervene in resource allocation decisions of the *Cassa* (Felice 2007). Finally, the peculiar institutional design of the *Cassa* isolated the bureaucrats working on this policy from ministerial bureaucracies and were composed mainly of administrative personnel who followed rules quite different to those followed in other policy sectors: the strong connection between the central bank and *Cassa* personnel guaranteed implicit 'management by objectives' bureaucratic behaviour, which characterized the early years of the *Intervento Straordinario per il Mezzogiorno* (ibid.). In comparative terms, the bureaucratic personnel of the *Cassa* were highly qualified (D'Antone 1995) and specifically trained to reach performance targets and the top bureaucrats of the *Cassa* managed to develop autonomous political authority that shielded the organization from external interference. Put another way, with respect to regional cohesion policy the bureaucracy was much more in line with 'goal attainment', which would characterize future post-1998 European regional cohesion implementation in Italy.

4.2.3 A falling star: the Cassa per il Mezzogiorno, 1965–1992

Originally the *Cassa per il Mezzogiorno* was planned to operate only for ten years, but already in 1952 an extension to 12 years was guaranteed. In fact, the *Cassa* was considered to be a major player in the funding of infrastructures that could be beneficial for industrial production and the take-off of economic (and social) development in Southern Italy. The first decade of fund allocation was not highly disputed since the need for infrastructural upgrading was shared by all the key institutional, political, social and bureaucratic actors. Since the late 1950s, however, greater funding competences were allocated to the *Cassa* since most of the infrastructural projects had been implemented (D'Antone 1995). The *Cassa*'s competence expansion was soon followed by the expansion of political constraints over its functioning: more specifically, Law 717/1965 increased the powers of the ministerial committee, whose chair became the 'extraordinary intervention' ministry, by introducing the 'conformity opinion' (*parere di conformità*) that was needed in order to provide a 'green light' to development programmes. This paved the way for increasing political interference in the development programmes' ideation and management. More specifically, from 1965 the ministerial committee (and especially the ministry coordinating the committee) would have had the final word over the approval or rejection of the funding of development programmes (Cafiero 1996).

Furthermore, since the early 1970s, which were characterized by the first oil shock and subsequent economic difficulties, the overall activity of the *Cassa* started to be heavily criticized. On the one hand, the results in terms of reducing regional disparities were very limited and therefore the overall effectiveness of the programmes funded by the *Cassa* was questioned; on the other hand, the increasing politicization of the funding policy was increasingly blamed (ibid.). In other words, for the first time since the early 1950s the existence of the *Cassa per il Mezzogiorno* was endangered. Law 183/1976 tried to recalibrate the overall functioning of the institution by introducing some innovations, such as: greater multi-annual programming capacities (five-year plans with specific growth and occupational targets were introduced), better formulation of overarching objectives regarding regional industrial policy, enhanced coordination between ordinary interventions and extraordinary interventions – those put forward by the *Cassa* – and the formulation of specific criteria and guidelines that were supposed to be followed by the recently established regions (La Spina 2003). Nevertheless, the results were judged unsatisfactory and criticism continued to grow. The overall interference of the legislative were accentuated by the creation of a bicameral commission, which had the prerogative not only to issue recommendations and exercise consultative powers, but also perform monitoring and controlling functions over the programming and implementation of the development programmes funded by the *Cassa per il Mezzogiorno*.

The Italian government and legislative decided that the experience of the *Cassa* should be called to an end and passed a law (64/1986) that would have radically restructured the institution, if not cancelled it definitively. The overarching goal, thus, was to 'downsize' the institution and cancel the programming–projecting–funding–implementation sequence that had until then governed the activity of the *Cassa per il Mezzogiorno* (Cafiero 1996). A new institution was created – the Agency for the Development of the South (*Agenzia per lo sviluppo del Mezzogiorno*), which was further placed under the control of the 'extraordinary intervention' minister (Article 1.6, Law 64/1986).

During this second period of Italian regional cohesion policy several institutional and policy features had changed with respect to the previous period. Although the overall *objectives* had not changed (the basic goal of a 'harmonious socio-economic advancement' remaining at the heart of the policy), as regards the *principles* a more nuanced approach had been followed because – together with the concentration principle – the programming principles were also placed at the heart of the overall intervention. Nevertheless, programming remained on paper only, because after the 1976 law few concrete steps in the direction of a fully-fledged programming capacity were taken (ibid.). The *financial instruments* had not been altered with respect to the previous period, whereas a significant change had been implemented: through the creation of the 'conformity opinion' (*parere di conformità*), greater political (e.g. ministerial) control was enacted and greater discretion in the approval of the programmes' funding was introduced.

As regards the institutional configuration, quite similar to the previous period the power relationship between the executive and the legislative remained balanced since the former maintained the power to coordinate policy implementation and the latter maintained power to allocate the resources via the approval of multi-annual budgets. Nevertheless, increasing the years of funding (such as in the case of Law 64/1986, which approved a nine-year funding programme) meant providing more autonomous power to the government – and especially to the 'extraordinary intervention' ministry – which therefore enhanced progressively its power over the legislative.

Although regional authorities had been created in the 1970s, they still did not have any relevant power with respect to regional cohesion policy formulation or implementation, and therefore – as in the early years of the evolution of the policy – the relationship between the central government and the sub-national authorities was strongly balanced in favour of the former. As regards bureaucratic behaviour, the peculiar management of the *Intervento Straordinario* left a very limited role for the central public administration, which was not involved in 'project management' activities and continued to primarily guarantee the formal validity of administrative acts. In fact, the professionalized bureaucratic personnel who operated within the Cassa also lost their autonomy due to the greater control of the executive and therefore lost their capacity to continue the 'management by objectives' behaviour that had characterized the previous intervention period (ibid.).

Finally, partisan control over the allocation of funds grew significantly because the appointed minister of infrastructure – which had since the 1960s been a representative of the Christian Democratic party – was capable of approving (or not approving) the programmes via the above-mentioned 'conformity opinion'. Clearly, partisan control was limited to the governmental parties since no role could be performed by the opposition parties, if not within the legislative. Interest groups continued to be fully supportive, although their specific influence related to the adoption and implementation of the policy was greatly limited by governmental power concentration and the increasing role played by governmental parties. Summing up, no particular increase in the power of the interest groups was connected with the 1965–1992 period, which became even more characterized by the (governmental) party predominance over the interest groups in the field of regional cohesion policy.

4.2.4 The end of the Cassa per il Mezzogiorno and the emergence of the European regional policy framework: (slow) policy transformation, 1992–2010

In 1992, in a period of great systemic turmoil within the Italian political system (Fabbrini et al. 2000; Fabbrini and Piattoni 2008) and following the mounting criticism regarding the management of public funds that was amplified by the electoral emergence of the Lega Nord, which was strongly against policies for the development of the South, seen as a hopeless source of corruption and a waste of public money (Diamanti 1993), the *Cassa per il Mezzogiorno* was abolished. Meanwhile, the reform of the European regional cohesion policy had offered new opportunities for the development of multi-level cohesion policies. With respect to the total funds allocated by the EC/EU in the first programming period,

> during 1989–1993 the European Community [has] spent for the development of the weakest regions about 400,000 billion 1993 Italian lira, of which 50,000 billion was for the Mezzogiorno. [...] The famous Marshall Plan aimed at the reconstruction of Europe during the 1950s would now require from the United States 130,000 billion 1993 Italian lira. The overall funding of the Italian 'extraordinary intervention' [implemented via the *Cassa per il Mezzogiorno*] was worth 250,000 billion 1993 Italian lira, which have been allocated during the 42 years of funding activity.
>
> (Solima 1996: 277, author's translation)

These claims show how relevant the new European regional cohesion policy was in terms of overall fund allocation: in a five-year span (1989–1993), almost 20 per cent of the total amount allocated in 42 years by the *Cassa per il Mezzogiorno*. Nevertheless, the relevance was mainly in theory since it appeared almost immediately that 'the CSF methodology had not been understood neither at the central domestic level nor at the regional level' (Leonardi and Nanetti

Table 4.1 EU structural funds expenditure

Member State	Expenditure (%)
Belgium	30
Denmark	33
Germany	33
Greece	31
Spain	36
France	29
Ireland	39
Italy	23
Luxembourg	34
Netherlands	31
Austria	25
Portugal	40
Finland	20
Sweden	17
United Kingdom	39
Total	33

Source: Author's calculation on Commission reports (various years) on Structural funds expenditure in member states.

2001: 346, author's translation). In fact, one of the most striking features of the implementation of the first programming periods was the limited expenditure capacity of EU funds. By the mid-1990s, also due to a relayed adoption of EU documents, the overall Italian capacity to spend EU funds was very limited in comparative terms, as highlighted by the hearings conducted by a special Parliamentary commission dedicated to the issue (*Camera dei Deputati – Commissione speciale per le politiche comunitarie* 1996: VII). The suppression of the 'old' *Cassa per il Mezzogiorno* had not automatically given birth to an improved capacity to follow EU guidelines and therefore, notwithstanding the availability of EU funds, for almost a decade expenditure capacity remained extremely low in comparative perspective (see Table 4.1).

To be sure, the overall architecture of the European regional policy was extremely challenging for the domestic public administration, which was also experiencing intense political pressure because of the above-mentioned 'political turmoil'. Nevertheless, until the second half of the 1990s no significant institutional change within the ministries was adopted in order to better cope with the new European opportunities and domestic expenditure capacities remained particularly limited. Put another way, the degree of misfit between the 'old' Italian regional policy (which was basically implemented by an external authority – the *Cassa* and the Agency for the *Mezzogiorno*) was so high that, notwithstanding the increasing adaptational pressure applied by the Commission, both formally (through the monitoring and 'naming and shaming' procedures contained in the annual report on the implementation of the Structural Funds) and informally (interview), it took several years to fully adapt to the new European policy structure. The policy misfit was very high because the policy objectives at the EU level were much better defined (e.g. standardized) than for the previous Italian policy, the principles were much more numerous and sophisticated (programming, partnership, additionality and concentration) with respect to the 'old' territorial concentration, the EU procedures were standardized and automatic and particularly demanding of domestic public administration structures (both national and regional) in terms of monitoring and implementation, and a substantial increase in the structural funds (ESF, ERDF, FEOGA-Guidance Section) made the domestic *Intervento Straordinario per il Mezzogiorno*, prior to its suppression, less relevant. For almost a decade, central and regional public administrations were not capable of effectively implementing the new European regional cohesion policy, although increasingly the domestic policy structure formally changed in order to accommodate European requirements. In fact, over the 1990s a full substitution of the 'old' policy with the new EU policy occurred but implementation required more time since in the transition period from a domestic policy to EU policy (1992–1998) 'great disorganization' prevailed within the central, ministerial public administration (interview).

On the implementation front, since the end of the *Intervento Straordinario*, a Regional Policy Observatory (*Osservatorio delle politiche regionali*) within the Treasury Ministry was created in 1993 and soon after (1995) transformed to a Coordination Room (*Cabina di Regia*), which was aimed at monitoring and coordinating the overall implementation of EU regional policy for which several ministries became sectorially responsible. The most important innovation, though, was introduced in 1998 when – within an overall organizational change at the Treasury – a dedicated department was created (*Dipartimento delle Politiche di Sviluppo e Coesione* – DPS), which took the lead with respect to policy coordination and implementation. The new department immediately became a crucial player in both policy formulation – helping the Italian government in turning from EU policy-taker to EU policy-adaptor in the policy field (see Chapter 2) – and policy implementation, facilitating institutional and policy adaptation. More specifically, the DPS took quite seriously the new EU policy structure principles and tried to assure better programming functions and partnership implementation. In fact, one of the first acts of the new department was to put together a report on territorial development, which took stock of the existing policies and tried to put forward a 'road map' that would enable the Italian central and regional governments to avoid losing EU funds – since the EU procedures required that expenditure took place during a given period (prior to the end of December 2001, in the case of the second programming period, 1994–1999). Together with an increase of the overall capacity of the funds managed at the ministerial level, pressure on greater regional performance was exerted by the ministerial team led by a former top bureaucrat of the Italian central bank (interviews). If compared to the previous programming period, the results obtained by the Italian government at the end of the second programming period were particularly impressive: although in comparative terms Italy did not stand out as a 'best performer', it had spent more than the Netherlands and not much less than the UK and Finland (see Figure 4.1 and Table 4.2).

94 *Europeanization and Italian regional cohesion policy*

Table 4.2 Financial execution by member state, 1994–1999.

Member State	Cumulative expenditure (%)
Belgium	71
Denmark	80
Germany	78
Greece	73
Spain	81
France	73
Ireland	87
Italy	63
Luxembourg	73
Netherlands	61
Austria	77
Portugal	89
Finland	65
Sweden	70
United Kingdom	66

Source: European Commission, *Relazione annuale sui Fondi Strutturali*, different years.

Furthermore, the overall new ministerial coordination capacities were also beneficial with regards to the acceleration of expenditure of EU funds that were managed at the regional level (Graziano 2004: 96).

In 1999, the Commission also praised the new expenditure capacities experienced by the Italian government, acknowledging the improved Italian performance. Although expenditure has also continued to be somewhat problematic in recent years, during the 2000–2006 period overall performance improved (Barca

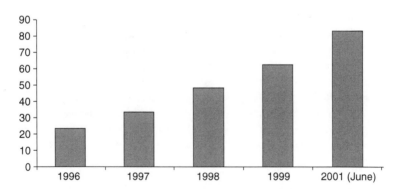

Figure 4.1 EU structural funds expenditure, Italy, 1996–2001* (source: author's calculation on Commission reports (various years) on structural funds expenditure in member states; *Ministero del Tesoro, Bilancio e Programmazione Economica* 2001: 256).

Note
* As for 2001, data refer exclusively to Objective 1.

2011: 33–34). However, in the implementation of the 2007–2013 programming period, the overall expenditure capacity was less satisfactory, especially with respect to the regional programmes (ibid.: 30–31), although the delay was primarily connected with conjunctural (budget uncertainties connected with the 2008–2009 crisis) rather than structural reasons – as in the case of 1989–1993 and the first implementation of the 1994–1999 period. Furthermore, at the central level overall administrative capacities were upgraded (unlike the *Cassa* period, the main implementing authorities of regional policy are ministries and regional governments) and the method of domestic expenditure data collection – which further differentiates among intermediate expenditure targets – and monitoring emphasizes the new administrative capacity attained by the Italian public authorities.

In sum, the domestic institutional innovations of the late 1990s provided better administrative capacities for implementing the new EU regional policy. Not only had the domestic policy structure radically changed in order to adapt to European requirements, but also institutionally the Italian government was in a better position to interact with the EU commission in the negotiation of the third programming period discussed between 1999 and 2001, acting as a policy-adaptor (since preference formation became better fixed and supported by domestic institutional and social actors, whereas policy bargaining capacities remained confined to the implementation dimension and the Italian government was not able to fully 'shape' the policy at the EU level) and not a passive policy-taker as had occurred in the past. Put another way, the policy misfit led to adaptational pressures, which were then translated into substantial (and not only formal) policy structure change and institutional innovations.

4.3 Mechanisms of Europeanization and political-institutional effects

If we focus on the mechanisms of Europeanization, with respect to cohesion policies two main mechanisms were in place: *imposition* and *non-formalized pressure*. Europeanization followed an imposition route since European regional policy was governed by regulations that were binding for all member states. More specifically, the introduction of a new level of government in cohesion policy paved the way for a hierarchical reorganization of multi-level interactions in the field of cohesion policy. Until the 1988 reform, supranational institutions (such as the Commission) were not capable of imposing their strategies on the member states because the allocation of powers in the multi-level setting was still clearly tipped in favour of member state governments. Since the reform, however, the overall situation has changed significantly because the Commission expanded its powers substantially due to its new binding programming role vis-à-vis member state governments (Marks *et al.* 1996). This power rebalance had overarching institutional effects: the 'imposition' of the new EU-based cohesion policy rules obliged the Italian government to create a new institution – the DPS discussed in the previous section – whose primary aim was (and still is) to interact with Commission officials in both policy formulation and implementation. Such institutional innovation also had substantial repercussions for the new coordinating role played by the Treasury with respect to the regional implementation of EU cohesion policy: even when EU policy implementation responsibilities were delegated to the regions, the DPS maintained a strong intermediating role between the regional and European levels. Furthermore, unlike the previous periods of domestic regional cohesion policy implementation, the government did not have complete freedom to draft its own preferences since they were constrained by (a) the other member state governments within the Council of Ministers; (b) the interpretation of the EU regional cohesion rules, which may not coincide with the reading desired by the governmental representatives. In the Italian case, even when – after the institutional change of the late 1990s – preference formation capacities increased, on several occasions negotiations with the Commission over technical, but relevant, policy details were not successful (for an example with respect to the Objective 2 territorial selection, see Gualini 2003). And this represents a further imposition on governments (in this specific case, on the Italian government) that goes beyond the already complicated regulation governmental negotiations that took place within the Council of Ministers. Therefore, in the case of cohesion policy, Europeanization involved both *political* (Council of Ministers level) and *administrative* (Commission) imposition.

The other mechanism that can be highlighted with respect to EU regional cohesion policy was *non-formalized pressure*. It was a more indirect mechanism, which went beyond mere adaptation to new EU policy requirements – as in the case of the above-mentioned regional policy. The Italian case is quite telling in this respect since other domestic regional policies, not directly involved with or connected to EU cohesion policies, changed their policy structure in order to be more in line with the prevailing EU approach. From 1986 – prior to the design and implementation of the reformed EU regional policy – Italian laws incorporated European objectives, principles and procedures. For example, the laws that completely ended the *Intervento Straordinario* experience (Laws 64/1986 and 488/92) continually referred to the European procedures and principles, and the same occurred with reference to the 'negotiated programming' initiatives that were launched in 1995 but 'refreshed' at the end of the 1990s when the European regional cohesion became a stable part of the Italian policy menu (Cocozza 1999). This Europeanization mechanism was clearly softer than the previous one since it was not directly linked to a piece of EU legislation, but it was strongly connected with the acknowledgement that the adoption of a European approach, even in relation to non-EU constrained policies, may be beneficial to governmental action. And this was precisely the case of innovative local development policies that gained further legitimation by being connected to EU policies. To a certain extent, the non-formalized pressure mechanism enabled EU institutions and policy ideas to have a greater impact – far beyond the formal reach of EU-regulated policies.

As regards the institutional effects triggered by Europeanization in relation to regional cohesion policy, all four dimensions have been concerned: executive–legislative, political parties–interest groups, centre–periphery and bureaucratic behaviour. First, the political and decision-making weight of the executive has increased significantly since the early 1990s. The upgrading of the institutional capacity of the Treasury (and then Economic Development, which currently hosts the DPS) has been accompanied by increasing formulation, coordination and implementation powers. Since the main package decisions are adopted at the EU level at which governmental representatives are the only domestic players, the preference formation and bargaining role of the legislative has been strongly limited. Whereas in the *Intervento Straordinario* Parliament had to vote on the multi-annual regional cohesion policy budget, currently the legislative can mainly be informed and discuss the regional cohesion policy budgetary decisions adopted at the EU level but not amend or radically change them. The budget decisions passed by Parliament are linked to overall domestic contribution to the EU, and therefore there is no political space left for the legislative to play a key role in the formulation of EU cohesion policy. The residual legislative powers are mainly Parliamentary scrutiny functions, which have also been exerted with respect to other European policies (for example, as already mentioned, between 1994 and 1996 a Parliamentary committee was set up in order to investigate the reasons for poor European regional cohesion policy expenditure in Italy and the debate provided further legitimation for the reorganization of the ministry aimed at increasing greater domestic institutional capacities in the formulation and implementation of the policy). In other words, the legislative is no longer capable of using relevant bargaining power with the aim of influencing one of the key features of regional cohesion policy – its budget – as it used to (although not on a yearly basis) during the *Intervento Straordinario* years.

Also with respect to the centre–periphery (e.g. regional) dimension, the power balance has changed over the past 20 years. This has occurred in both the policy formulation and implementation phases. Within the policy formulation phase, since the creation of the DPS an extensive concertation process – involving regional authorities – has been pursued by the ministry. Following the launch of the national initiative *Cento idee per lo sviluppo* (One Hundred Ideas for Development), a 'concertation' conference has been organized by the ministry in preparation for the domestic formulation of the new programmes that would have been funded under the 2000–2006 regional cohesion policy programme. Ever since, the regional governments have been involved in the formulation of the policy, although initially they were quite weak in forming fixed regional preferences due to the lack of experience in the field (interviews). Also in the domestic implementation phase a power rebalancing has occurred. One of the best indicators of such a process is the percentage of funds managed at the regional level with respect to the centrally managed funds. Since the 2000–2006 programming period, over 70 per cent of the total funds are managed by the regional governments and for the 2007–2013 period the share of regional expenditure has remained at the same level (interview). This reallocation of funds has offered new opportunities for the regions to become crucial actors in the formulation of regional development programmes. To be sure, not all regions were ready for the accomplishment of such a complex task: regional variation in expenditure capacities emerged in the early 2000s in relation to programming, coordination and implementation capacities (Milio 2007, 2008; Graziano 2010; interviews). Put another way, the outcomes from this reallocation of powers have differed in the various Italian (Southern) regions, but the overall process of power reallocation has been evident for all regional authorities since the early 2000s.

As a consequence of Europeanization, the ministerial bureaucracy also experienced significant changes. First, the creation of a new department and the recruitment of new bureaucrats in top positions with different professional profiles (economics and management specialists) from the traditional ministerial bureaucrats (holding generalist degrees such as law and political science; see also Mortara 1992) provided personnel change at the top level of the ministerial bureaucracy (interviews). Second, the organization of the department and the reallocation of administrative tasks within the ministry increased the effectiveness of targeted administrative actions performed by better qualified personnel. Furthermore, the European regional cohesion policy rules left very limited discretionary power to the political layers of the ministries (e.g. the ministers) and provided greater legitimation to the expertise provided by the bureaucrats (interview). Training initiatives were also implemented at the lower levels in order to upgrade the competences of the bureaucrats. For example, the RAP 100 programme was a governmental initiative aimed at increasing the administrative capacities of decentralized and regional public administration staff involved in the management of European cohesion policy. The programme provided assistance mainly to local authorities and paved the way for the recruitment of 'development agents' throughout the territories where the European regional cohesion policy was implemented. Another example is the SFERA programme, which offered training opportunities for young professionals who were interested in pursuing a career in public authorities managing the European regional cohesion policy both at the national and sub-national levels.

Finally, the traditional balance between political parties and interest groups in the field of cohesion policies was also challenged by the policy transformation induced by Europeanization. As mentioned previously, since 1965 (governmental) parties had become increasingly influential in the formulation of domestic cohesion policy by exerting the discretionary power available both within institutions (executive and Parliament, with the 'conformity rule' and the regional cohesion budget allocation votes) and without (during the implementation phases by influencing the decisions regarding the final allocation of cohesion policy resources). The new policy setting reduced the discretionary powers of the political parties, and enhanced – via the partnership principle – the role of interest groups. Until the late 1990s, virtually no major interest group had specific offices – and competences – dedicated to regional cohesion policy (interviews). From the early 2000s, all the major interest groups (trade unions such CGIL, CISL and UIL, and business associations such as *Confindustria*) but also interest groups previously even more marginalized (such as the institutional interest group ANCI, representing Italian municipalities, or environmental associations such as *Legambiente*) created specialized offices that could interact on a continuous basis with the key political authorities involved in European regional policy. Furthermore, also at the sub-national level the interest groups reorganized in order to become more effective in preference formation and negotiation at the regional level (interviews). To be sure, the main political parties also reorganized in order to increase their knowledge (and possibly influence) regarding policy formulation and implementation (interviews), but the partnership mechanisms supported by the European policy and implemented by the central domestic administration did not include political party representatives. For example, the 'programming sectorial and regional tables' that were created both at the national and regional levels did not include party representatives but did include interest groups. Some traditionally weak interest groups (such as environmental associations and third sector organizations) were included for the first time in policy formulation and over the years managed to increase their influence capacities at both national and regional levels. Put another way, the power balance between interest groups and political parties with respect to their capacity to (a) be included in European regional cohesion decision-making processes and (b) be influential in the processes has been reversed by Europeanization-induced policy change.

4.4 Europeanization and regional cohesion policy change in Italy: an overall assessment

Sixty years after its inception, Italian regional cohesion policy is now fully included within a wider European regional cohesion strategy. Domestic policy has changed significantly over the past 20 years, and change has gone in the direction supported by the European Union. In this chapter, we analysed the main features of the development of Italian regional cohesion policy and illustrated the growing interplay between the EU and domestic levels. We argue that the new Italian regional policy has been radically modified by Europeanization and its specific mechanisms – imposition and non-formalized pressure. As Table 4.3 illustrates, the current structure of the Italian cohesion policy fully conforms to EU policy.

Over the past 20 years, Italian governments have increasingly followed European objectives, principles and procedures and used EU financial instruments in order to try to reduce regional disparities throughout the country. The key objectives of domestic regional policy are those developed at the EU level – and also those policies that are not directly connected to the EU regional cohesion policy – that is, the principles of programming, partnership, additionality and concentration of interventions. EU-based procedures are adopted in the various phases of policy implementation and the key resources come from the EU budget. After a first phase of slow 'formal adaptation' (1992–1998), the pace of policy transformation accelerated (1998–2011).

Put another way, not only are the rules followed more strictly by the Italian government and the Italian regions and the overall expenditure capacity increased, but the *politics* of cohesion policy are also quite different from those prior to Europeanization. We will discuss the politics of policy transformation in

Table 4.3 Italian and EU regional cohesion policy structures: domestic evolution and policy transformation

	Italy (1945–1962)	Italy (1962–1992)	Italy (1992–2010)	EU (1989–2010)
Objectives	Socioeconomic development	Socioeconomic development	Overcome the 75% GDP per capita threshold in underperforming regions	Overcome the 75% GDP per capita threshold in underperforming regions
Principles	Geographic concentration	Geographic concentration Programming (residual)	Geographic concentration Programming Partnership Additionality	Geographic concentration Programming Partnership Additionality
Procedures	Standardized and automatic	Discretionary	Standardized and automatic	Standardized and automatic
Financial instruments	Domestic funds	Domestic funds (predominant) EU structural funds (residual)	Domestic funds (residual) EU structural funds (predominant)	Domestic funds (residual) EU structural funds (predominant)

greater detail in Chapter 6 when we will compare the three policy study objects of this study, but at this stage – following the analysis presented in this chapter – we can characterize the new Italian regional policy as a product of European regional policy, especially in its consolidated multi-level and inclusive nature. This holds true particularly with respect to the various interests that have a stake in regional cohesion policies – including both institutional (regions, provinces, municipalities) and non-institutional actors (social partners, non-profit organizations and environmental associations). The change witnessed within the cohesion policy field was neither rapid nor automatic. The institutional and political resilience to change was quite strong prior to 1992. As we will discuss in greater detail in Chapter 6, until the conclusion of the *Intervento Straordinario* implementing EU regional policy was politically inconvenient, at least according to the 'traditional' standards when public resource allocation was seen as a way to maintain political clients in order to consolidate or expand electoral consensus (Cafiero 1996). At the end of the 1990s, political actors still did not (want to) understand that standardization of the cohesion policy fund allocation could not easily be circumvented (interview). Especially in the 1980s, Italian regional cohesion policies were 'captured' by national and local politicians. As La Spina noted, from the 1960s 'not only did we register the failure and termination of the Intervento Straordinario, but more generally it emerged as a consolidation of increasing *subordination* of Southern economy and society to the national but especially local political élite' (2003: 252–253).

If we take a broader perspective, however, we realize that some of the most relevant policy features of the 'new' policy could be found in the first setting of the policy (1950–1965). To a certain extent, the European Commission is now playing a similar role to that played by the authority managing the *Cassa per il Mezzogiorno*, being somewhat external to the political dynamics of electoral competition that have governed for several years the functioning of Italian cohesion policy (1965–1992). Put another way, Europeanization has helped Italian regional policy return to its original configuration, although within an overall context of increased resources and complexity with respect to the past. Especially as regards policy procedures that characterized the first 15 years of Italian regional cohesion policy, European policy refreshed methods and approaches that had been developed only partially in the early days of the *Intervento Straordinario*. Therefore, in the long term we may consider the 1965–1998 period as a parenthesis between the original design and implementation of the Italian regional cohesion policy (with a sort of external, technical institution – the *Cassa per il Mezzogiorno* – that was in charge of policy implementation) and the most recent period (1998–2011) whereby national and regional implementation takes place within a supranational policy formulation and adoption. To be sure, the role played by the *Cassa* and the European Commission should not be confused: whereas the *Cassa per il Mezzogiorno* performed a key function in the policy implementation phase, the European Commission played a key role in policy formulation and design. There is some resemblance between them, however, since in both cases an overall shield against excessive partisan interference was created.

5 Europeanization and Italian employment policy

5.1 European employment policy

Unlike the other policies analysed in this book, employment policy was not at the heart of the early policy goals of the European Community. As Falkner very effectively summarized: in the 1960s 'the dominant philosophy was that welfare would be provided by the economic growth stemming from the economics of a liberalised market and not from the regulatory and distributive capacity of public policy' (1999: 84). Employment concerns increased over the years as a result of the 'permanent austerity' (Pierson 2001) faced by European economies since the mid-1970s and became central in EU decision making during the late 1990s. In the following subsections we will provide a summarized description of the main features of the evolution of European employment policy.

5.1.1 Facilitating workers' freedom of movement: 1960–1970

The first decade of European integration was marked by a poorly developed employment policy structure. As a result of domestic resistances to delegating powers over such a relevant policy that had been domestically managed over the previous decades, no autonomous specific goals were set out with respect to employment policy, the only 'derived' goal being connected to the creation of the common market and to the overarching objective of supporting individual (and therefore also workers') freedom of movement throughout the EU territory. No specific principles were adopted at the EU level and the only existing procedures were connected to the adoption and implementation of the financial instrument, the European Social Fund (ESF) – the only policy structure element available since the early 1960s. The ESF was introduced in 1960 but, as mentioned in the previous chapter, its scope was extremely limited since it could be exclusively used for unemployed workers' vocational training and travel expenses connected to the transferral of the (long-term) unemployed or underemployed workers to any European territory offering greater employment opportunities. The procedures connected to the management of the ESF provided an important implementation role for the Commission, since the European institution was in charge of implementing the allocation of funds, but the decisions regarding the beneficiaries were adopted at the central domestic level (Pavan Woolfe 1998). The main beneficiaries of the fund's allocations were countries where economic development had already been strong during the 1950s – e.g. Germany and France – but the main beneficiaries (65 per cent during the first ten years of ESF implementation) of the fund's expenditure were individuals of Italian citizenship who moved from 'underdeveloped' regions (in Italy) to 'developing' or fully developed regions (especially in Germany). To be sure, in the words of one of the Commission representative who was involved in the early phase of ESF management, 'the results obtained during this phase of the Fund [1960–1970] were limited in all countries, especially looking at Italy' (ibid.: 18, author's translation). In broader terms, one of the main limitations of employment policy in the early days of European integration was that there was no articulated employment policy (or strategy) and the few elements present at the time were fully subordinated to the common market creation goal and domestic decision making. In times of sustained economic growth, this limitation was overlooked but the policy answers changed once the overall economic situation deteriorated and unemployment started to become a severe challenge for European and domestic policy-makers. In sum, the only existing policy structure components in the 1960s were the financial instruments represented by the ESF resources and specific procedures connected to ESF allocation, whereas no other components of the policy structure – objectives, principles, procedures linked to an overarching European employment strategy – were developed at the EC level.

5.1.2 The rise of common employment concerns: 1971–1991

In 1970 the overall employment situation was not particularly worrisome. In some countries that were soon going to join the European organization there was full employment (as in the case of Denmark, with a 0.7 per cent unemployment rate) similar to other EU members (such as Germany with a 0.6 per cent unemployment rate), whereas the only country to have an unemployment rate that was more than double the other EC countries was Italy (5.3 per cent), soon joined by the new EU member Ireland (1973), whose unemployment figure was 5.8 per cent.

In 1971 the European institutions realized that, notwithstanding the implementation of common market policies, the employment disparities throughout the EC needed to be targeted via the enhancement of existing EC policies. The European Commission pressured for a reform of the ESF aimed at increasing the centrality of employment concerns in other EU policies, if not yet to develop a fully-fledged European employment strategy (Falkner 1999); more specifically, the decision adopted by the Council of Ministers (Decision 66/1971) provided greater power to the Commission in the implementation of the ESF, which would soon become completely managed by the Commission in both the programming and implementation phases. Prior to the 1971 decision, the Commission was mainly involved in reimbursing expenditure related to ESF programmes adopted by the member states; after 1971, the Commission would be involved much more strongly since it had 'the possibility to evaluate (...) the projects submitted and to define (...) objective selection criteria' (Pavan Woolfe 1998: 26–27, author's translation). Between 1973 and 1977, 90 per cent of the ESF budget was allocated to vocational training courses – although the overall ESF budget package was only 3 per cent of the EC budget.

During the 1970s, EU social concerns went beyond the ESF and also considered social assistance and industrial relations issues. In 1974 the first 'social action plan' was approved and inaugurated, the first (timid) attempt to move towards more comprehensive employment and social policies. The launch of the 'social action plan' was linked to the consideration that European social policy should have played a greater role in the overall EU policy menu by defining specific policies or at least by setting European objectives for domestic social policies, without trying to regulate in a uniform way social problems nor transferring at the EU level competences that could have been guaranteed more effectively at other levels of government.

Furthermore, also as regards industrial relations, the European level tried to become more relevant by launching tripartite *fora* (with the European representations of trade unions – European Trade Union Confederation, ETUC – and business associations – Union of Industrial and Employers' Confederation of Europe, UNICE, now Businesseurope) with the aim of helping to guarantee policy coordination among domestic employment policies and streamline them with the emerging, general EU goals. More specifically,

> [a] new tripartite institution was set up in 1970 to deal with employment issues: the Standing Employment Committee, composed of Ministers of Labour, the social partners and the Commission. The aim was to coordinate national employment policies and make them compatible with Community objectives; but it was ineffective because of the number of participants and the very formal character of its proceedings. Moreover the Ministers of Labour were reluctant to facilitate its functioning, believing that employment should remain a national prerogative. Four 'European Tripartite Employment Conferences' took place between 1975 and 1978 under pressure from the ETUC in a period when the economic situation was deteriorating. These were supposed to pave the way for a joint approach to economic and employment issues, but faded away through the lack of national follow-up measures and the negative attitude of UNICE.
>
> (Goetschy 1999: 118)

Clearly, the member state labour ministers were not ready to share further sovereignty with European institutions and business associations were not willing to reach agreements with the trade unions at the EU level (see also Falkner 1999: 86). Therefore, the 1970s were not marked by a full European employment strategy, although – especially in the 'social action plans' – several of the ingredients that would be at the heart of the future European Employment Strategy and the Open Method of Coordination were already laid out in this period.

The 1980s were years of increasing unemployment, but those affected were primarily the unemployed young and female population. Individual aspirations and family household restructuring (considered by Pierson (2001) as endogenous pressures to welfare states) had made the unemployment problem more acute than ever. The European Commission, especially since the Delors presidency (1985–1994), became substantially more involved in social and employment issues. In Goetschy's words, 'The European Social Dialogue was relaunched by Jacques Delors in 1985, involving regular meetings between the three social partner organizations which could agree non-binding joint opinions' (Goetschy 1999: 118). More specifically, first vocational training was also further promoted and funded at the EC level through a constant increase of the dedicated ESF resources; second, more intense discussions – if not true negotiations – were held among social partners and the Commission which managed to strike an agreement among the Commission, social partners and 11 member states (only the UK refused to sign it), which developed into the Community Charter of Fundamental Social Rights of Workers adopted in 1989. Although not formally binding, the Social Charter was the first relevant step towards the creation of a European social dimension, which would be substantially expanded during the 1990s. To be sure, since the Community Charter was not unanimously approved by the member states and was not legally binding, it basically consisted of a 'checklist' of principles that the member states could respect in their employment and social policy design but no coordination or evaluation powers were granted to the Commission. Such powers were provided only in the second half of the 1990s when the European Employment Strategy was crafted. In short, still in the late 1980s the EU employment policy structure was limited to financial instruments and related specific procedures, whereas no other component of the policy structure was adopted nor adequately supported by European institutions. The Community Charter was a mere declaration of principles, but was not linked to any specific EU public policy.

5.1.3 Building the European employment strategy: 1991–1997

Since the early 1990s, also due to the persistence of a growing concern over the capacities of EU member states to cope with higher levels of unemployment, the EU entered solidly into the scene with relevant subsequent actions aimed at developing a European employment strategy. Although formally the European Employment Strategy (EES) was launched at the 1997 Luxembourg Jobs Summit in September, in the literature there are different views on the birth of the EES. Some authors considered it to be launched in Essen in 1994 (Goetschy 1999), others look to the Employment Title contained in the Amsterdam Treaty in 1997 (Kenner 1999; Lönnroth 2000). Here, we suggest that the origins of the EES could already be traced in the annexation of the Community Charter to the Maastricht Treaty (under the form of the so-called Social Protocol) for two reasons: first, the annexation was a clear success of the Delors Commission, although it had not actually insisted on it and since the 1990s the EES can only be understood by making constant reference to the entrepreneurial role played by the Commission, supported by new member states (such as Sweden) that were in favour of the enhancement of a 'social Europe'; second, the 'Social Protocol' gave some coordination powers to the Commission, a similar procedure to the one then further institutionalized in the Amsterdam Treaty and in the conclusion of the Lisbon Summit (2000) with the launch of the Open Method of Coordination (OMC; de la Porte and Nanz 2004; Zeitlin and Pochet 2005). Furthermore, the adoption of the White Paper on 'Growth, competitiveness, employment' (the so-called 'Delors White Paper'; Commission 1993) by the Commission also contributed to opening a discussion on the role of European institutions in social policy fields – especially in employment:

> [T]he White paper (…) attempted to combine contradictory elements. (…) The ambition was to meet the convergence criteria for EMU, the implications of which were deflationary, and yet to achieve higher levels of employment. (…) The objective was to integrate employment policy with other policy issues (fiscal, social protections, environment, equality of opportunities for men and women, new family patterns, demographic change), linking Keynesian and supply-side economics.
>
> (Goetschy 1999: 120)

Furthermore, since the early 1990s the Commission had managed to increase the available ESF funds (also as a consequence of the 1988 regional cohesion policy reform discussed in the previous chapter) and increased its capacity to craft EU legislation (e.g. directives) regarding employment conditions and regulations such as European work councils (1994), part-time work (1997) and fixed-term work (1999; for further details, see Falkner 2000). Put another way, the Commission (and especially the Directorate General in charge of employment and social affairs, former DG IV) became a key motor in all the initiatives that were aimed at increasing European tools for employment and industrial relations issues. Since the early 1990s the Commission managed to obtain a key co-ordination position, although the main decisions adopted prior to the Amsterdam Treaty (1997) were very limited in scope. In short, although the Commission became more relevant over the years, by the mid-1990s there was still no fully-fledged comprehensive employment policy structure characterized by specific goals, principles, procedures and financial instruments – the only policy area where shared sovereignty occurred was vocational training.

5.1.4 *The consolidation of the European employment strategy: 1997–2010*

In 1997, the Employment Title introduced by the Amsterdam Treaty set a number of specific goals among which the most important was to pursue a high level of employment by committing the member states to the promotion of a skilled, trained and adaptable workforce. The Amsterdam Treaty also established a specific country surveillance procedure according to which member states' employment policies were examined through a yearly Joint Employment Report issued by EU institutions. Moreover, the Commission proposed, and the Council of Ministers yearly adopted, specific employment guidelines for the member states on the basis of which each member state developed national action plans for employment. Finally, the Commission could propose and the Council could adopt recommendations of selected member states. In this respect, the Luxembourg Jobs Summit of November 1997 anticipated the entry into force of the Treaty and further consolidated the emerging EES, developing four guiding pillars (or principles): employability, entrepreneurship, adaptability and equal opportunities. Specific goals were related to these principles:

> employability: within five years the member states should offer every young person within the first six months of unemployment an opportunity for training, retraining, work experience, or participation in an employment scheme; similar opportunities should be provided for adults within the first year. (...) entrepreneurship: member states should make it easier to start up and run businesses. (...) adaptability (...) social partners were invited to negotiate agreements at sectoral and company level designed to modernize work organization, make firms more competitive and ensure a better balance between flexibility and security for workers. (...) equal opportunities (...) with the aim of reducing discrimination against women in the labour market.
>
> (Goetschy 1999: 127)

By the end of the 1990s the profile of a fully-fledged policy structure was taking shape: principles were adopted, complex benchmarking procedures were set and the ESF continued to be the main financial instrument used for vocational training and domestic employment services reorganization. Yet, specific objectives were missing. The Commission had tried to include a 65 per cent employment rate EU objective and a 7 per cent EU unemployment target in the Luxembourg Summit conclusions, but the member states decided to avoid such quantified goals (ibid.: 128). Only in the Lisbon Special European Council (2000) was the overarching quantified goal an EU employment rate 'as close as possible to' 70 per cent.

Between 2000 and 2003, a midterm review and impact evaluation was carried out. This exercise illustrated (some) procedural strengths and (substantive) weaknesses of the overall process. According to the Commission (2002a), among the positive procedural aspects, the EES had created a common, integrated framework for structural reform, increasing especially the involvement of numerous actors at various levels of government (European, national, subnational). Greater focus was also put on the creation of 'more and better jobs' (Commission 2003), although towards the end of the 1990s – prior to the 1998 economic and financial crisis – it became quite clear that the EES was not going to meet its expectations. In fact, from a substantive point of view, the strategy did not seem to be as effective as expected, since regional differences in labour market performance remained significant and had become even wider in some member states. Furthermore, the implementation of the four pillars of the EES was uneven, and regional and local levels of administration were not participating in the overall process as expected (Commission 2002b). Finally, if we take a broader perspective,

> in the wider context of employment policy as a whole [...] the changes pale into insignificance compared with the short-term threats to employment posed by both global economic developments and risks, and the inability to reach agreement [...] on the reforms to endow Europe with an economic governance regime that would promote the output stability and growth that are needed to bring about a sustained rise in employment.
>
> (Watt 2004: 135)

Other critics have also emphasised that:

> the EES has been unable to promote 'quality in jobs' and, instead, pleads for the development of part-time and temporary jobs. Also, while praising Denmark and Sweden for their high levels of employment, the EES criticizes them for their high level of taxes and unemployment benefits. The coherence of these social and economic systems, which articulate social cohesion with economic efficiency, is not understood by the Commission and the Council.
>
> (Raveaud 2007: 430)

Put another way, the limited changes made to the European Employment Strategy were even more limited if compared with the increasing external challenges posed to employment creation. Furthermore, the apparently balanced European approach to employment issues suggested by the above-mentioned ambitious goal to link Keynesian and supply-side economics seemed by the end of the 1990s not to function properly, since 'the orientation of the EES can be understood as deriving from mainstream economics' (ibid.: 411) and not from a Keynesian–supply side economics compromise.

Summing up, between 1997 and 2010 (when the Lisbon 2020 Strategy – which will be discussed in the concluding chapter of this book – was launched), some procedural adjustments took place (such as 'streamlining the annual economic and employment policy coordination cycles'; Commission 2002b) in order to make the EES more coherent and coordinated with the annual economic guidelines. The substitution of annual national action plans for employment with triennial national reform programmes significantly reduced the length of the employment-focused documents with respect to the overall Growth and Employment Strategy. The Lisbon Strategy was also given a 'new start' with some substantive changes, within which three overarching objectives were introduced:

full employment, quality and productivity at work, cohesion and an inclusive labour market. But the overall policy structure did not change substantially since over the years only incremental changes – primarily limited to objectives and only partially to principles – occurred.

The key objective of the EES over the past 15 years has primarily been full employment (with quantified and standardized employment rate targets since 2000); its main principle – summarizing the four pillars – could be labelled flexibility and, since 2007 (Commission 2007), flexicurity with a particular emphasis on activation; the most important financial instrument was and continues to be the ESF; and the main standardized procedure is the Open Method of Coordination, which determines the periodic interactions among the various actors involved: Commission, Council, member state governments and social partners.

5.2 Italian employment policy

In order to provide a systematic illustration of the trajectory of domestic employment policy and its interplay with the EU guidelines, inspired by Clasen and Clegg (2011), we will focus on the three key components of employment policy: income protection, employment protection and employment services and training. First, income protection is aimed at providing *income maintenance*, e.g. the institutional configuration and protection level provided by the unemployment protection system; second, employment protection legislation is aimed at providing *job security*, e.g. labour market regulations, with a particular reference to hiring rules and employment protection legislation; third, employment services and training is aimed at supporting *employment opportunities*, e.g. measures aimed at providing the necessary skills to workers in order to ease their job inclusion or re-inclusion. Using the widely diffused OECD (Organisation for Economic Co-Operation and Development) classification, income protection regulations can be considered as passive policies, whereas the others may be considered as the most relevant active policies.

As regards income protection, comparing the Italian system of unemployment benefits with those of other European countries illustrates some of the long-lasting features of the country. In most EU members states income protection is organized around three pillars: *unemployment insurance* (UI) – a contributory scheme, providing earnings-related benefits with a maximum duration; *specific unemployment assistance* (UA) – a non-contributory scheme for the unemployed who either do not fulfil contributions requirements sufficiently to be entitled to first-pillar benefits or are no longer entitled to ordinary benefit; and *general social assistance* (SA) – which operates as a safety net by guaranteeing a minimum or basic income (ISFOL 2002).

Combining these policy-specific analytical lenses with the more general policy structure lense presented in Chapter 1, in the following sections we will provide a description of the evolution of Italian employment policy and its interplay with the emerging EES.

5.2.1 The development of the Italian policy structure: 1945–1968

In a nutshell, traditional Italian employment policy has relied on: (a) a limited universal first pillar scheme (income protection) and special programmes introduced in 1949 providing 'short-term compensation benefits' in the case of temporary working-time reduction without definitive dismissal (*Cassa integrazione guadagni ordinaria e straordinaria – CIGO*) – the comprehensive second (UA) and third (SA) pillar schemes for the most disadvantaged groups were never set; and (b) increasing employment protection – though limited to 'insiders', a problem that would become crucial with the emergence of numerous 'outsiders' from the 1980s and mid-siders from the 1990s (Jessoula *et al*. 2010) – and increasing comprehensive (albeit often ineffective) public employment services and training opportunities.

As regards employment benefits, the ordinary unemployment benefit, UB (*Indennità ordinaria di disoccupazione*), was introduced in 1919 for blue-collar workers and subsequently extended to all other categories of dependent worker. This scheme has always been financed through contributions, and benefits have traditionally been very low, though varying significantly across economic sectors. The high level of income protection in case of job loss for the 'insiders' – i.e. workers in central and unionized sectors of the economy, employed in medium and large firms – was also reinforced by employment protection legislation that supported 'guaranteed' employment (e.g. high employment protection). The only policy innovation introduced in 1962 – that allowed fixed-term contracts – was limited to 'seasonal' workers, who constituted a marginal part of the working force and therefore did not alter the main features of the overall employment protection legislation. On the employment services and training front, the post-Second World War period was characterized by the provision of a public monopoly over employment services – which limited employers' ability to choose workers and proved to be mostly ineffective (Ichino 1982) – and the lack of a well-organized system of higher level vocational training. Only one specific subsidized employment contract type was introduced, in 1955 (Law 25/1955 – apprenticeship contract – *contratto di apprendistato*), which provided 'on the job' training opportunities to workers, typically the young and inexperienced (Gualmini 1998).

Therefore, in the first period of the evolution of Italian employment policy the income protection system in case of unemployment was aimed at primarily supporting the 'insiders', who could also rely on both a high level of job security, due to an overall high degree of protection in employment legislation terms, and a rewarding system of 'short-term compensation benefits' for income replacement in case of unemployment. Between 1945 and the late 1960s, overall employment policy was not severely challenged because the overall unemployment rate was low, the main mode of job inclusion being through a standard contract and the overall economic situation was still booming.

If we adopt the policy structure analytical lense, the overall objectives of the first 20 years of the post-Second World War Italian employment policy were full employment (although no specific targets were set in this respect); the guiding principle was security (in terms of employment protection legislation); the procedures were very limited and automatic because they were primarily related to employment services and not fully structured training services, whereas 'short-term benefits – not provided on an automatic basis – were residual; and the financial instruments were specific national funds primarily aimed at supporting income protection of the unemployed through unemployment benefits and CIGO benefits.

Focusing on the institutional features of employment policy, as a result of the limited political salience of employment policy issues, the analysed period was characterized by an overall power balance between the executive and the legislative because policy implementation was exclusively in the hands of the executive and the legislature had great room for manoeuvre in the adoption phase of the policy process. Furthermore, the policies were fully centralized, because employment services and training – and not only unemployment benefits management and employment protection legislation – were also a prerogative of the central government (and legislature). With respect to the power balance between various interests, between 1945 and 1968 business association interests prevailed over workers' interests since they managed to positively interact with the most representative party both in the executive and in the legislature (the Christian Democratic party; see Mattina 1991) and the trade unions were particularly weak during this period (Reyneri 1990; Feltrin 1991; Carrieri 1995). Parties were capable of maintaining great autonomy in decision making, remaining unchallenged crucial actors in the executive and in the legislative and greatly controlling interest groups (Morlino 1991a: 484). Finally, the overall orientation of the bureaucratic personnel – who performed limited functions within a context of undemanding employment policy implementation and an overall low unemployment rate – was limited to controlling the fulfilment of unemployment benefit requirements and therefore not focused on specific targets of unemployed 'activation' (Graziano 2004).

5.2.2 The rise and fall of workers' enhanced protection: 1968–1983

From the second half of the 1960s, employment policy was embedded within a political and social context. The intense trade union movement protests between 1968 and 1975 determined greater interest group representation and improved capacity to shape the agenda and policy formulation of the Italian government. The 1968 (Law 115) introduction of the 'extraordinary' CIGO (*Cassa integrazione guadagni straordinaria – CIGS*) and the adoption of the Workers' Statute (*Statuto dei Lavoratori*) in 1970 were signs of the increased power of worker representation (Regalia 1984; Romagnoli 1995). The overall consequences of these policy changes were the further consolidation of an employment policy that protected 'insiders' from dismissal (CIGO and CIGS) and unionization rights in the workplace that went beyond mere worker contractual agreements (Romagnoli 1995: 156). These indisputable trade union successes, though, developed within an overall deteriorating context of employment opportunities. On the one hand, the first post-Second World War economic turbulence hit Europe (the first and second oil crises; see Graziani 2000) and, on the other hand, the expectations of the new entrants – young, trained and increasingly female – into the employment world increased the unemployment rate by almost 50 per cent, from 5.3 per cent in 1970 to 7.5 per cent in 1980. By the second half of the decade, the policy salience of employment increased dramatically and some policy changes that were not in favour of trade union interests were adopted. The decline in enhanced worker protection had started.

First, a new policy targeted on the younger population was approved in 1977 (Law 285): a 'training' non-renewable contract (*contratto di formazione*) of limited duration (maximum two years) was introduced aimed at facilitating the job inclusion of young people between 15 and 26 years of age (29 for female workers and graduates). The approval of the 'training' features was delegated to a tripartite regional authority wherein the recently created regional governments sat together with trade unions and business association representatives. Nevertheless, due to the constraints connected to the unchanged placement mechanisms (nominal recruitment was still prohibited), the effectiveness of the policy was extremely limited (Cadeddu and Midena 2000). Furthermore, on those occasions when the new contract was adopted, similar to the case of apprenticeship contracts, since no sanctions were foreseen for employers who did not implement the training component of the contract, the overall result was that a less-costly contract was available for employers – and often no training activities were guaranteed. It must be noted, however, that – at least in principle – the training component of the contracts was funded jointly by domestic (national and/or regional) and European (ESF) funds. It was a first (timid) sign of the 'penetration' of European resources in domestic vocational training policies.

Second, a further opportunity for dismissal was approved by Law 675/1977, which was aimed at facilitating worker job transition or mobility via specific incentives. The law was not successfully implemented, not as the result of poor administrative capacities (as in the case of public employment services), but rather due to the complex procedures envisaged by the regulation that did not set specific criteria regarding the formation of the so-called mobility lists (*liste di mobilità*), which ultimately tended to be made up of 'undesirable' people such as the elderly, the sick and trade union activists (Reyneri 1987: 165). Therefore, although conceived as a policy mix aimed at supporting job transition by also guaranteeing income protection, the law turned out to be ineffective within the overall context of unemployment growth.

Third, vocational training was radically reformed. Law 845/1978, following the creation of the regional authorities, delegated vocational training competences to the regions – as foreseen in the Italian constitution (Article 3). Vocational training is particularly relevant for our purposes since it reveals a first sign of the institutional redefinition of competences in employment policies and it involves a greater role for European financial instruments – namely, the ESF. In fact, the administrative capacities proved to be quite well differentiated with respect to implementing vocational training policies (ISFOL 2002), the regional authority role was limited to 'co-implementation' since the main guidelines and funds still had a centralized (e.g. governmental) origin but the available ESF resources started to enter permanently into the domestic policy structure – although only as regards vocational training.

The first years of the new decade were still characterized by the consequences of the second oil shock, which had created severe occupational problems: in 1980 the unemployment rate was 7.5 per cent whereas in 1983 it rose to 9.4 per cent, and the employment rate slightly decreased from 56.2 to 55.7 per cent. The decade opened with large firms in severe crisis and a subsequent reduction of jobs. The case of FIAT – one of the most important Italian companies – is of particular interest: in 1980 the 'company crisis' was announced and more than 20,000 workers benefited from a CIG programme. The trade unions (with the support of the Italian Communist Party) tried to react and mobilize FIAT workers, but after 35 days the occupation of the biggest FIAT plant (Mirafiori) had to stop: a decisive 'march of the 40,000' FIAT cadres who wanted to 'go back to work', in opposition to the workers on strike and in support of FIAT's management goals, made clear that the times were changing and no further trade union protest was going to prevent the company's management implementing job reduction strategies (for further details, see Revelli, 1989).

The crisis faced by large firms determined also the crisis of the trade unions that were particularly active in those firms. Initially, the government responded to the problematic situation through the expansion of already existent income maintenance programmes and, like the French and German governments, managed the rising unemployment in large companies with the adoption of a new piece of legislation (Law 155/81), aimed at subsidizing exit from work through early retirement benefits. The 'early retirement' law gave male workers aged over 55 and female workers aged over 50, dismissed by large industrial companies, the right to an 'earlier' access to retirement. As a result of the great success of the policy measure, the law – originally valid only for 1981 – was extended to the 1990s and remained part of Italian legislation for over two decades (Gualmini 1998). The trade unions retreated and enhanced protection for workers was ended: the workers who benefited from Law 155/81 were among the last to benefit from the intense post-1968 trade union successes.

Summing up, during the 1968–1983 period 'insiders' remained at the core of income and employment protection guaranteed by Italian legislation, whereas no step forward with respect to social assistance was taken. Nevertheless, 'outsiders' became increasingly relevant because the unemployment rate grew significantly and the oil crises had also created severe problems for small and medium enterprises that did not benefit substantially from the CIG and CIGS unemployment benefit systems, which were targeted primarily at big companies. Overall employment legislation protection remained high, although the cost of dismissals via pre-retirement or mobility policies was supported by public budgets. The vocational training system was reformed and decentralized, which provided more (but still limited in diachronic perspective) powers to regional authorities.

In terms of policy structure changes, the key objective remained full employment (still no better specified and nor were unemployment rate targets); the key policy principles remained security – although it became increasingly costly for both companies and the public budget; the policy procedure became somewhat discretionary because of the increased use of the CIGO and CIGS and the new laws introduced throughout the decade; and the financial instruments came from both central government and the European Community via the ESF.

As regards institutional features, the centrality of the government was reduced because legislative production became much more relevant than in the past: new fundamental laws were adopted (CIGS, Workers' Statute, Training Contract, etc.) and sincee the legislature was the key actor in passing the laws the government primarily co-managed – together with the specialized social security agencies such as INPS (*Istituto Nazionale per la Previdenza Sociale*) – the implementation of the existing employment policies. The government was also challenged as a unitary actor since the deterioration of the economic situation and the accentuation of the crises faced by companies made prime ministerial offices and the economic and budget ministries more relevant than that for employment and social affairs (Reyneri 1990). Furthermore, notwithstanding the decentralization process – especially as regards vocational training policies – the overall employment policy was still primarily managed at the central level since crises faced by companies were primarily discussed (and solved) at the central and not the regional level. Also with respect to employment services, competences remained centralized because regional authorities were still in the making and therefore not fully prepared to cope with an occupational and economic crisis such as that which hit European countries at the end of the 1970s. Although by the end of the analysed period the trade unions had lost some of the bargaining power that had characterized their actions between the late 1960s and early 1970s, the assessment of the overall power balance for this period is favourable to union interest, especially if evaluated in a diachronic perspective: neither prior to this period nor later would the trade unions be so powerful in relation to business associations. During this period, political parties lost some of their grip on interest groups, which were somehow imposing their political agenda on Parliamentary debates.

Finally, the (central) bureaucracy was not significantly challenged in its traditional functioning since the main tasks regarding employment policy remained similar to those of the previous period and therefore no reorientation towards 'management by objectives' occurred during 1968–1983. Changes in administrative behaviour were still to come.

5.2.3 Partial deregulation for 'outsiders' and income security maintenance for 'insiders': 1983–1992

The mid-1980s were characterized by an overall amelioration of the economic situation but the same cannot be said with reference to the occupational situation. The increase in unemployment, due also to the continuous entry of women and skilled young potential workers into the world of employment, made it impossible to simply rely on short-/medium-term interventions and on income support subsidies that had been designed for standard contracts applied in large companies. Especially in the Southern part of Italy, it became increasingly clear that there was a need to change overall employment policy strategies in order to expand the productive capacity of firms and foster job creation. To pursue such ambitious goals, the idea of a new social agreement among interest groups was launched by the government. In 1983 the national trade unions, the national employers' associations and the Ministry of Labour signed an important social pact that gave birth to Law 79/83. The outcome of the negotiation was a complex political exchange involving income, fiscal and incentive policies. Fiscal policy had to tackle the effects of inflation, income policy had to slow down the dynamic of labour costs, and tax relief (especially on social security contributions) had to gain employers' approval (Ferrera *et al.* 2000). Furthermore, companies were allowed to directly hire up to 50 per cent of their workers. This was a clear break with the past when – at least formally – companies could not directly hire workers but had to hire those who were on the unemployed list managed by the public employment services.

The 'concerted' action of 1983 was followed by an attempt to strike a second social agreement among various actors (national governments and social partners, in particular the three most important trade unions: the CISL, UIL and CGIL). Because of the increasing conflict between the various trade unions and left-wing parties (on one side were the Socialist Party – led by Prime Minister Craxi – and CISL and UIL; on the other side were the Communist Party and the communist and socialist trade union – CGIL) the agreement failed. Given the reluctance of the communist party to reach an agreement with the socialist party, the Prime Minister Craxi decided to reduce wage indexation with the so-called *Decreto di S. Valentino* (which later became Law 863/84). Although various trade unions interpreted and responded to them differently, new flexible employment contracts for young workers (*contratti di formazione e lavoro*) and work-sharing, part-time and solidarity contracts (*contratti di solidarietà*) were introduced. The aim was to stimulate the creation of employment opportunities for 'outsiders', in particular women and the young unemployed, and at the same time reduce the costs of standard contracts via the elimination of automatic indexation.

More specifically, the *contratti di formazione e lavoro* reformed the 1977 law that had already introduced the training contracts (*contratti di formazione*) and presented a related idea: a non-renewable two-year contract that could be adopted by companies that had not dismissed workers in the previous 12 months. These contracts were widely used by companies because overall conditions were particularly favourable in economic terms and the training could be organized 'in-house'; however, this meant that the training component of the contract was implemented without any external control and therefore was often either not guaranteed or guaranteed only partially.

Also part-time contracts were introduced and deregulated since it was left to the companies to determine which percentage of employees could benefit from such contracts. Although the contract did respond to some specific needs of the new (young and female) labour force, the contract was not widely diffused since it was particularly costly in relative terms with respect to full-time contracts and also because it required an overall company reorganization that was little appreciated by both public and private companies (Gualmini 1998).

The solidarity contract was also introduced with the aim of limiting collective dismissals in large companies and was implemented in a 'concerted' way because the contract could be issued only after a preliminary agreement between the company and the most representative trade unions was reached. The solidarity contract was not particularly diffused until the early 1990s, when – after a reform that will be discussed in the next section – due to increased company needs and the aggravation of the economic crisis the usefulness of such a contract type was better appreciated by both employers and workers.

The new 'activation' trend was further followed by other two important laws under new Employment Minister Gianni De Michelis, which gave greater consideration to the emerging European context (let us recall that between 1985 and 1987 the Single European Act was negotiated) and adopted a ten-year employment plan that took into account in a more comprehensive way the challenges posed by the new economic situation that was developing within the EU. One of the key points raised in the ten-year plan was 'entrepreneurship': in a brief chapter by De Michelis in an edited volume, significantly entitled 'Job(s) can be created. Entreprise and Work: Job Creation in Europe', the minister underlined the relevance of considering Italian employment creation challenges within the emerging EU guidelines by also suggesting the creation of a European Employment Fund, which could have been central in the creation of an European employment strategy – 12 years prior to the official launch of the EES (AA.VV. 1986).

The first law that attempted to deal with job creation was Law 44/1986, aimed at supporting young entrepreneurs (between 18 and 29 years of age), especially in the Southern regions of the country. Incentives were not granted to all the business plans submitted, but only to those selected by a specific external selection committee that evaluated the sustainability of the entrepreneurial project. Furthermore, it was the first law that considered the monitoring and evaluation of a project as central in the implementation phase – in line with the emerging regional cohesion policy procedures, especially with respect to ESF resources.

Another policy reform was introduced in 1987 (Law 56), which further deregulated employment protection legislation and introduced changes in the organization of the monitoring of company employment requirements by introducing regional employment observatories aimed at producing and elaborating detailed information on employment and employer need trends. Also the ministry was supposed to produce annual reports on the evolution of employment trends using the data provided by the regional observatories. The law also contained a specific 'benchmarking' reference to the use of such procedures in other EU countries (Article 8), inferring that if such a practice was adopted (successfully) elsewhere it would also be beneficial to the Italian employment policy governance system.

The 1990s saw the enactment of Law 223 (1991). According to this law, employers could directly select employees to hire, whereas in the past (as already mentioned, at least formally) severe limitations were placed on this procedure. Although this procedure already existed in practice, such decisions consolidated the 'activation' and employability trend that had already emerged at the end of the 1980s. Furthermore, and even more importantly with respect to income protection purposes, a new scheme was introduced: the mobility benefit. This benefit was extremely important because, unlike the ordinary and special short-term wage replacement benefits (CIGO and CIGS), it was aimed at dismissed workers and was supposed to help them transition (due to a two-year, or in some cases four-year, transitional period) from one job to another. The new benefits were (and still are) provided in the case of collective dismissals by firms that are eligible for benefit from the CIGS and in the case of individual dismissal of workers already in the CIGS. Also, such benefits are usually limited to collective dismissals in the manufacturing sector, excluding small firms. This new benefit covered 100 per cent of the CIG's short-term wage replacement benefit for 12 months and 80 per cent for other years. Its duration varies according to the age of the worker and the region where the firm's plant is based: under specific conditions, it could last up to 48 months, meaning that in some cases workers might be entitled first to the CIG(S) and then for the mobility benefit for a period of a maximum of eight years.

In terms of policy principles, the mobility allowance represented quite a change because – unlike the CIGO and CIGS, which were considered temporary benefits for workers formally still employed – the mobility allowance was granted to workers who were technically considered dismissed and had no chance of being reintegrated into their previous job. As Fargion noted:

> Law 223 is couched in the language of supply-side adjustments and touches on the basic elements that make up the workfare logic. By discouraging the passive collection of benefits and promoting unemployed workers' 'employability' emphasis has clearly shifted to reintegrating the unemployed into the workforce as swiftly as possible.
>
> (2002: 6)

In short, because of increasing unemployment pressures and the context of the crises faced by large firms, the policy reforms followed a path that combined recalibration of old measures aimed at ensuring continuity in the protection of 'insiders' and a (very timid) start at adopting new policies aimed at providing new opportunities for 'outsiders' and the increasing mid-siders – which in the 1980s were still primarily workers in small and medium enterprises not benefiting from the available income protection schemes targeted at workers in large companies. Furthermore, although a European strategy had not yet developed, in the mid-1980s increasing references to European (if not EU) practices were made, especially in the 1986 and 1987 laws. The overall policy structure remained anchored to generic objectives (full employment) and the overall guiding principle remained job security (for insiders). However, entrepreneurship (e.g. job creation) also started to become a new policy principle, at least with respect to the still somewhat limited laws targeted at 'outsiders'. The procedures remained discretionary when applied to the most relevant income protection measures (CIGO and CIGS), whereas more automatic and standardized procedures were adopted with respect to the 'young entrepreneurship' programmes. Finally, an increasing role was played by the ESF resources within the implementation of training programmes, although the resources aimed at guaranteeing income protection (which were predominant in the overall public expenditure on employment policies) were still domestic funds.

The overall income protection schemes were not altered during this period, although in the industrial sector the unemployment subsidy was calculated as a percentage of previous earnings only after 1988, and the replacement rate was extremely modest – e.g. 7.5 per cent at the end of the 1980s. This measure regarded an important component of what we have labelled the mid-siders, e.g. those workers employed in small and medium enterprises, which were typically non-unionized. Instead, insiders could benefit from the CIGO and CIGS schemes, which provided high wage replacement – 80 per cent of last wage – in the case of (partial or total) working-time reduction without definitive dismissal. However, these schemes covered only about 40 per cent of dependent workers (Geroldi 2005), mostly employed in large companies in the industrial sector and the provision of these benefits continued to follow a bargaining process among the government, unions and employers.

From an institutional perspective, the executive gained predominance over the legislative with respect to the previous period (for example, in bargaining with social partners in the formulation of policy reforms) but Parliament was still crucial in adopting the laws and therefore the overall power balance was even. Although the above-mentioned reform regarding the creation of regional employment observatories did offer more evaluating powers to regional authorities, the overall centralized employment policy decision-making process was not substantially altered; political parties (both majority and opposition) became central to decision making once more; and the power balance between business associations and trade unions, after the defeats of the latter between 1984 and 1985, was increasingly favourable to business associations. Political parties became more relevant than in the previous period since legislation between 1983 and 1992 was particularly intense and controversial. As regards bureaucratic orientation, because the overall policy menu was not altered substantially by activation measures bureaucratic behaviour remained in line with the previous period since only the job creation policy adopted by Law 44/1987 was particularly demanding in terms of performance-based administrative capacities, whereas the other did not require a 'management by objective' bureaucratic orientation.

In short, the second part of the 1980s and the early 1990s represented an important decade with respect to employment policies since new active and flexible policy measures were introduced. In general, however, these innovations were very limited and did not change the overall structure of employment policy – which remained orientated in favour of 'insiders' – nor did they contribute to the reduction of unemployment or an increase in the employment rate. The European dimension timidly became part of the cognitive framework of some of the key decision-making actors (for instance, in the promotion of active employment policies such as vocational training and specific policy provisions targeted at the young unemployed – such as Law 44/1986). In institutional terms, the most significant change concerned the role of the government: from a mediator role, the government (in particular, the Craxi government) tried to foster a more autonomous 'policy proposition' capacity that created some upset in the trade unions. But no significant administrative change took place in the employment policy area. As a result, the existing system of short-term wage replacement benefits helped to reduce the collateral effects of the industrial restructuring that took place in those years, and at the same time the new active policy measures remained institutionally timid, poorly implemented and not systematically funded (Ferrera *et al.* 2000).

European ideas became an increasingly important point of reference – as the 1986, 1987 and 1991 laws demonstrate. In the words of former minister, De Michelis:

> [T]he occupational situation in Italy, the opportunities for a re-equilibrium of our labour market, the choices that the system will have to make in the near future, locate the economic problems of our country in the broader context of Europe. Political, economic and social reasons justify the inclusion of the debate regarding the Italian labour market, and more in general the various economies of the European states, in a broader conceptual frame where the various [employment] systems are placed in a unitary European dimension.
>
> (AA.VV. 1986: 201)

It seems therefore quite clear that the European cognitive framework supported the inclusion of an 'activation' approach in the Italian policy menu. And, European policies being very limited at that time (especially with respect to the income protection dimension), such a framework did not promote a significant reform of the system of unemployment benefits – which remained very similar to its original configuration of the late 1940s – but rather introduced some 'activation' and marginal evaluation features that would then be reinforced after the launch of the EES in 1997.

5.2.4 Adapting to the European employment strategy (1992–2010): between policy adjustment and policy transformation

In general, the 1990s were an extremely active decade, characterized by important reforms in the employment policy field (Treu 2001; Tiraboschi 2006; see Table 5.1).

Table 5.1 Major changes in employment policy regulation and unemployment benefits, 1990–2008

Law no. 223/1991	• introduction of a new unemployment benefit scheme: *indennità di mobilità* (mobility allowance) targeted to dismissed workers already covered by *CIGS* (workers of big firms mainly in the industrial sector). It provides generous benefits (replacement rate: 80 per cent) for 12 months (extendable to 48 months with a consequent reduction of the replacement rate of the subsidy).
Law no. 236/1993	• ordinary unemployment benefit: replacement rate increased to 25 per cent of previous wages, but duration (six months) and eligibility requirements (at least two years of insurance seniority and contributions paid for at least 52 weeks in the two years prior to unemployment) unchanged.
Law no. 451/1994	• ordinary unemployment benefit: replacement rate increased to 30 per cent of previous wages, but duration (six months) and eligibility requirements (at least two years of insurance seniority and contributions paid for at least 52 weeks in the two years prior to unemployment) unchanged.
Law no. 196/1997	• introduction of new flexible measures of labour contracts (i.e. temporary work) and expansion of previously existing flexible measures (part-time, apprenticeship and continuous collaboration contracts). Furthermore, a reorganisation (i.e. re-launch) of vocational training is regulated by the Law.
Law no. 388/2000 (2001 budget law)	• ordinary unemployment benefit: replacement rate increased to 40 per cent of previous wages; duration increased to nine months for workers aged 50 and over (it remained six months for the under-50); eligibility requirements (at least two years of insurance seniority and contributions paid for at least 52 weeks in the two years prior to unemployment) unchanged.
Law no. 30/2003 and L. Decree 276/2003	• introduction of new flexible contracts (project, job on call, etc.) and further promotion of part-time contracts.
Law no. 80/2005	• ordinary unemployment benefit: replacement rate increased to 50 per cent of previous wage for the first six months (40 per cent for the following three months and 30 per cent for the remaining months), duration increased to seven months for workers under-50 and to ten months for workers over-50, eligibility requirements unchanged.
Law no. 247/2007 (2008 budget law)	• ordinary unemployment benefit: duration increased to eight months for the under-50 and 12 months for the over-50, replacement rate increased to 60 per cent of previous wage for the first six months (50 per cent for the following two months in the case of the under-50 and 50 per cent for the following three months and 40 per cent for three months in the case of over-50), eligibility requirements unchanged
	• unemployment benefit with reduced eligibility (*indennità di disoccupazione a requisiti ridotti*): replacement rate increased to 35 per cent of previous year daily average wage for the first 120 days, 40 per cent for the following, maximum duration increased to 180 days, eligibility requirements unchanged (at least two years of insurance seniority and at least 78 days of work in the year).

Source: Jessoula *et al.* 2010: 573.

If the 1980s were characterized by some changes (in particular, with respect to the principles and, to a limited extent, the procedures of the overall policy structure), during the 1990s the policy change was even more evident. Change occurred in the following directions (Graziano 2007): (a) increase in ordinary unemployment benefits and contextual restriction of 'unemployed' status (Law 236/93, Law 388/2000, Law 80/2005, Law 247/2007); (b) creation (1994) of the social useful jobs programme (*Lavoratori socialmente utili*); (c) decentralization (and progressive privatization) of employment services (Legislative Decree 469/97); and (d) introduction of new flexible contracts (Law 196/97, Law 30/2003).

First, ordinary unemployment insurance benefit was raised to 25 per cent of the previous wage of the unemployed, substituting the previous predetermined daily allowance benefit. It was still not in line with other European countries, but nevertheless its augmentation began and would continue in following years; currently it replaces up to 50 per cent of the average gross earnings received over the last three months. After 1999 the benefit was no longer provided in the case of voluntary dismissal of the worker, and in 2000 a redefinition of the status of 'unemployed' occurred. According to Legislative Decree 185/2000, in order to be entitled to unemployment benefit, the unemployed had to cooperate with the new employment services, be available for informative interviews and participate in recommended vocational training courses. Therefore, on the one hand, some activation principles were introduced in the Italian policy setting but, on the other hand, an adjustment in the replacement rate (more in line with the other European countries) was guaranteed to the unemployed.

In 1994, an already existing policy instrument aimed at combating long-term unemployment was reformed: the Useful Social Jobs (*Lavori socialmente utili* – LSU). The LSU programme, first introduced in 1981, consisted of specific insertion programmes, created by the government and sub-national authorities, which lasted for a maximum of 12 months and required a part-time job (20 hours weekly) and a net wage of about €450. Originally considered an 'active measure' of insertion in the labour market, the programme turned into a masked 'social assistance scheme' (Fargion 2002; Barbier and Fargion 2004). The number of LSU workers rose to almost 150,000 in 1999, when a new 'stabilization' programme aimed at the creation of small LSU cooperatives made the programme move towards an end.

Another feature of the 1990s was the further decentralization of employment services: since 1997 sub-national authorities (regional and provincial) had become relevant actors in the implementation of employment policies. In addition, the same law gave the opportunity to private firms to manage employment services, widening the number of employment service actors and de facto opening an employment services market. Therefore, a new multi-tiered governance of employment policy was emerging: income protection and employment protection legislation was still provided at the national level, whereas employment services and vocational training were increasingly delegated to sub-national authorities.

122 Europeanization and Italian employment policy

Furthermore, the introduction of new flexible or 'atypical' contracts (in particular, temporary and other non-standardized work contracts) and the relaunch of part-time work were among the most recent employment protection legislation reforms approved by the Italian governments. First, until 1997 temporary work was illegal in Italy; only following the so-called Treu (taken from the name of the Employment minister) reform under the centre-left coalition were such contracts made possible. Over five years several multinational (as well as 'purely' Italian) temporary work agencies grew constantly and, according to the Ministry of Employment and Social Affairs, currently over 1,000 agencies are operating in Italy (for further details on the 'take-off' of temporary employment agencies in Italy, see Nannicini 2006). Furthermore, after the Treu reform the subsequent Biagi (named after the labour law consultant who actively collaborated on drafting the law) reform – Law 30/2003 – further increased the number of non-stardardized contracts, making employment legislation for temporary work much more flexible than in the past (see Figure 5.1).

It is also useful to mention that both reforms were in line with the 'European' flexibility imperative (as already argued, the guiding principle for the first ten years of European Employment Strategy) and fostered similar flexibility principles (Accornero 2006), although the governments that approved them were different: centre-left (Treu reform) and centre-right (Biagi reform). Finally, especially since the discussion of the *White Book on Employment* (*Ministero del Lavoro e delle Politiche Sociali* 2001), the overall objectives of the Italian employment policy fully embraced the standardized European objective of a 70 per cent total employment rate by 2010.

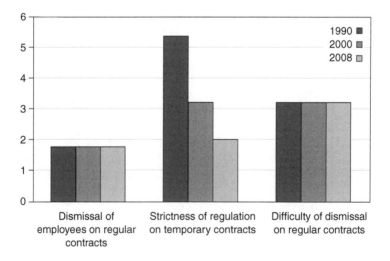

Figure 5.1 Employment protection legislation index, Italy, 1990–2008 (source: OECD online labour market programmes database).

Note
Indicators are on a scale from 0 (least restrictions) to 6 (most restrictions).

More generally, however, together with some relevant innovations regarding flexibility, during the 1990s the traditional pattern of income protection and employment protection legislation continued. Furthermore, it seemed also particularly difficult for 'active' measures to function effectively in an 'active' fashion: for example, the above-mentioned active policy measure, the LSU (socially useful jobs, introduced in 1991 but fully used in the second half of the decade), which was clearly inspired by a workfare principle, during implementation turned into a passive policy measure used especially in areas characterized by high unemployment, such as the Southern regions (see also Boeri 2000): in other words, it provided means to ameliorate social exclusion rather than to enhance employment opportunities. Nevertheless, in particular during the second part of the decade and in the early 2000s, if we look at the overall expenditure for active and passive policies between 1993 and 2008 (Table 5.2), there had been an impressive increase in the expenditure for active employment policies and a stabilization of passive employment policies. To be sure, the overall expenditure on employment policy remained generally low (especially in comparative perspective), but the trend is nevertheless remarkable. Even if we look at the number of beneficiaries during recent years, there are significant changes: the number of beneficiaries of active employment policies has almost doubled, whereas a reduction in the number of beneficiaries of passive employment policies has occurred (Table 5.3). This shows how much the traditional

Table 5.2 Italian passive and active employment policies expenditure, in percentage of GDP – 1993–2009

	1993	1996	1999	2001	2008	2009
Passive measures	1.2	1.0	0.7	0.6	0.8	1.4
Active measures	0.1	0.4	0.5	0.5	0.5	0.4
Total	1.3	1.4	1.2	1.1	1.3	1.8

Source: OECD, Social Indicators Database; OECD, *Employment Outlook 2006*: 273.

Table 5.3 Beneficiaries of 'active' (excluding training) and 'passive' policies (excluding agricultural beneficiaries), Italy, 1996–2009

	1996	1999	2001	2006	2009
Active measures	924,587	1,708,917	2,023,516	1,327,496	1,555,641
Passive measures	–*	–*	672,565	752,919	1,484,913
Total	–	–	2,512,659	2,080,415	3,040,554

Source
Ministero del Lavoro e delle Politiche Sociali 2003: 24, 43; Ministero del Lavoro, della Salute e delle Politiche Sociali 2008: 43; Ministero del Lavoro e delle Politiche Sociali 2012, statistical appendix.

Note
* Data not available.

policy configuration has changed over the years, moving away from a predominantly 'passive' policy toward a more equilibrated policy mix in which active policies become increasingly relevant – even though during the 2008–2009 crisis expenditure on passive policies increased dramatically for obvious conjunctural reasons.

Finally, even during the 2008–2009 economic crisis the overall policy menu consolidated by the above-mentioned reforms has not substantially changed. In fact, though the government has acknowledged the risks for social cohesion that recent employment trends may bring in the light of Italian employment policy shortcomings (the employment rate decreased by 1.3 points during the 2008–2010 period, and unemployment increased from 6.7 to 7.4 per cent), the Berlusconi cabinet (2008–2011) had not exploited the severe recession (2009 GDP growth was –5.4 per cent) in order to put forward an encompassing reform of the income protection scheme for the unemployed. Rather, it expanded the existing income protection instruments that were well used for 'insiders' even though it was the mid-siders who were particularly hit by the crisis (Jessoula et al. 2010).

The Berlusconi government had in fact privileged a strategy that relied on existing programmes to tackle the social consequences of the economic and employment crises. More specifically, the measures adopted aimed at allowing companies to temporarily reduce the employed labour force without definitive dismissal while compensating workers in case of working-time reduction. This was pursued through two measures: the extension and decentralization (through the so-called *ammortizzatori social in deroga*) of short-term wage replacement benefit schemes (CIGO and CIGS) to sectors/firms previously not covered, and the provision of unemployment benefits also in cases of temporary suspension from work.

In short, the policy changes of the 1990s were quite substantial, but differentiated with respect to the three key components of employment policy: income protection, employment protection, and employment opportunities through public (and private) employment services and training. With respect to income protection, incremental adjustments had been adopted in order to expand coverage and benefits. In the employment protection policy subfield, significant changes had been adopted – primarily with respect to new entrants into employment, one of the components of the 'mid-siders' (ibid.) – whereas no changes had affected the employment protection legislation of 'insiders' (see Figure 5.1). In the services employment policy and training subfield changes had occurred: a service employment market (e.g. enabling private companies to deliver employment services) had been created, vocational training had been increasingly regionalized and ESF funds had become increasingly central. If we take an overall picture of the new policy structure, the objectives incorporated in the Italian documents were the same as the EES (previously a target 'close' to a 70 per cent total employment rate by 2010, and now a national target of 67–69 per cent of total employment by 2020[1]). The guiding principle had been a selective mix of the EU pillars, which can be summarized in the overarching principle of flexibility and more recently flexicurity. The procedures had varied; still discretionary with respect to income protection, but increasingly automatic with respect to vocational training. The financial instruments had become even more centred on the ESF. In a nutshell, whereas with respect to vocational training the overall policy structure had radically changed from the previous Italian vocational training configuration (e.g. *policy transformation* had occurred), in the case of employment protection legislation and income protection changes had been more limited with respect to procedures but still quite significant in diachronic perspective (e.g. *policy adjustment* had occurred).

Summing up, during the 1990s relevant changes progressively characterized Italian employment policy, making it simultaeously more flexible and more orientated towards 'activation'. Traditional passive policies, which still remain at the core of the distributive side of the employment policy coin, had been accompanied by increasingly relevant active policies. As we shall further discuss in the following chapter, the reorientation of Italian employment policy was facilitated by the (re)launch in the beginning of the decade of the *concertazione*, i.e. a corporatist pattern of decision making that involved all social partners and in particular the trade unions and employers' associations. This method, providing a 'double legitimation' (social and political) for the decisions adopted by the centre-left governments, facilitated the adoption of policies (such as the Treu reform of 1997 and the Biagi reform of 2003 – although in this case without the support of one important social partner, the CGIL) that probably would not have occurred in other circumstances (Mania and Sateriale 2002; Ferrera and Gualmini 2004).

From an institutional standpoint, the reforms had determined: (a) greater power concentration in the hands of the executive since the employment reforms were fully supported by the government and, in the case of the Biagi law, the legislative approved an 'enabling' decree that de facto gave significant legislative autonomy to the government; (b) greater power balance with reference to the centre–periphery relationship (the regions and other sub-national authorities – provinces – substantially increased their power in employment services and vocational training implementation (interview) and, in some limited cases, income protection via the introduction of regional unemployment assistance schemes such as in the case of *Friuli Venezia Giulia*, *Basilicata*, *Campania*, *Lazio* and *Sardegna*, but the central government remained in full control of employment protection legislation); (c) greater power in the hands of interest groups over political parties because of the legitimizing '*concertazione*' (or social dialogue, in the case of the Biagi reform) practice; and (d) greater orientation towards administrative results for the bureaucracy, increasingly involved in new performance-based functions with respect to public employment services and vocational training management programmes and – more generally – in the function of employment data collection and analysis (unlike the early 1990s, data was much better quality and was updated regularly). Furthermore, collaboration among different statistical sources (INPS, Ministry, ISTAT) also greatly improved – as the most joint II Report on Social Cohesion in Italy demonstrates (*Ministero del Lavoro e delle Politiche Sociali* 2011).

5.3 Mechanisms of Europeanization and political-institutional effects

At first glance, many of the policy innovations introduced within the Italian employment policy menu have to do with Europe and the launch of the EES: together with defining fixed employment rate targets, supporting new policy principles and providing the European Social Fund resources, the role of the European Union institutions can be fully appreciated in the 'benchmarking' procedure regarding employment policies that was launched in Luxembourg in 1997 and has recently been relaunched by the Lisbon 2020 initiative. In fact, as already mentioned, following the Delors Commission White Paper (Commission 1993), the European Employment Strategy (EES) was created in order to foster the 'social' dimension of the European integration process. Although the 'paradigmatic' change may still be consolidating, it is quite clear that since the mid-1990s Italy has been increasingly tied to European policy patterns that lead policy transformation (private employment services and training reform) and policy adjustment (employment protection legislation change only for 'newcomers' in employment).

But how did Europeanization enter the Italian scene? Through four different mechanisms. First, non-formalized pressure. Similar to regional cohesion policy, although not to the same extent, ECC/EU employment policy ideas were incorporated in the Italian policy menu even prior to the formal launch of the EES. For example, in Law 223 (1991), the adoption of a more flexibility-orientated approach was in line with some of the ideas circulating within EC institutions. Although not formalized, the pressures emanating from Europe began to be felt by Italian policy-makers who wanted to be more in line with emerging European 'approaches' (AA.VV. 1986: interviews). The more effective mechanisms, though, were imposition (with respect to training), direction and coordination (with reference to employment protection legislation and employment regulations). Especially after 1997 (but to a certain extent also previously; for further details, see Graziano 2004), imposition concerned specifically domestic vocational training activities, which were increasingly funded by the ESF – recent calculations estimate that 80 per cent of Italian vocational training activities are co-funded by the EU (interview). Not complying with Europe meant losing relevant economic resources, thus adjustment was fully supported in order not to lose European funding opportunities. Although, with respect to the ESF, the overall expenditure capacity of the Italian government and regions has not been always effective (see Chapter 4 on the regional cohesion policy), in the case of vocational training policy the Italian authorities had no choice: either they accepted EU rules in formulating and implementing vocational training activities or they lost the ESF resources. At a time when budgetary limitations faced all the Italian authorities, there really was no alternative: the ESF resources had to be used (following EU rules) or vocational training would not have been adequately funded. An even more stringent imposition mechanism is related to the rulings of the European Court of Justice, especially with reference to opening up the employment services market. The Job Centre I and II rulings – especially the second issued in 1997 – were particularly crucial in determining the 1997 Treu reform that legalized temporary work agencies in Italy. Finally, and even more significant than the above-mentioned mechanisms, in the case of employment policy (especially with reference to part-time and fixed term-work) and coordination, relevant Europeanization mechanisms in the Italian case over the past 15 years including several directives regarding employment regulation (parental leave, atypical work, part-time and fixed-term work) set the domestic political agenda, which progressively incorporated the directives in the 1997 and 2003 employment policy reforms. As regards coordination, the EES and the OMC were completely based on the 'soft pressures' that were channelled by standardized procedures of peer review, benchmarking and best practice analysis, which became a constant point of reference for the Italian ministry. The National Action Plans for Employment and then the National Progress Report were based on monitoring and evaluation exercises that were not performed previously by the Italian public administration (for further details, see Sacchi 2008). Therefore, since 1997 the coordination Europeanization mechanism – inbuilt in the EES – was also one of the main, continuous sources of pressure on Italian policy-making.

From an institutional perspective, the effects of Europeanization seem less relevant than in the case of regional cohesion policy or agricultural policy. This may be linked to the specific nature of employment policy, which was more controversial, less technical and more recently developed at the EU level than the other two. First, employment policy has traditionally been quite controversial at the domestic level: the long-lasting European class cleavage between business and labour interests was particularly acute in the case of employment policy since this was one of the main contested fronts – not only in Italy. Employment protection legislation has historically been a battleground for the long-lasting conflicts between capital and work – as is well-known, this legislation is one of the most significant cleavages within European political and party systems. The domestic embeddedness of the conflict was thus more difficult to change via European policies even when – especially under the Delors Commission and prior to the EES – they were more equilibrated with respect to the various interests involved. Second, unlike regional cohesion policy and agriculture, the policy is less technical and can be more easily communicated to members of interest groups or the general public. In the other policy fields analysed in this book, not only were the interests much more concentrated, but also the overall technicalities were greater. Thus, in the case of employment policy, no specific actor could effectively use an expertise-based competitive advantage over the other players in the policy game. Third, the EES is more recent than the others and therefore may not yet have fully displayed all its potential in terms of institutional effects.

Nevertheless, if we look at the power balance between the executive and the legislature, we register the greater centrality of government. Not only was the fundamental 1997 reform strongly supported by the government, but the 2003 reform was also reached through an enabling law (Legge Biagi), which left

Table 5.4 Italian and EU employment policy structures: domestic evolution, policy adjustment and transformation

	Italy (1945–1968)	Italy (1968–1983)	Italy (1983–1992)	Italy (1992–2010)	EU (1992–2010)
Objectives	Full employment	Full employment	Full employment	Increasingly quantified employment rate, employment services and vocational training goals	Increasingly quantified employment rate, employment services and vocational training goals
Principles	Job security	Job security	Security (predominant) Flexibility (residual)	Security (insiders) Flexibility (outsiders and mid-siders)	Flexibility Flexicurity (after 2007)
Procedures	Discretionary	Discretionary	Discretionary (income protection) Automatic (vocational training and employment services)	Discretionary (income protection) Automatic (vocational training and employment services)	Benchmarking (income protection) Automatic (vocational training and employment services)
Financial instruments	Domestic funds	Domestic funds	Domestic funds (predominant) ESF (residual)	Domestic funds (income protection) ESF (vocational training and employment services)	ESF (vocational training and employment services)

ample room for manoeuvre to the government. Also, in the political reactions to the European Court of Justice rulings (for example, the Job Centre I and II cases), the government was the main actor to promote a new policy more in line with EU-based obligations.

Furthermore, several interviews conducted pointed out the increasing role played by the government in the EES as a key driver for enhanced power exercise vis-à-vis the Parliament – excluded from negotiations regarding domestic preferences at the EU level. With respect to the centre–periphery relationship, European recommendations systematically supported a power rebalancing (Commission 2000; FORMEZ 2001), which was also in line with the new regionalistic ideas and policy goals circulating both in the centre-left and centre-right coalitions (Fabbrini and Brunazzo 2003; interview). Interest groups again became central in decision making after the brief parenthesis of the 1980s, and their participation in decision making (interviews; Ferrera and Gualmini 2004) – strongly supported by the partnership principle enacted by European institutions with reference to employment as well as regional cohesion policy (Commission 2003: 8; interviews) – reduced visibly the autonomous role played by political parties. Table 5.4 summarizes the domestic policy changes with reference to the EU policy structure.

5.4 Europeanization and employment policy change in Italy: an overall assessment

More than 60 years of employment policy have shown that radical policy changes in this policy field are particularly rare in the Italian context. Although the pressure created by the problem (unemployment *in primis*) has significantly increased over the past 40 years, the most important reforms regarding employment protection legislation have been introduced in the past decade or so. Is it a mere coincidence that this happened after the intensification of European pressure – although not as binding as in the case of the European regional cohesion policy? The sequencing and content of the most recent policy changes prove that it was not by chance that, in the past 15 years, Italian employment policy has adopted new (EU-based) objectives, new flexibility principles, increasingly standardized procedures and used ESF resources for the reorganization of the vocational training system. As illustrated above, through various mechanisms Europeanization has clearly played a strong role in redefining Italian policy. Although the politics of Europeanization still remain to be investigated and a more specific discussion will be presented in Chapter 6, the narrative presented in this chapter shows striking similarities between the EU employment policy trajectory and the Italian trajectory. Italy was – in the mid-1990s – a clear case of policy misfit and therefore the transformation requested in order to comply with Europe did not happen suddenly but took about a decade and a series of subsequent reforms. As a matter of fact, the only Italian employment policy component that has not been significantly altered is income protection and employment protection legislation regarding 'insiders'. Again, is it by chance? As we shall further argue in the next chapter, the 'selective' changes that occurred in the Italian context were a product of the politics of policy adaptation: the only Europeanization-driven changes adopted and implemented at the domestic level were those which were fully supported by the key institutional, political and social actors. Especially in the employment policy field, trade union support has been crucial in all the reforms; the Biagi reform would probably not have been adopted without the strong support provided by two of the most representative trade unions (CISL and UIL). Because of the Italian configuration of interest group representation, whereby – unlike other European countries (Baglioni *et al*. 2008a, 2008b) – the unemployed were not represented in the decision-making system and trade unions were primarily concerned with their members' (e.g. largely 'insiders' or pensioners) preoccupations, innovation in income protection was extremely limited, especially if compared to the changes that occurred in the other two employment policy components – employment protection legislation for the 'newcomers' and employment services organization. In short, there were no relevant endogenous pressures regarding income protection change, and the exogenous pressures being levied by the EU – via the abovementioned different Europeanization mechanisms – set the scene. Clearly, European pressures did not lead automatically to policy change since domestic actors – interest groups, political parties, public institutions – were in charge of formulating, adopting and implementing policies primarily concerned with domestic competence and developing specific interests relating to the various employment policy issues. The patterns of domestic adaptation will be discussed in the following chapter.

6 Europeanization and the politics of domestic adaptation

In the previous chapters of this book the multi-level dynamics of policy change have been investigated with respect to agricultural, regional cohesion and employment policy. More specifically, the degree of policy fit has been assessed by adopting a policy structure approach (e.g. focusing on policy objectives, principles, procedures and financial instruments), and a diachronic analysis of both European and domestic policy developments has been provided. We now turn to the politics of domestic adaptation where an in-depth analysis of the role played by the mediating factors is given, the aim of this section being to provide evidence of the political dynamics of domestic adaptation by focusing on key domestic institutional and non-institutional actors and their relationship with policy change.

6.1 The politics of domestic adaption

Prior to the illustration of the politics of domestic adaptation, some preliminary remarks derived from the overall research design are needed. First, the specification of the initial research hypotheses and the use of the policy structure analytical tool have enabled us to highlight the main sources and mechanisms of Europeanization by linking more precisely the evolution of the EU policy structure and the domestic policy structure. Hence, focusing on the notion of policy fit/mid-fit/misfit has allowed us to systematically test the research hypotheses illustrated in Chapter 1. Second, the distinction between policy continuity and various types of policy change (policy adjustment and policy transformation) provided greater accuracy in the analysis of the dynamics and content of policy change patterns. Third, clearly distinguishing between the process (Europeanization) and its effects (in terms of political-institutional relationships) has allowed a better understanding of the differential impact of Europeanization in the various policy areas scrutinized. More generally, together with the in-depth description of the dynamics of specific policy change patterns, an overall analysis of the sources of European adaptation pressures has been offered. In the following sections, we first summarize the main findings regarding the patterns of adaptation and then discuss for each policy the specific role played by the domestic institutional and non-institutional actors.

6.1.1 Differential patterns of adaptation

The guiding hypotheses put forward in Chapter 1 were the following. First, the greater the policy-shaping capacities of the domestic government, the lesser the policy misfit will be. Second, the greater the policy misfit between EU and domestic policies, the greater adaptational pressures will be and the greater the policy changes (if in line with key domestic institutional and non-institutional actors) that will occur. Third, the greater the coerciveness of the legislative foundations of the policy, the greater the adaptational pressures will be. Therefore, in cases of misfit of policies regulated in a binding fashion (e.g. through the Europeanization mechanism of imposition and direction), it is more probable that a policy transformation will occur and that political-institutional effects will be particularly relevant. In contrast, when policies are regulated by a non-coercive Europeanization mechanism (such as coordination and non-formalized pressure), it is more probable that policy adjustment or policy continuity will occur in connection to limited or non-existent overall institutional effects.

The findings presented in the previous chapters show that, in the case of both regional cohesion and employment policy, the degree of misfit was high. In the case of agriculture, for three decades (1960–1992) there was a misfit (mid-fit) but not as marked as in the other two policy cases. During the most recent period of agricultural policy (1992–2010), the overall degree of misfit – as the result of the policy changes occurring at the EU level – transpired to be high.

Can the policy mid-fit (in the case of agricultural policy) and misfit (in the case of the other two policies) be explained by poor policy-shaping capacities? The evidence presented in Chapter 2 fully supports the hypothesis that low fit is linked to low policy-shaping capacities. And, as also discussed in Chapter 2, this is not mere coincidence because policy formulation at the EU level too often did not include Italian preferences (when available) and therefore the policy adopted was more in line with other member states' policy structures. In more general terms, our research suggests that the policy fit/misfit is not predefined but often is the end point of a process wherein domestic preferences have not been articulated or bargained for effectively. Put another way, no country is per se 'unfit' for Europe: the politics of preference formation and bargaining at the EU level will define which country is fit or unfit for Europe. Furthermore, the evidence presented in Chapter 2 also shows that, if policy-shaping capacities are limited, 'downloading' adaptation may be particularly difficult because the required degree of 'compliance' is higher than it would have been if greater domestic policy-shaping capacities were available.

This specific policy configuration, in line with the above-mentioned hypotheses, had determined *policy transformation* in the cases of regional cohesion policy, temporary employment regulation, training and public employment services (active policies), whereas it determined *policy adjustment* in the case of standard employment regulation and income protection (passive policies). The case of agricultural policy is different because, unlike the other two policies that have been characterized by greater continuity of the policy structure at the EU

Europeanization and politics of domestic adaptation 133

level, since the mid-1980s and in particular after the MacSharry reform (1992) it was only moderately changed (*policy adjustment*). Furthermore, being binding but not particularly relevant with respect to existing agricultural policies at the domestic level, in terms of domestic policy the first period (1960–1992) was a case of *policy continuity*, whereas during the most recent period (1992–2010) agricultural policy also experienced a radical change that can be labelled a case of *policy transformation*. More specifically, in the case of regional cohesion policy a full policy structure substitution has occurred and currently the Italian policy menu profile has fully adapted to the EU policy structure by being characterized by mainly the same policy objectives, principles, procedures and financial instruments. Nevertheless, the process of *policy transformation* did not occur immediately as a period of incremental adaptation (1992–1996) but preceded the full policy change registered after 1996. We will come back to this peculiar form of policy change in the final section of this chapter. In the case of employment policy, the situation was more complicated by the complex nature of the policy and its political salience for several institutional and non-institutional actors. As regards income protection and temporary employment regulation, only *policy adjustment* occurred, whereas in the case of (public and private) employment services and training, a full policy transformation characterized the Italian case. Finally, with respect to agricultural policy, after a long period of continuity – notwithstanding increasing European adaptational pressures connected to the long-lasting condition of policy mid-fit – from 1992 policy transformation occurred, e.g. all the various policy structure dimensions were increasingly altered and became increasingly similar to the European policy structure.

Can such differential patterns of policy adaptation be explained only by reference to degree of misfit and the legislative foundations (binding versus non-binding) of EU policies? In accordance with the research hypotheses developed in Chapter 1, the findings tell us that it is not the case. No automatic link between policy misfit, adaptational pressures and degree of policy change has been revealed by the empirical analysis provided in the previous three chapters. In order to provide a full explanation of the different patterns of adaptation, we need to focus on crucial mediating factors such as political and social actors, coalitions among the actors and formal (mediating) institutions. In short, we need to focus on the domestic politics of policy adaptation.

6.1.2 The politics of domestic adaptation: the agricultural policy case

The CAP was one of the first policies to be adopted at the EU level and, especially because of the pressures exerted by the French government, it developed a very specific policy structure that progressively challenged domestic political and social actors. In the Italian case, for over 40 years Europeanization has been poorly felt because European policy was added to more relevant available domestic policies and the political advantages of implementing the CAP were limited if compared to the existing Italian policies. Also, the CAP policy structure was not radically different from the Italian one (mid-fit) and the adaptational pressures were therefore limited. Put another way, for a long period of time, a *residual implementation* of the CAP took place in the Italian context. First, no institutional political actor was particularly supportive of Europeanization since domestic policies were more adaptable to their needs, e.g. distributing agricultural resources for social assistance purposes rather than mere agricultural development goals (Lizzi 2002). Furthermore, no multi-level coalition favourable to Europeanization emerged until the early 1990s, when the public budgetary constraints established at the EU level and the 'old' domestic agricultural resource allocations were put under the spotlight. Finally, unlike regional cohesion policy, which will be discussed in Section 6.1.3, no formal facilitating factors were available. In sum, for over 40 years the CAP was timidly implemented, domestic policies were poorly connected to European policies and no relevant political-institutional effects derived by Europeanization can be detected.

From the early 1990s, however, the overall situation changed substantially. The CAP policy changes, which had slowly emerged since the mid-1980s, introduced at the EU level a new policy structure that was significantly different from the Italian one, and therefore, in this case of policy misfit, the adaptational pressures became increasingly stronger. Furthermore, the overall budgetary constraints became increasingly stringent and therefore the implementation deficiencies in both domestic and European policies were more evident than ever (interview). Finally, the 'political earthquake' that hit Italy in the early 1990s (Cotta and Isernia 1996) left less room for the old social assistance-orientated domestic policies because of the crisis within the old political party configuration. New political actors emerged (especially in the context of Prodi's governments, 1996–1998 and 2006–2008) and social actors started to look differently at the CAP because the constraints became more binding (the dairy product quotas) and the opportunities more promising in comparative terms because of the increasing domestic cuts. Therefore, through the launch of the concertation method during the Prodi government under the De Castro ministry, a new coalition among political and social actors was set and Europeanization was fully supported (interviews). Finally, although not specifically aimed at supporting agricultural policy reform, the ICB became increasingly supportive of a more effective use of EU funds, which were also relevant for agricultural policy and therefore, implicitly, it became a pro-Europeanization actor with respect to domestic agricultural policy adaptation (interview). A specific, and relevant, formal mediating factor was represented by Italian regional governments, which, by supporting further regionalization of agricultural policy, also supported policy adaptation with respect to the new, innovative goals of the CAP such as rural development and environmental protection. In fact, since the early 1990s the Italian government had been more capable of both exerting policy-shaping capacities at the EU level and implementing the CAP domestically. The reform of the ministry and the reorientation of the main goals of Italian policies that were increasingly aligned with the CAP are rough indicators of the more favourable attitude and behaviour of the élite with respect to Europeanization. Although the overall concertation methods have not been dismissed in more recent times, subsequent Italian governments have been less effective, especially with respect to shaping EU policies (Lizzi 2008). Nevertheless, from residual implementation, in more recent years more effective implementation has been guaranteed. Furthermore, European goals and guidelines are a constant point of reference for domestic governmental activity: one of the most recent ministerial guidelines is strongly anchored to European guidelines by focusing on enhancing international competitiveness and farms' multi-functionality (*Ministro delle Politiche Agricole Alimentari e Forestali* 2011: 4–5).

In short, in more recent times the modifications of preferences of the main political and social actors have also remained substantially favourable to the new policy structure induced by Europeanization. Those actors against Europeanization – who emerged during the 1990s in the autonomous protests against the full implementation of the dairy product quotas, for example – increasingly lost relevance. Within the changing overall multi-level political and policy environment (new CAP policy structure, the Maastricht criteria, the Italian political earthquake), institutional and non-institutional actors fully appreciated the relevance of European policies and became facilitators of Europeanization, fully supporting the policy transformation that has characterized Italian agricultural policy over the past decade or so.

6.1.3 The politics of domestic adaptation: the regional cohesion policy case

The analysis of the case of Italian regional cohesion policy evolution has illustrated how, until the early 1990s, no significant political or social actors were particularly in favour of supporting Europeanization with respect to policy change. The prevailing domestic policy – funded by the *Cassa per il Mezzogiorno* – left enough political room for manoeuvre to all the key domestic actors. More specifically, within the relevant ministerial offices and the top governmental bureaucracy there was no specific preference in changing the overall policy structure in order to 'comply' with the post-1998 EU regional cohesion policy reform. On the one hand, the lack of a pro-Europeanization preference formation depended on the limited political convenience of changing a domestic policy that was paying high political dividends as a result of its overall discretionary functioning (see also Giuliani 1996, for a similar argument regarding overall limited Italian compliance). On the other hand, the lack of a pro-Europeanization preference formation depended on the limited knowledge available to the social actors; not being fully aware of the new opportunities offered by the European structural funds, they thus did not 'use' them in order to support full compliance. Especially with respect to bureaucratic preference formation, the traditionally weak programming tradition of the ministerial bodies involved also did not offer specific capacities to promote bureaucratic expansion by means of greater competences – such as those that could have been connected to a transformative form of domestic policy change and its full implementation. In other words, the actors involved in domestic cohesion policy were more inclined to use the still existing (discretionary) domestic policies rather than set new preferences over a (selective) new regional cohesion domestic policy structure in line with that of the EU. The limited bureaucratic capacities can be effectively illustrated by the low expenditure rates of European funds until the second half of the 1990s. Since no relevant actor was pro-Europeanization, no coherent élite coalition could be organized in order to facilitate the process. The only actor that fully supported the new European policy structure was the Italian central bank, which did not have the political power to impose its preferences over those of the other actors. Only during the second half of the 1990s, after the collapse of the 'First Republic' (Cotta and Verzichelli 2007), did new political and institutional actors (Minister Ciampi, former governor of the ICB), top ministerial ranks (the new DPS led by Barca, a former research director of the ICB) and policy experts from academia (mainly economists who helped the ministry in the preparatory work that led to the new formulation capacities of the Italian government experienced between 1998 and 1999) manage to facilitate Europeanization. Furthermore, the new Parliament (which between 1994 and 1996 had experienced an unprecedented turnover and was increasingly populated by anti-public expenditure members, as in the case of the Lega Nord representatives: Albertazzi and McDonnell 2005; Cotta and Verzichelli 2007), following the Parliamentary investigation into the limited expenditure of EU funds, also supported greater political action in favour of Europeanization. Such increased institutional and non-institutional support paved the way for the full incorporation of the European policy structure into the Italian policy structure. Finally, trade unions and regional authorities also realized that the new policy configuration could offer them new political opportunities and therefore decided to support the new diffused pro-Europeanization attitude and political behaviour. Put another way, although incrementally, all the key actors acknowledged that the 'old' discretionary domestic regional cohesion policy could not survive under the new EU-constrained Parliamentary and governmental action and that Europeanization could be a 'positive sum' game because they could all benefit from it in terms of political (electoral support) and social dividends (investment and employment opportunities for the members of business associations and trade unions). The new institutional actors and their coalitional capacities enabled them to overcome residual resistance to full Europeanization (such as that expressed by pre-existing bureaucratic bodies like the *Cabina di Regia*, which was largely marginalized by the new actors' activity; interview) and they were further supported by increasing pro-Europeanization statements made by the ICB (interview). In sum, Europeanization occurred incrementally during the second half of the 1990s and policy transformation was the end result because the preferences of the key institutional and non-institutional actors were increasingly in favour of Europeanization-induced policy changes.

6.1.4 The politics of domestic adaptation: the employment policy case

Employment policies (in relation to their three main components – income protection, employment legislation and employment services and training) have also gone through great changes over recent decades. Although domestic policy had changed several times prior to the launch of the EES and its consolidation between the 1990s and 2000s, the overall policy structure was quite different from that which emerged at the EU level during the 1990s. As discussed in Chapter 2, Italian preference formation and bargaining capacities were traditionally very low and therefore the Italian government could not be considered a policy-shaper. After the EES, in the presence of increasing adaptational pressures channelled through Council (and Commission) guidelines and recommendations, the Italian policy structure in the field of major European interventions (concerning employment legislation and employment services and training) has been substantially modified, as described above. In the traditional domestic policy-making configuration, the political game was played primarily by the government (and the key party leaders performing governmental functions), the legislature and social partners; and the key goal was to guarantee full protection to insiders via 'passive' policies (Gualmini 1998; Graziano 2007). The emergence of (a) new European ideas in the 1980s and (b) a new European policy structure determined new constraints and opportunities, which were differentially evaluated by the actors involved. Since the 1980s, the socialist representatives (particularly crucial since they held the prime ministership with Craxi and the Labour Ministry in various governments) were more inclined to follow European ideas and started to adopt (still marginal) policies that were strongly opposed by trade unions and other opposition political parties (such as the Communist Party). The real governmental orientation change, however, happened during the 1990s when first the Prodi government and thereafter the Berlusconi governments (II and III) fully supported the redefinition of Italian employment policy – especially with respect to non-standard employment regulation, public services and training. Furthermore, from the early 1990s the economic and budgetary policy changes required by the new Maastricht criteria meant that the overall relationship between the dominant actors started to change format – mainly through the launch of concertation practices that resembled 'old' neo-corporatist patterns, although with some fundamental differences (Regini 2000). The trade unions made several concessions between 1992 and 1993 in order to help the government fulfil the new European obligations and obtained in exchange a (limited) increase in income protection schemes (Mania and Sateriale 2002). Furthermore, with the Prodi government – and under Labour Minister Treu, who had in the past been a consultant for one of the leading trade unions, CISL – the concertation produced the 1997 reform that was formulated primarily following Europeanization imposition mechanisms (the Job Centre rulings with respect to liberalizing employment services) and 'softer' mechanisms such as coordination (which was at the heart of the new, formalized European employment strategy). Put another way, new institutional actors (the Amato government in 1992 and the Prodi government between 1996 and 1998) strongly in favour of Europeanization managed to create pro-Europeanization coalitions with trade unions and business associations in order to adopt policy changes with respect to non-standard employment regulation and liberalization of employment services and training.

138 *Europeanization and politics of domestic adaptation*

This specific part of the overall employment policy constituted a 'positive sum' game since there were no costs or losses for the key constituents of the institutional and non-institutional actors and new EU-based funding opportunities – especially in the training field – were made available. It is not by chance that no substantial 'subtractive' reform – notwithstanding the increasing EU recommendations and guidelines – occurred in the field of income protection (including CIG and CIGS) or in standard employment regulation: in these fields, trade unions would have been 'losers' with respect to the prevailing interests of their constituents – mainly standard workers and pensioners (Jessoula *et al.* 2010) – and therefore would have strongly opposed any 'subtractive' reform.

The 2003 reform (the so-called Biagi Law), although approved under a different government (Berlusconi II), was another 'deregulative' reform that was strikingly close to the European policy guidelines and recommendations. To a certain extent, the Berlusconi governments (2001–2006) continued what had been started by the previous government, although rather than corporatist arrangements, the government maintained a 'social dialogue' with the social partners. The tripartite concertation, which had characterized the Prodi government, was heavily criticized and labelled as ineffective and barely innovative in the first important employment policy document released by the Berlusconi II government (2001–2005), the *White Book on the Italian Labour Market* (*Ministero del Lavoro e delle Politiche Sociali* 2001: V). Such orientation was in accordance with the overall approach to economic and social policy of the government, which

> criticized the *concertazione* for its low effectiveness and innovation potential. Rather than new, trilateral, corporatist agreements, the *White Book* advocated a new method of interaction with social partners, dubbed as 'social dialogue' (...), basically consisting of milder forms of consultation and preventive negotiations on economic and social policy, in which the executive reserved for itself wider margins of manoeuvre and the role of 'ultimate' policy-maker.
>
> (Ferrera and Gualmini 2004: 43)

In fact, between 2001 and 2003, the unions had been on the defensive, particularly after the governmental delegation draft bill – which followed the presentation of the above-mentioned *White Book* – regarding, among other things, the deregulation of employment contracts and the reform of Article 18 in the Workers' Statute of 1970. This article, which protected workers from unmotivated dismissal, was applicable only to firms with more than 15 employees. This issue was raised in the delegation decree, providing further opportunity for a derogation in three specific cases: if a firm 'emerged' from the black economy and had a clear intention to settle its contributive position; if a firm overcame the 15 employees threshold as a result of hiring new 'standard' employees; and if a firm transformed temporary workers into permanent ones.

This proposal, strongly supported by the leading business association – *Confindustria* – could not be easily accepted by all the trade unions. In March 2002, the biggest Italian trade union (CGIL) called a general strike that turned into a massive demonstration (3 million people marched in Rome), whereas neither CISL nor UIL participated. During the following months, both UIL and CISL (but not CGIL) decided to negotiate with the government and approve a new social agreement (*Patto per l'Italia*, July 2002). The pact was clearly permeated by 'activation' jargon, explicitly citing the policy objectives set at the European level in Lisbon (2000) and Barcelona (2001). Furthermore, among the annexes, there was also a new article of the delegation decree, which contained a 'softer' version of the government's proposal regarding the reform of Article 18. In response to the pact, a broad coalition composed of minor trade unions and parts of the CGIL promoted a referendum aimed at the extension of Article 18 to firms with fewer than 15 employees. It was clearly a political move, in stark contrast to the governmental proposals, but it failed because the required quorum of 50 per cent of the voters was not reached. This event showed that CGIL was the only main 'loser' of the employment policy reforms since it failed to consolidate through the referendum the employment security principle, whereas the governmental coalition – which included the main business association, *Confindustria*, and the other two trade unions, CISL and UIL – was successful in adopting new flexibility-inspired employment regulations. Nevertheless, thanks to the above-mentioned intense mobilization, CGIL managed to block any initiative aimed at reforming Article 18 – which, in the early 2000s circumstances, could be seen as a (partial) success. Put another way, unlike the other two policies covered by this study, with specific reference to the 2003 employment policy reform, social and political support were more controversial; nevertheless, the pro-Europeanization coalition (government, *Confindustria*, CISL, UIL) managed to overcome the resistance of CGIL and therefore acted as a favourable factor with respect to Europeanization-orientated policy changes that further deregulated employment contracts. CISL and UIL would probably have been less in favour of the policy changes if their core constituencies (standard and public employment workers) had been involved. The political (and social) costs of the reforms were placed on the non-'represented': the mid-siders and the outsiders; in other words, the unemployed and non-standard workers (Baglioni *et al*. 2008a, 2008b). The narrative points out the controversies inspired by employment policy reform largely inspired by European guidelines and recommendations. Furthermore, the role of mediating formal institutions – such as the ICB, which was generally in favour of employment policy reform – was more nuanced since it never took a clear-cut position on the abolishment of Article 18. Nevertheless, the ICB did support employment services and vocational training reform – which were *transformed* during the late 1990s and early 2000s. Therefore, *policy adjustment* and not *policy transformation* occurred in income and standard worker employment protection regulation, whereas *policy transformation* (supported by all the key institutional and non-institutional actors) occurred in the fields of non-standard worker employment regulation, employment services and training.

6.2 Toward greater policy-shaping capacities? A contrasted landscape in recent policy developments

In March 2010, the Commission issued a communication entitled 'Europe 2020: A Strategy for Smart, Sustainable and Inclusive Growth', which set the overarching economic and social goals for the next decade. Furthermore, in October 2011 the Commission made a proposal for the future of CAP, and in December 2011 issued a proposal for regulation of regional cohesion policy for the future programming period (2014–2020). All three policy areas studied in this book are under revision since the new programming period (2014–2020) is currently at the heart of the EU's political agenda. As usual in EU decision making, the main motor of policy proposals is the Commission, and between 2009 and 2010 public responses to the first Commission documents regarding Europe 2020 were analysed by it. Between 2012 and 2013 the main institutional actors in the EU will adopt the new regulations regarding agriculture and regional cohesion policy. How has the Italian government been reacting to the new policy opportunities provided by the European institutions? Has policy transformation also led to increasing policy-shaping capacities as hypothesized by some scholars (Brunazzo 2010, with reference to regional cohesion policy)?

The first policy to be assessed and reformed has been employment policy, although within the broader framework of overarching social and economic goals. In February 2010, an overall assessment of the Lisbon Strategy was issued by the Commission, which laid down the main challenges that were then addressed by the Europe 2020 initiative. Although several achievements have been reached with respect to the original goals, the Commission also acknowledges that 'implementation has suffered from variable ownership and weak governance structures' (Commission 2010a: 6). Put another way, beyond the Italian case, differential adaptation – especially with reference to implementation – to the EES has also characterized other member states because 'the performance of some Member States already exceeded the target, whereas for others targets were set at such a level that meeting them within the available time-frames appeared unrealistic' (ibid.). The Italian case is one of those in which the targets have not been met, although a policy transformation has occurred: in 2010 the overall employment rate was 56.9 per cent whereas the overall European goal was set at the 70 per cent mark, and even prior to the economic and financial crisis of 2008 the figure was 58.7 per cent (Eurostat online database). The same could apply to other employment targets that were not met by Italian governmental action. Clearly, the economic crisis did not play a facilitating role, but nevertheless looking at the rough Italian employment indicators after ten years of implementation of the Lisbon Strategy the results are meagre. As stated by the Commission, probably the overall targets set in 2000 were too ambitious for some countries – such as Italy – but after a decade of domestic policy adjustment and transformation in the field of employment we could expect greater capacity to form specific domestic preferences in the European arena. To be sure, Italy was not the only country not to meet the Lisbon employment rate goals since only five member states (Austria, Denmark, Germany, the

Netherlands and Sweden) managed to do so; two others (the UK and Cyprus) were very close (ibid.). Therefore, in both evaluation of the Lisbon Strategy and the new Europe 2020 initiative the Commission acknowledged that in several countries more coordination and flexibility in meeting the targets was needed (Commission 2010a, 2010b).

But how have the Italian governments interacted with reference to the most recent EU developments? Have the specificities of the Italian employment situation been 'uploaded' by governmental actors? First, if we look at the formal capacity to represent domestic preferences at the European Union level beyond the (very limited) success obtained in the early 1990s (Sacchi 2008: 160), evidence suggests that not much has changed. In the words of a top trade union representative: 'In the past ten years [the Italian government] has played a minor role' (interview). The same impression has been shared by other trade union representatives (interviews), and by the leading business association, *Confindustria* (interview). Beyond a general appreciation of European initiatives, the overall perception is that Italian governments have been 'following, rather than leading' (interview) even in recent developments in EU employment policy. According to the interviewees, this specificity is linked to the variable 'Euroenthusiasm' of governments over the past 15 years (seemingly, more in favour of Europe in the case of centre-left governments and the converse with centre-right governments; interview), and also to the difficulties of the Italian employment situation with respect to the European targets (interview). In short, even in the most recent EU policy development negotiations the Italian government has not been able to exert a relevant influence on the EU decision-making process because the sharing of preference formation has been limited. For example, with respect to the domestic targets in the Europe 2020 strategy, lower targets have been fixed with respect to the 75 per cent total employment rate (20–64) but no discussion among the key social actors had been organized prior to its communication to the Commission (interviews). Furthermore, not only has the overall contribution to the launch of the Europe 2020 initiative been very limited with respect to employment issues, responses to the Commission's preliminary documents were also particularly general and vague (see the Italian response to the consultation for the future EU 2020 strategy – 'The case for a better European economic governance' (2010) – where the most developed claim regarding employment issues is the following:

> As far as employment policies are concerned, deep changes in the international division of production and labour have already occurred because of globalisation. (…) Modern and appropriate education and training systems are therefore essential to provide the knowledge resources and competences needed for workers to sustain employment and growth).
>
> (Ministero per le politiche europee 2010: 2)

In the case of employment policy, the evidence regarding preference formation and bargaining with respect to the Europe 2020 initiative suggests that Italy still falls strongly in the 'policy-taking' category.

Also the CAP is in the process of being redefined with respect to the 2014–2020 programming period. Following the institutional innovation introduced by the new Lisbon Treaty, which includes agriculture among those policies that have to be adopted following the ordinary legislative procedure (former co-decision procedure), the policy is today at the centre of a more involved multi-level decision-making process whereby the member state governments remain particularly relevant in the Council of Agricultural Ministries where bargaining capacities are essential and further bargaining capacities will be required with respect to the European Parliament. The policy process that will lead to the new CAP was initiated by the Commission in 2010, with the issuing of a communication entitled: 'The CAP towards 2020: Meeting the Food, Natural Resources and Territorial Challenges of the Future' (Commission 2010c). Explicitly referring to the overarching Europe 2020 strategy, the document focuses on the overall aim of 'green growth in the agricultural sector and the rural economy as a way to enhance well being by pursuing economic growth while preventing environmental degradation' (ibid.: 6). The overall policy structure remains anchored to its two complementary pillars (annual, mainly decoupled, direct payments, on the one hand, and multi-annual rural development measures, on the other), with the further aim to respond to three overarching challenges: food safety in the EU and beyond, environment and climate change and territorial balance (ibid.: 4–5). Furthermore, in October 2011 the Commission produced an accompanying document ('impact assessment') and a proposal for regulation of the CAP. In the 'impact assessment' document the Commission takes stock of the results obtained in the current (2007–2013) implementation of the CAP and cites an OECD evaluation of the European agricultural policy, which states that the subsequent CAP reform process over the past 30 years 'led to a significant decrease in the distortion of production and trade and in an increase of income transfer efficiency' (Commission 2011a: 12). Within the context of an overall increase in decoupled direct payments and rural development expenditure and a decrease in export subsidies and coupled direct payments, today's CAP policy structure is very different to that of the early 1980s. The document continues by stating the key objectives for future action:

> Today's challenges to EU agriculture have become broader and more complex in particular due to economic pressures such as the deterioration in agricultural terms of trade, the erosion of the sector's competitive potential and the challenge of further liberalisation of agricultural markets; increased environmental threats such as climate change and the loss of biodiversity; and territorial needs such as keeping the great diversity of rural areas in the EU-27 vital and attractive. In the context of the contribution of agricultural policy to the Europe 2020 strategy, the three broad policy objectives for the future CAP are: Contributing to a viable, market oriented production of safe and secure food throughout the EU by acting on drivers related to income derived from the market (improving farmers' capacity to add value to their production, improving the functioning of the food supply

chain in a pro-competitive way, providing a safety-net in case of excessive price drops), promoting sustainable consumption, enhancing the competitiveness of agricultural holdings (innovation, modernisation, resource efficiency, addressing production difficulties in areas with natural constraints) and helping farmers to deal with income volatility and the below average income and productivity of the sector (income support, risk management for economic and public health risks). This is related to the smart growth objective of the Europe 2020 strategy; Ensuring the sustainable management of natural resources, such as water and soil, and the provision of environmental public goods such as preservation of the countryside and biodiversity, integrating and promoting climate change mitigation and enhancing farmers' resilience to the threats posed by a changing climate, fostering green growth through innovation and reducing environmental damage by agriculture. This contributes to the sustainable growth objective of Europe 2020 with the aim of contributing to a low carbon economy, an expanding bioeconomy and protecting the environment; Contributing to the balanced territorial development and thriving rural areas throughout the EU by responding to the structural diversity in farming systems and assuring positive spill-over effects from agriculture to other sectors of the rural economy and vice versa, improving their attractiveness and economic diversification. This is related to the inclusive growth objective of Europe 2020 considering the relatively lower level of development of rural areas and the aims of social and territorial cohesion within and also between Member States.

(Commission 2011a: 35–36)

The Italian reaction to the Commission's proposals has been quite critical since, according to recently appointed Minister Catania when he was still a top ranking bureaucrat in the Agricultural Ministry, by continuing to support primarily decoupled direct payments 'the policy proposed by the Commission does not seem to be orientated to firms that produce and invest in their activities. It seems to favour landed property which may decide to reduce its production capacities, whereas in some regional contexts it tends to turn into a purely assistentialistic policy. In fact, decoupled direct payments, only linked to the agricultural area, end up being exclusively functional to [land] revenue, and therefore totally unrelated to the agricultural firms' needs.

(Catania 2011: 8, author's translation)

Furthermore, also the agricultural associations have expressed similar fears. In the words of the Coldiretti President:

(…) it is to be avoided that, after the abandonment of a regime centered on coupled direct payments, a change to a new land surface coupled regime is established. This would in fact poorly reasonable to citizens' and would create perplexities among agricultural firms.

(Marini 2012: 165–166 – author's translation)

The president of the other important agricultural association, *Confederazione Italiana Agricoltori* – CIA, has also criticized the Commission's proposal:

> For the CIA, the new Cap has to have specific objectives: market efficiency; agricultural producers' support; contractual economy diffusion; relevant initiatives supporting intergenerational transfer; support towards financial instruments (…) aimed at reducing price volatility and market crises.
>
> (Politi 2012, author's translation)

For CIA, the current Commission's proposal also risks heavily supporting agricultural revenue rather than focusing on productive activities (ibid.).

Finally, *Confagricoltura* – which represents bigger firms than the other two associations – is critical in the same vein as CIA and Coldiretti, and also criticizes the overall reduction in funds envisaged by the proposal (Guidi, President of Confagricoltura, 2012). Put another way, all the key institutional and social actors involved in domestic agricultural policy decision making are opposed to the Commission's proposal and largely share a common interest and preference that is supported by the current Italian government (interviews). Preference bargaining is still to come but, similar to regional cohesion policy, in the agricultural field stronger preference formation capacities currently also characterize Italian governmental action. More generally, over the past 15 years – because of the CAP's increasing relevance to domestic agricultural policies – the capacity to share and steer domestic preferences has increased significantly (interviews). Unlike employment policies, conflicts among the key institutional and non-institutional actors have been very limited and over time the concertation method has consolidated and supported a coherent preference that has been (and probably will be further) negotiated at the EU level. Although until now bargaining capacities have remained limited, preference formation is much more coherent and inclusive than in the past when European decisions were simply 'taken' by domestic actors. Nevertheless, no real fully 'shaping' capacity has been registered over recent years because the overall governmental approach has been reactive rather than proactive (interviews). Therefore, in the case of agricultural policy, Italian governmental representatives have merely moved away from the 'old' *policy taker* profile to a more nuanced *policy adapter* profile.

The case of regional cohesion policy is similar to agricultural policy since the policy transformation analysed in the previous sections has given birth to long-lasting changes in the preference formation capacities of the competent ministry. Since the creation of the new Department of Development and Cohesion Policies (DPS) in 1998, the government has been capable of creating greater consensus among the various institutional and social actors in order to better represent the needs of the territories that are eligible for regional cohesion fund allocation:

> During the 2001–2006 reform negotiations, Italy promoted its national preferences much earlier and much more effectively than during any previous negotiation round. This is acknowledged also by the Commission (…) in

the First Periodic Report on Economic and Social Cohesion. (...) The document the Commission refers to is the First Memorandum on the Reform of EU Regional Cohesion Policy, published in July 2001, just seven months after the informal negotiations had started at the EU level. A coordination board – involving DPS, regions, trade unions, and employers' representatives, the so-called *comitatone* (large committee) proposed to the Commission to develop cohesion policy with the aim of achieving three objectives: first, ensure that EU cohesion policy would have an impact on the competitiveness of the developing regions; second, target particularly the needs of candidate countries; third, ensure higher quality, greater simplification, and more extensive subsidiarity for the developing regions of the EU-15 member states. A Second Memorandum followed in December 2020: in it Italy identified eleven more specific goals.

(Brunazzo and Piattoni 2008: 58–59)

Furthermore, in the definition of domestic priorities for the 2007–2013 programming period, the Italian government also shared its goals with the main institutional and social actors involved at the various levels of government – trade unions, business associations, agricultural associations and regional authorities (interviews). The inclusive strategy of the DPS also supported the creation of so-called 'special purpose institutions', which were ad hoc coalitions derived from the implementation of European initiatives such as urban or other EU-(co)funded territorial projects (interview). Put another way, the coordinated preference formation mechanisms continued during the decade and were not only episodic – although some criticism has been put forward with respect to the Berlusconi IV government, which was characterized as having decoupled domestic and European regional cohesion policy and drastically reduced the consultation activities implemented by the previous centre-left governments (interview). Another specific feature of the last decade of regional cohesion policy implementation is that learning occurred within the social partner representatives, which progressively appreciated the overall territorial strategy supported by the EU regional cohesion policy and refocused their preferences accordingly: for example, the leading business association, *Confindustria*, acknowledged that incentive allocation could not be the best way to promote development because of its 'distorted implementation mechanisms', that is, discretionary allocation would not lead to a long-lasting impact in terms of development support (interview). Other social actors have learned to appreciate the institutionalization of the programming principle, which currently enables permanent consultation among the various actors having a specific interest in regional cohesion policy (interview), e.g. primarily regions, trade unions and business associations. In other words, the past decade has institutionalized preference formation and enhanced overall preference coordination capacities, although with respect to preference bargaining the overall capacities expressed until now have been limited because, in the various programming rounds, the Italian contribution consisted mainly of reacting to policy proposals developed at the EU level by the Commission or by other member state representatives (interview).

More recently, though, following the Commission regulation proposal on the future programming period of EU regional cohesion policy, the Italian government has promptly reacted and proposed substantial amendments to the overall strategy. The Commission proposal (Commission 2011b) highlights several key points for the future programming period: strengthening research, technological development and innovation; enhancing access to and use and quality of information and communication technologies; and enhancing the competitiveness of small and medium-sized enterprises, the agricultural sector (for the EAFRD) and fisheries and aquaculture sector (for the MFF); supporting the shift towards a low-carbon economy in all sectors; promoting climate change adaptation, risk prevention and management; protecting the environment and promoting resource efficiency; promoting sustainable transport and removing bottlenecks in key network infrastructures; promoting employment and supporting labour mobility; promoting social inclusion and combating poverty; investing in education, skills and lifelong learning; and enhancing institutional capacity and an efficient public administration (ibid.: 7–8). Furthermore, the management features of regional cohesion policy implementation were a source of concern:

> Experience suggests that in the current programming period, the diversity and fragmentation of rules governing spending programmes are often perceived as unnecessarily complicated and difficult to implement and control. This imposes a heavy administrative burden on beneficiaries as well as on the Commission and Member States, which can have the unintended effect of discouraging participation, increasing error rates and delaying implementation. This means that the potential benefits of EU programmes are not fully realised.
>
> (ibid.: 2)

The reaction of the Italian government was swift. In a document presented in December 2011 several specific proposals for amendments to the Commission's proposal were made as follows: greater guarantees regarding the implementation of result-orientated indicators; simplification and better focusing of the programming documents; streamlining of the reporting of results in order to further involve the European Parliament through the support of greater public debates; further enhancement of ex ante conditionalities in order to better support the regional cohesion policy implementing institutions; better targeting and identification of the initiatives aimed at the territories that would enhance the inclusion of cities, citizens' networks, workers, universities and firms with the aim of providing more 'uploading' opportunities in the programming with respect to their needs and preferences; creation of a European partnership code of conduct guaranteeing the full and effective contribution to decisions by organized citizens; and a further guarantee of adequate, fair and efficient sanctioning measures with respect to the Stability Pact recommendations (Barca 2011: 26–27). It is clearly too early to reach any conclusion with respect to the bargaining process that will develop during 2012, but the Italian government has shown a greater capacity to react to the Commission's proposals and during recent years has already further developed its preference formation capacities. Therefore, over the years the overall 'upgrading' of regional capacity to 'upload' policy has been continuous, notwithstanding the enduring limited implementation capacities that are still characterizing Italian regional cohesion policy. In sum, together with *policy transformation* in the case of regional cohesion policy, the Italian government has also become a *policy adaptor*, evolving from the more traditional pattern of being a *policy-taker*. At the end of the 2012 negotiations concerning the new 2014–2020 programming period, it will be possible to see whether the Italian government has further developed into a *policy-shaper*.

In short, over recent years the three policies analysed have evolved in a differentiated way with respect to overall domestic ability to form coherent preferences and to negotiate for them at the EU level. In the field of employment policy, *policy adjustment* and *policy transformation* have not been coupled with greater preference formation or bargaining capacities, whereas in the case of agricultural and regional cohesion policies *policy transformation* is strongly linked to increasing coherent and coordinated preference formation – although still limited bargaining capacities. Therefore, in the case of employment policy the Italian representatives can still be labelled policy-takers, whereas in the other two policy objects of this study they can be labelled policy-adaptors and not (yet?) policy-shapers since their bargaining capacities are still limited. It must be noted that Europeanization-induced policy transformation – made possible through the support of domestic institutional and non-institutional actors – has increased Italian preference formation capacities, which in turn may be in contrast to European institutional preferences, as in the case of the Commission's proposals in the fields of both agricultural and regional cohesion policy. This should not be surprising because there is no difference between supporting Europeanization and trying to increasingly shape European policies. Put another way, supporting Europeanization-induced policy change with respect to past policies does not automatically entail further support of *whatever* policy is adopted at the EU level. As already underlined in the literature (Brunazzo 2010), one unintended consequence of Europeanization may be a greater domestic willingness – and ability – to shape EU policies: greater appreciation (and overall support) of the existence of a multi-level decision-making system leads domestic institutional and non-institutional actors to further engage in EU-level decision making in order to 'shape' EU opportunities and policies, and at the same time avoid mere implementation of decisions that are not in line with domestic preferences. To a certain extent, this phenomenon – at least with respect to agricultural and regional cohesion policies – makes Italy more similar to other important EU member states (such as France and Germany), where policy misfit was generally limited by preference formation and bargaining capacities (Webber 1998) or cancelled through the power of changing the EU rules which had generated such policy misfit (as in the case of the redefinition of the Maastricht criteria between 2003 and 2004 put forward by the German and French governments; Della Sala 2008). Furthermore, the comparative approach adopted throughout this study has shown that in cases of greater coerciveness (agricultural and regional cohesion policy), the overall consequences of Europeanization are relevant not only with respect to political-institutional relationships as argued in the previous chapters, but also to fostering policy-shaping capacities: the more binding EU rules are, the more domestic institutions will adapt in both the 'downloading' and 'uploading' phases by supporting greater preference coordination, which will then be bargained for at the EU level. For the moment, it suffices to conclude this section by stating that the recent developments in the EU policy objects of this study fully confirm the idea that preference formation capacities need to be clearly distinguished from preference bargaining capacities. The Italian case illustrates that, even when preference formation capacities are fairly high (as in the case of recent decades with particular reference to agricultural and regional cohesion policies, but not in the case of employment policy), bargaining success rests on different features that may go beyond the reach of institutional and non-institutional actors' preferences. Put another way, the competitive advantage of member states that have been particularly successful in the above-mentioned policy fields (France, Germany, Spain) did rest on preference formation coordination but also on other more general bargaining features: in the context of EU decision making, a 'two-level game' (Putnam 1988) needs to be played effectively at both levels of government, since policy preference coherence and coordination at the national level may not be a sufficient condition for successful bargaining at the EU level. In the concluding section of this book we will further discuss the broader implications of these findings related to the Italian case.

6.3 Europeanization and the politics of domestic adaptation: an overall assessment

The three policy cases presented in this book have all been involved in Europeanization processes, although domestic adaptation has varied with respect to the intensity of policy change and political-institutional effects. In all the cases analysed, Europeanization did not occur automatically since it was supported – again, in a differentiated fashion – by domestic institutional, political and social actors that have progressively acknowledged the political advantages of fully adapting to European regulations, directives, recommendations, communications and guidelines in both agricultural and regional cohesion policy (*policy transformation* and relevant institutional effects). In contrast, in the case of employment policy, support was differentiated: high in the case of 'outsider' and 'mid-sider' employment protection legislation, employment services and training management reforms (*policy transformation*), limited in the case of 'insider' protection legislation (*policy adjustment*), and the overall institutional effects connected to Europeanization were limited. In other words, in all the policies analysed, Italy by the early 1990s was characterized by policy misfit, and adaptational pressures (stronger in the case of binding policies such as agriculture and regional cohesion, weaker in the cases of less binding policies such as employment policy) were followed by policy changes in both the domestic adoption and implementation phases of the policy process.

Furthermore, a clear link between policy changes and policy-shaping capacities (e.g. preference formation and bargaining) has emerged from our analysis. More specifically, in the case of agricultural and regional cohesion policies, policy transformation has been matched by greater preference formation capacities (turning Italy into an overall policy-adaptor), whereas in the case of employment policy overall policy adjustment has been accompanied by continuity with respect to preference formation capacities. Nevertheless, no policy analysed has (yet?) given birth to full policy-shaping capacities since preference bargaining at the EU level remains limited, at least in comparative terms. In order to explain this specific trait of the Italian role in EU decision making, we need to go back to the key factors discussed in Chapter 2 with respect to domestic systemic agenda-setting capacities. Following Tallberg's (2007) work, we identified crucial variables in explaining the evolution of the systemic preference formation and bargaining capacities of the Italian government since the early years of European integration. It emerged that political authority and expertise (e.g. individual sources of power) were the crucial factors that could explain the successes and failures of Italy as an EU systemic agenda-setter (systemic meaning 'high politics' decisions such as new treaties or treaty amendments). Since 1992 Italy has been predominantly a policy-taker with reference to systemic agenda-setting capacities because limited governmental continuity could be detected and the overall budgetary constraints derived from the Maastricht Treaty put Italy in a critical position. Only between 1996 and 2001 did it seem that the Italian government was more capable of coordinating preferences and interacting more fruitfully with EU institutions, acting as a *policy-adaptor* (interviews). But even in this case, at its best Italy could merely 'comply' with European policies rather than fully shape its agenda through an ad hoc coalition with other member state representatives. This does not mean that Italian governments have not tried to be systemic agenda-shapers, as the attempt to introduce the aggregated debt indicator within the 2010–2012 Growth and Stability Pact reform – drafted as a new treaty approved by the European Council in early March 2012 – shows. As regards this specific issue, the Berlusconi IV government's Economy Minister Tremonti tried to shape the Growth and Stability Pact reform by introducing the notion of 'aggregated debt', which includes household and corporate debt, an indicator that would have been much more advantageous for Italy. To be sure, a first apparent success was obtained at the meeting of the Group of 20 (G20) finance ministers held in Paris in February 2011, and the success of the Italian initiative was further consolidated in Washington, DC in April 2011 as, within the overall G20 strategy aimed at addressing financial and economic imbalances, a set of indicators was considered to be relevant, among them the 'private savings rate and private debt' (Meeting of Finance Ministers and Central Bank Governors 2011: 1). Nevertheless, following the exacerbation of the Greek crisis, in the final outcome of the EU variant of 'addressing the imbalances' process (e.g. the 'fiscal compact' treaty signed in early March 2012), no reference is made to 'aggregate debt' nor to 'private savings rate' or 'private debt' in the targets. Put another way, no successful preference bargaining at the EU level was carried out prior to the Berlusconi IV government crisis, and the new preferences expressed by the Monti government (2011–) are less conflictual as regards the notion of 'debt' considered in the so-called 'fiscal compact' treaty, which was signed by 25 government leaders, including Monti.

More generally, as regards systemic agenda-setting capacities, even in the presence of personal authority and expertise, in cases when Italian preferences are not in line with mainstream preferences at the EU level very limited room for manoeuvre is available, possibly because of the limited credibility that has characterized several Italian governments over the past decade (Tallberg 2007; interviews). With the new Monti government (2011–) things are apparently changing (see, for example, *Financial Times*, 27 January 2012), but it is clearly too early to assess if preference bargaining capacities are also in the process of changing. Until very recently, however, even when the mix of personal authority and expertise was available (as in the case of the Prodi government), governmental bargaining capacities as regards systemic agenda setting remained very limited. And this may also contribute to explaining why policy-based bargaining capacities also remained limited even in cases – such as in agricultural and regional cohesion – where policy transformation has been followed by greater preference formation capacities.

Summing up, over the past 20 years in the Italian case – characterized by high policy misfit – adaptation in the form of *policy transformation* has occurred because of the full support of domestic institutional and non-institutional actors in those policy areas that were less conflictual (agricultural and regional cohesion). In contrast, in the employment policy field – traditionally more conflictual than the other two – adaptation has been more limited since *policy transformation* occurred only in the (limited) cases in which the key institutional and non-institutional actors shared the advantages of Europeanization, whereas in other employment policy subfields only EU *policy adjustment* was detected.

7 Conclusion

The research presented in this book was aimed primarily at understanding Italy's patterns of adaptation in three relevant policy areas: agriculture, regional cohesion and employment. The results show that all the Italian policies have been characterized by Europeanization-induced policy changes (at varied degrees of intensity) and that political-institutional relationships have also been – at least partially – modified as a consequence of Europeanization. Furthermore, beyond the Italian case, the analysis has covered three key elements: the conceptualization and operationalization of Europeanization; policy structure and policy change; and the 'goodness of fit' hypothesis. In this concluding chapter we will illustrate the main analytical – if not theoretical – implications of our study.

7.1 Europeanization and its effects: conceptualization and operationalization

As discussed in Chapter 1, the first 'wave' of Europeanization research was primarily interested in defining the object of study (Radaelli 2000, 2003a; Olsen 2002). Beyond a mere evocative use of the notion, Europeanization may be an important analytical tool enabling the full understanding of policy (and politics) change at both the EU and member state level. Furthermore, research design and operationalization are of particular relevance in such studies, because in Europeanization studies '[a]wareness of research design is still low' (Exadaktylos and Radaelli 2009: 526). Our policy-based study shifted from a simple definition of Europeanization as the process of construction and diffusion of EU policies, by also considering the 'uploading' and 'downloading' stages.

The second step taken regarded the operationalization of the concept: for this purpose, an in-depth description of policy construction and policy diffusion was provided. Put very simply, in the case of public policy, Europeanization can be detected if construction and diffusion of EU public policy has occurred. The illustration of agricultural, regional cohesion and employment policies has shown – although with different mechanisms and at different moments in time – that Europeanization has affected all three policy areas analysed.

The third analytical step consisted of understanding the prerequisites and policy and political-institutional effects of Europeanization. For this purpose, we proceeded as follows: first, by distinguishing between EU agenda- and policy-setting capacities (shaping, adapting, taking) and variants of domestic policy adaptation (policy transformation, policy adjustment and policy continuity) we tried to substantiate empirically the 'uploading' dynamics and policy/political-institutional effects of Europeanization. To be sure, once political-institutional changes were detected we tried to specify as clearly as possible the Europeanization-induced changes, without assuming that domestic and political-institutional changes were 'automatically' linked to Europeanization. By specifically focusing on the dimensions and politics of change, we tried to illustrate the European added value in domestic change processes.

This research design has proved particularly fertile since, through in-depth process tracing and qualitative sequencing analysis, it revealed how Europeanization mattered in domestic change processes. The evidence presented in the previous chapters illustrates the differential adaptation that occurred in the three policy areas, with respect to both the 'construction' and 'diffusion' stages. Although limited to policy analysis, we consider that the research strategy used in the investigation of three specific policies in the Italian case could also be used for a better understanding of Europeanization patterns in other member states and policy areas.

7.2 Policy structure and policy change

Another important contribution to the literature concerns the analysis of policy change. Prior to the problem of 'measuring' Europeanization, one of the key challenges of the policy analyst is to measure policy change. In fact, policy change is often ill-defined because the dimensions of analysis are either implicit or not fully explicit. Even in Radaelli's widely cited, path-breaking contribution on 'Europeanization of public policy' (2003a), the conceptualization of policy change is not fully explicit: although the notion of 'magnitude of policy change and its direction' is introduced (p. 37) and direct reference is made to Hall's 'third order change' (pp. 37–38), there is no specification regarding the *dimensions* of policy change. Interestingly, Radaelli identifies the possible types of policy 'outcome' (retrenchment, inertia, absorption and transformation; p. 37) but the measurement criteria are not spelt out.

More generally, and even beyond Europeanization studies, we argue that by 'unpacking' policy structure according to four key dimensions (objectives, principles, procedures, and financial instruments), the analysis of different forms and intensity of policy change can be more accurate. Clearly, as already mentioned in Chapter 1, the policy structure approach adopted in this study is heavily indebted to Peter Hall's (1993) path-breaking contribution, but we claim that the policy analysis has benefited substantially from the use of the policy structure approach because: (a) it facilitated the policy evolution description; and (b) it also facilitated a clear qualification of policy change (policy adjustment versus policy transformation) by looking at 'standardized' analytical dimensions that go beyond the specificities of the policies analysed in this book and therefore could also be applied to other policies. To be sure, within the definition of the objectives, principles, procedures and financial instruments, some room is also left for the researcher's discretionary reading of reality (e.g. assessing policy continuity or degree of change). However, unlike more impressionistic policy descriptions, we argue that anchoring the analysis to four simple dimensions has the main advantage of making the subjective interpretation of reality more limited than in less well-defined approaches. Possibly, other sub-dimensions could be added to the four overarching ones used in this study, but the main added value of the policy structure approach is that it clearly defines the key elements of the policies under scrutiny and facilitates an in-depth analysis of public policies.

7.3 The 'goodness of fit' hypothesis

The most important theoretical element developed so far in Europeanization studies regards the 'goodness of fit' hypothesis. In the most comprehensive critical assessment of the validity of the hypothesis, Mastenbroek and Kaeding state that: 'as the original hypothesis has been rejected on several occasions, we argue that we should go beyond the degree of fit in theorizing EU adaptation. We have argued that the hypothesis is too deterministic, leaving no room for domestic politics' (2006: 347; for further evidence-based criticism, see also Falkner et al. 2007). This holds particularly true if we take the clearest and simplest definition of misfit as the one formulated by Duina and Blithe, who:

> hypothesize that implementation of common market rules depends primarily on the fit between rules and the policy legacy and the organization of interest groups in member states. Rules that challenge national policy legacies and the organization of interest groups are not implemented fully and on time; they are normally rejected, typically reaching domestic systems only partially and long after the official deadlines.
> (1999: 499)

In this definition there is indeed an implicit 'automatism' in the adaptational process following 'misfit'. Furthermore, we may add that if the empirical analysis is confined to directive implementation, then implicitly the hypothesis is related to only one Europeanization mechanism (direction) and not to other mechanisms (regulation, coordination and non-formalized pressures), and this limitation may be problematic for the full testing of the hypothesis. One way to avoid excessive determinism in implementation analysis has been to focus qualitatively on the directives transposition – as very thoroughly done by Falkner and others (Falkner et al. 2005; Falkner and Treib 2008; for a debate on this specific research approach, see also Toshkov 2007; Thompson 2009). Another strategy is to provide a more nuanced version of the 'goodness of fit' hypothesis by further focusing on the domestic politics of adaptation (as originally suggested by Risse et al. 2001) in various policy fields. This is the research strategy followed in this study and we claim that – although somewhat revised as regards its original formulation – we should maintain the 'goodness of fit' hypothesis since domestic preferences may differ under conditions of misfit, mid-fit or fit. As a reply to the question raised by Mastenbroek and Kaeding – '[i]f domestic preferences or beliefs can overcome a misfit, what is the added value of this variable?' (2006: 338) – we would answer that our research suggests that high or low degree of misfit may also shape the *domestic politics of adaptation* because, in cases of misfit, more support will be needed from domestic actors who are in favour of Europeanization, whereas in cases of low misfit overall domestic support may be weaker. Put another way, different degrees of misfit may determine different domestic politics of adaptation in terms of domestic institutional and non-institutional actors' coalitional strategies and multi-level interaction with the EU. Without taking seriously into consideration the goodness of fit hypothesis, it would have been much more difficult to understand the patterns of domestic adaptation presented in Chapter 6 of this book. Domestic actors may use European policies in order to increase their 'competitive advantage' at the domestic level in order to overcome resistance with respect to their preferences (see also Woll and Jacquot 2010; Graziano *et al.* 2011a, 2011b). Therefore, if the 'goodness of fit' hypothesis is well-defined and operationalized, and accompanied by a fully-fledged consideration of the domestic actors and their preferences both in the construction and diffusion stages of Europeanization, it may hold valuable theoretical potential for future Europeanization research.

Appendix 1   Synoptic table
Italian governments 1992–2011

Synoptic table Italian Governments 1992–2011

Legislature	Government	Prime Minister	Economic affairs			Treasury	Budget and Economic Planning	Agriculture	Social policies and employment	Development and territorial cohesion
			Finance							
1992–1994 XI Legislature	AMATO (28.6.1992–28.4.1993) *Center-left*	Giuliano AMATO	Giovanni GORIA			Piero BARUCCI	Franco REVIGLIO	Gianni Angelo FONTANA	Nino CRISTOFORI	
	CIAMPI (28.4.1993–10.5.1994) *Center-left*	Carlo Azeglio CIAMPI	Vincenzo VISCO Franco GALLO (since 4.5.1993)			Piero BARUCCI	Luigi SPAVENTA	Alfredo Luigi DIANA	Gino GIUGNI	
1994–1996 XII Legislature	BERLUSCONI (10.5.1994–17.1.1995) *Center-right*	Silvio BERLUSCONI	Giulio TREMONTI			Lamberto DINI	Giancarlo PAGLIARINI	Adriana Poli BORTONE	Mario Clemente MASTELLA	
	DINI (17.1.1995–17.5.1996) *Technical*	Lamberto DINI	Augusto FANTOZZI			Lamberto DINI	Rainer MASERA Augusto FANTOZZI, interim (12.1.1996–16.2.1996) Mario ARCELLI (since 16.2.1996)	Walter LUCHETTI	Tiziano TREU	
			Finance		*Treasury, budget and economic planning*					
1996–2001 XIII Legislature	PRODI (17.5.1996–21.10.1998) *Center-left*	Romano PRODI	Vincenzo VISCO			Carlo Azeglio CIAMPI			Michele PINTO	Tiziano TREU	
	D'ALEMA (21.10.1998–22.12.1999) *Center-left*	Massimo D'ALEMA	Vincenzo VISCO			Carlo Azeglio CIAMPI Giuliano AMATO (since 13.5.1999)			Paolo DE CASTRO	Antonio BASSOLINO Cesare SALVI (since 21.6.1999)	
	D'ALEMA II (22.12.1999–25.04.2000) *Center-left*	Massimo D'ALEMA	Vincenzo VISCO			Giuliano AMATO			Paolo DE CASTRO	Cesare SALVI	
	AMATO II (25.4.2000–11.6.2001) *Center-left*	Giuliano AMATO	Ottaviano DEL TURCO			Vincenzo VISCO			Alfonso Pecoraro SCANIO	Cesare SALVI Livia TURCO, interim (since 6.6.2001)	

			Economics and finance	Productive Activities		
2001–2006 XIV Legislature	BERLUSCONI II (11.6.2001–23.4.2005) *Center-right*	Silvio BERLUSCONI	Giulio TREMONTI (until 3.7.2004) Silvio BERLUSCONI interim (3.7.2004–16.7.2004) Domenico SINISCALCO (since 16.7.2004)	Antonio MARZANO	Giovanni ALEMANNO	Roberto MARONI	Gianfranco MICCICHÈ (without portfolio)
	BERLUSCONI III (23.4.2005–17.5.2006) *Center-right*	Silvio BERLUSCONI	Giulio TREMONTI	Claudio SCAJOLA	Giovanni ALEMANNO	Roberto MARONI	
			Economics and finance	*Economic development*		
2006–2008 XV Legislature	PRODI II (17.5.2006–6.5.2008) *Center-right*	Romano PRODI	Tommaso Padoa SCHIOPPA	Pierluigi BERSANI	Paolo DE CASTRO	Cesare DAMIANO	
2008–Present XVI Legislature	BERLUSCONI IV (8.5.2008–16.11.2011) *Center-right*	Silvio BERLUSCONI	Giulio TREMONTI	Paolo ROMANI (since 4.9.2010) Claudio SCAJOLA (until 5.5.2010) Silvio BERLUSCONI interim (until 4.5.2010)	Luca ZAIA (until 14.4.2010) Giancarlo GALAN (until 23.3.2011)		
Francesco Saverio ROMANO (since 23.3.2011)		Raffaele FITTO[a] (without portfolio)					
	MONTI (16.11.2011–Present) *Technical*	Mario MONTI	Mario MONTI	Corrado PASSERA[b]	Mario CATANIA	Elsa FORNERO[c]	Fabrizio BARCA[d] (without portfolio)

Notes

a The name of the ministry is 'Relationships with the regions and territorial cohesion'.
b The name of the ministry is 'Economic Development, Infrastructure and Transports'.
c The name of the ministry is 'Employment, social policies with responsibility on equal opportunities'.
d The name of the ministry is 'Territorial Cohesion'.

Appendix 2   Interviews

Ministry of Employment and Social Affairs, 1999
Ministry of Treasury, Budget and Economic Programming, 2000
Ministry of Treasury, 2000
Ministry of Economic Development, 2009
Ministry of Economic Development, 2009
Ministry of Economic Development, 2009
Ministry of Employment and Social Affairs
Ministry of Employment and Social Affairs, 2003
Ministry of Agriculture, 2012
Ministry of Agriculture, 2012
Ministry of Agriculture, 2012
Prime Minister's office, Employment Policy Coordination Committee, 2003
EU Commission representation, Rome, 2009
Regional government, Puglia, 1999
Regional government, Puglia, 1999
Regional government, Puglia, 1999
Regional government, Campania, 1999
Regional government, Campania, 1999
Regional government, Campania, 1999
Regional government, Campania, 2000
Regional government, Calabria, 1999
Regional government, Calabria, 2001
Regional government, Calabria, 2001
Political Party, Alleanza nazionale, 2003
Political party, Democratici di Sinistra, 2003
Political party, Rifondazione Comunista, 2003
Political party, Forza Italia, 2003
Trade union, CGIL, 2003
Trade union, CISL, 2003
Trade union, UIL, 2003
Trade union, CISL, 2009
Trade union, CGIL, 2009
Trade union, UIL, 2009

Trade union, CISL, 2010
Trade union, CGIL, 2010
Trade union, UIL, 2010
Institutional association, ANCI, 2009
Agricultural association, COLDIRETTI, 1999
Agricultural association, CIA, 2012
Agricultural association, CONFAGRICOLTURA, 2012
Agricultural association, COLDIRETTI, 2012
Business association, CONFCOMMERCIO, 1998
Business association, CONFAPI, 1999
Business association, CONFCOOPERATIVE, 1999
Business association, LEGA DELLE COOPERATIVE, 1999
Business association, CNA, 1999
Business association, Confartigianato, 1999
Business association, CONFINDUSTRIA, 1999
Business association, CONFINDUSTRIA, 2009
Business association, CONFINDUSTRIA, 2010
Non-governmental association, FORUM DEL TERZO SETTORE, 1999
Non-governmental association, CILAP-EAPN, 2010

Notes

1 Europeanization and domestic policy change: a framework for analysis

1 Throughout this book we shall use the term European Union, although the European political organization has been labelled with different names since it was established in 1957: European Economic Community first and, since 1985, European Community. The European Union was introduced in 1992 with the Treaty of Maastricht.
2 It goes beyond the purpose of this short discussion to do justice to the richness of the theoretical debate regarding European integration. For such an account, among others, see Cram (1996) and Rosamond (2000).
3 As institutionalized modes of Europeanization, Sharpf (2000) considers also hierarchical direction but by distinguishing between 'construction' and 'diffusion' Europeanization mechanisms it seems more appropriate to further 'unpack' the hierarchical direction into two diffusion mechanisms – regulation and direction.
4 Appendix 1 provides general information on the governments that have ruled Italy from 1992 to 2011.

2 Italian politics and EU decision making

1 We will focus on other relevant dimensions (regions and interest groups) in the discussion of the various policies.

5 Europeanization and Italian employment policy

1 The new Lisbon 2020 strategy allowed domestic government to fix their goals within the overarching EU goal of 75 per cent. This is the reason why the Italian 2020 target is lower than the previous one, which was valid for all the EU member states.

Bibliography

AA.VV. (1986) *Il Lavoro si Crea. Impresa e lavoro* [*Job Creation in Europa*], Milano, Italy: Franco Angeli.

Accornero, A. (2006) *San Precario lavora per noi. Gli impieghi temporanei in Italia*, Milano, Italy: Rizzoli.

Albertazzi, D. and McDonnell, D. (2005) 'The Lega Nord in the Second Berlusconi Government: In a League of Its Own', *West European Politics*, 28(5): 952–972.

Albertazzi, D., McDonnell, D. and Newell, J. (2007) *Di lotta e di governo: The Lega Nord and Rifondazione Comunista in coalition*, paper presented at the 57th Annual Conference of the UK Political Studies Association, 11–13 April, University of Bath.

Amato, G. (1976) *Economia, politica e istituzioni in Italia*, Bologna, Italy: Il Mulino.

Ambler, J.S. and Reichert, M.S. (2001) 'France: Europeanism, Nationalism and the Decline of State Planning', in E.E. Zeff and E.B. Pirro, eds. *The European Union and the Member States: Co-operation, Co-ordination and Compromise*, Boulder, CO: Lynne Rienner.

Anderssen, S.S. and Eliassen, K.A., eds. (1993) *Making Policy in Europe: The Europeification of National Policy-making*, London and Thousand Oaks, CA: Sage.

Armstrong, H. (1995) 'The Role and Evolution of European Community Regional Policy', in M. Keating and B. Jones, eds. *The European Union and the Regions*, Oxford: Clarendon Press.

Bache, I. (2007) 'Cohesion Policy', in P. Graziano and M.P. Vink, eds. *Europeanization: New Research Agendas*, Basingstoke: Palgrave Macmillan, 239–252.

Bache, I. and Olsson, J. (2001) 'Legitimacy through Partnership? EU Policy Diffusion in Britain and Sweden', *Scandinavian Political Studies*, 24(3): 215–237.

Bachtler, J. and Méndez, C. (2007) 'Who Governs EU Cohesion Policy? Deconstructing the Reforms of the Structural Funds', *Journal of Common Market Studies*, 45(3): 535–564.

Baglioni, S., Baumgarten, B., Chabanet, D. and Lahusen, C. (2008a) 'Transcending Marginalization: The Mobilization of the Unemployed in France, Germany, and Italy in Comparative Perspective', *Mobilization*, 13(3): 323–335.

Baglioni, S., della Porta, D. and Graziano, P. (2008b) 'The Contentious Politics of Unemployment: The Italian Case in Comparative Perspective', *European Journal of Political Research*, 47(6): 827–851.

Balme, R. and Woll, C. (2005) 'France: Between Integration and National Sovereignty', in S. Bulmer and C. Lequesne, eds. *Member States and the European Union*, Oxford: Oxford University Press.

Barbier, J.-C. and Fargion, V. (2004) 'Continental Inconsistencies on the Path of

Activation: Consequences for Social Citizenship in Italy and France', *European Societies*, 6(4): 437–460.

Barca, F. (2009) *An Agenda for a Reformed Cohesion Policy: A Place-based Approach to Meeting European Union Challenges and Expectations*, Independent report prepared at the request of D. Hübner, Commissioner for Regional Policy.

Barca, F. (2011) *Relazione alle Commissioni Bilancio di Camera e Senato del Ministro per la coesione territoriale*, Roma.

Barca, L. (2004) 'Il PCI e l'Europa. Intervista con il Senatore Luciano Barca', *Menabò di Etica ed Economia*, 20 June, Rome.

Barnier, M. (2001) *Cohesion in the enlarged European Union*, Speech delivered at the Second European Cohesion Forum, 21 May, Brussels.

Bellucci, P. and Conti, N. eds. (2012) *Gli Italiani e l'Europa. Opinione pubblica, élite politiche e media*, Roma: Carocci.

Benz, A. and Eberlein, T. (1999) 'The Europeanization of Regional Policies: Patterns of Multi-level Governance', *Journal of European Public Policy*, 6(2): 329–348.

Beyers, J., Eising, R. and Maloney, W. (2008) 'Researching Interest Group Politics in Europe and Elsewhere: Much We Study, Little We Know?', *West European Politics*, 31(6): 1103–1128.

Bindi, F. and Cisci, M. (2005) 'Italy and Spain: A tale of Contrasting Effectiveness in the EU', in S. Bulmer and C. Lequesne, eds. *Member States and the European Union*, Oxford: Oxford University Press.

Boeri, T. (2000) *Uno Stato asociale. Perché è fallito il welfare in Italia*, Roma-Bari: Laterza.

Boerzel, T.A. (1999) 'Towards Convergence in Europe? Institutional Adaptation to Europeanization in Germany and Spain', *Journal of Common Market Studies*, 37(4): 573–596.

Boerzel, T.A. (2001) 'Non-compliance in the European Union: Pathology or Statistical Artefact?', *Journal of European Public Policy*, 8(5): 803–824.

Boerzel, T.A. (2003) 'Shaping and Taking EU Politics: Member State Responses to Europeanisation', Queen's Papers on Europeanisation, 2/2002.

Boerzel, T.A. (2007) 'Environmental Policy', in P. Graziano and M.P. Vink, eds. *Europeanization: New Research Agendas*, Basingstoke: Palgrave Macmillan, 226–238.

Borghetto, E. and Franchino, F. (2010) 'The Role of Sub-national Authorities in the Implementation of EU Directives', *Journal of European Public Policy*, 17(6): 759–780.

Borras, S., Font, N. and Gomes, N. (1998) 'The Europeanisation of National Policies in Comparison', *Southern European Politics and Society*, 3(2): 23–44.

Bouvet, F. and Dall'Erba, S. (2010) 'European Regional Structural Funds: How Large is the Influence of Politics on the Allocation Process?', *Journal of Common Market Studies*, 48(3): 501–528.

Brunazzo, M. (2010) 'From Policy-shaper to Policy-taker: The Europeanization of Italian Cohesion Policy', *World Political Science Review*, 6(1): 1–28.

Brunazzo, M. and Piattoni, S. (2008) 'Italy and Cohesion Policy', in S. Fabbrini and S. Piattoni, eds. *Italy in the European Union*, Lanham, MD: Rowman and Littlefield.

Bull, M. and Baudner, J. (2004) 'Europeanization and Italian Policy for the Mezzogiorno', *Journal of European Public Policy*, 11(6): 1058–1076.

Bulmer, S. (1983) 'Domestic Politics and European Community Policy-making', *Journal of Common Market Studies*, 21(4): 349–364.

Bulmer, S. (2007) 'Theorizing Europeanization', in P. Graziano and M.P. Vink, eds. *Europeanization: New Research Agendas*, Basingstoke: Palgrave Macmillan.

Bulmer, S. (2009) '*Politics in Time* meets the Politics of Time: Historical Institutionalism and the EU Timescape', *Journal of European Public Policy*, 16(2): 307–324.

Bulmer, S. and Burch, M. (1998) 'Organising for Europe: Whitehall, the British State and the European Union', *Public Administration*, 76(4): 601–628.

Bureau, J.-C. and Matthews, A. (2005) *EU Agricultural Policy: What Developing Countries Need to Know*, IIIS Discussion Papers, 91.

Buresti, C. and Marciani, G.E. (1991) 'L'esperienza dei programmi integrati mediterranei', *Rivista economica del Mezzogiorno*, 5(1): 7–54.

Bursens, P. (2007) 'State Structures', in P. Graziano and M.P. Vink, eds. *Europeanization: New Research Agendas*, Basingstoke: Palgrave Macmillan.

Cadeddu, S. and Midena, E. (2000) 'Il mercato del lavoro', in A. Cassese, ed. *Trattato di diritto amministrativo*, Milan, Italy: Giuffré.

Cafiero, S. (1996) *Questione meridionale e unità nazionale*, Rome: La Nuova Italia Scientifica.

Camera dei Deputati – Commissione speciale per le politiche comunitarie (1996) *Utilizzazione dell'Italia dei fondi strutturali*, Rome.

Caporaso, J. (2007) 'The Three Worlds of Regional Integration Theory', in P. Graziano and M.P. Vink, eds. *Europeanization: New Research Agendas*, Basingstoke: Palgrave Macmillan.

Caporaso, J. and Jupille, J. (2001) 'The Europeanization of Gender Equality Policy and Domestic Structural Change', in M. Cowles, J. Caporaso and T. Risse, eds. *Transforming Europe? Europeanization and Domestic Change*, Ithaca, NY: Cornell University Press.

Carrieri, M. (1995) *L'incerta rappresentanza*, Bologna, Italy: Il Mulino.

Casula Vifell, Å. (2009) 'Speaking with Forked Tongues: Swedish Public Administration and the European Employment Strategy', *European Integration online Papers*, 13/2009.

Catania, M. – Dipartimento delle politiche europee e internazionali del Ministero delle politiche agricole alimentari e forestali (2011) *Lo scenario verso la nuova PAC, relazione presentata al primo forum nazionale dell'agroalimentare*, 11–12 November, Cremona, Italy.

Cavatorto, S. (2005) 'Le élite politiche italiane nelle grandi scelte comunitarie', in M. Cotta, P. Isernia and L. Verzichelli, eds. *L'Europa in Italia*, Bologna, Italy: Il Mulino.

Cavatorto, S. and Fois, G.A. (2005) 'Le elites politiche italiane nelle grandi scelte comunitarie', in M. Cotta, P. Isernia and L. Verzichelli, eds. *L'Europa in Italia*, Bologna, Italy: Il Mulino.

Cazzola, F., ed. (1979) *Anatomia del potere DC. Enti pubblici e 'centralità democristiana'*, Bari, Italy: De Donato.

Checkel, J. (2001) 'The Europeanization of Citizenship?', in M.G. Cowles, J. Caporaso and T. Risse, eds. *Transforming Europe? Europeanization and Domestic Change*, Ithaca, NY: Cornell University Press.

Cini, M. and Mura, M. (2010) Promoting Cohesion in Europe: The Changing Role of EU Institutions, unpublished manuscript.

Clasen, J. and Clegg, D., eds. (2011) *Regulating the Risk of Unemployment: National Adaptations to Post-industrial Labour Markets in Europe*, Oxford: Oxford University Press.

Cocozza, F. (1999) 'Programmazione negoziata e il nuovo impulso al regionalismo economico', *Le istituzioni del federalismo*, 22(2): 259–281.

Cole, A. and Drake, H. (2000) 'The Europeanisation of the French Policy: Continuity, Change and Adaptation', *Journal of European Public Policy*, 7(1): 26–43.

Coleman, W.D. and Chiasson, C. (2002) 'State Power, Transformative Capacity And Adapting To Globalization: An Analysis Of French Agricultural policy, 1960–2000', *Journal of European Public Policy*, 9(2): 168–185.

Commission of the European Communities (1968) *Agriculture 1980*, Brussels, Belgium.

Commission of the European Communities (1969) *A Regional Policy for the Community*, Brussels, Belgium.

Commission of the European Communities (1985) *Perspectives for the Common Agricultural Policy*, Brussels, Belgium.

Commission of the European Communities (1993) *Growth, Competitiveness, Employment: The Challenges and Ways Forward into the 21st Century*, White Paper, Brussels, Belgium.

Commission of the European Communities (1997) *Agenda 2000: For a Stronger and Wider Union*, Brussels, Belgium.

Commission of the European Communities (1999) *The EU Budget*, Brussels, Belgium.

Commission of the European Communities (2000) *Acting Locally for Employment: A Local Dimension for the European Employment Strategy*, Brussels, Belgium.

Commission of the European Communities (2002a) *Taking Stock of Five Years of the European Employment Strategy*, Brussels, Belgium.

Commission of the European Communities (2002b) *Streamlining the Annual Economic and Employment Policy Co-ordination Cycles*, Brussels, Belgium.

Commission of the European Communities (2003) *The Future of the European Employment Strategy (EES): "A Strategy for Full Employment and Better Jobs for All'*, Brussels, Belgium.

Commission of the European Communities (2005) *Working Together for Growth and Jobs: A New Start for the Lisbon Strategy*, Brussels, Belgium.

Commission of the European Communities (2007) *Towards Common Principles of Flexicurity: More and Better Jobs through Flexibility and Security*, Brussels, Belgium.

Commission of the European Communities (2010a) *Lisbon Strategy Evaluation Document*, Brussels, Belgium.

Commission of the European Communities (2010b) *Europe 2020: A Strategy for a Smart, Sustainable and Inclusive Growth*, Brussels, Belgium.

Commission of the European Communities (2010c) *The CAP towards 2020: Meeting the Food, Natural Resources and Territorial Challenge of the Future*, Brussels, Belgium.

Commission of the European Communities (2011a) *Impact Assessment: Common Agricultural Policy towards 2020*, Brussels, Belgium.

Commission of the European Communities (2011b) *Proposal for a Regulation of the European Parliament and of the Council*, Brussels, Belgium.

Commission of the European Communities (n.d.) *EU Trade in Agriculture*, Brussels, Belgium.

Conti, N. (2010) 'European Citizenship in Party Euromanifestos: Southern Europe in Comparative Perspective', *South European Society and Politics*, 15(1): 119–141.

Conti, N. and Memoli, V. (2011) *L'Europa secondo i partiti: vincolo, scelta o opportunità?*, paper presented at the Annual Conference of the Italian Political Science Association – SISP, 8–10 September, Palermo, Italy.

Conti, N. and Verzichelli, L. (2005) 'La dimensione europea del discorso politico. Un'analisi diacronica delle preferenze partitiche in Italia (1950–2001)', in M. Cotta, P. Isernia and L. Verzichelli, *L'Europa in Italia*, Bologna, Italy: Il Mulino.

Conzelmann, T. (1998) '"Europeanization" of Regional Development Policies? Linking

the Multi-level Approach with Theories of Policy Learning and Policy Change', *European Integration Online Papers*, 4(2).
Corriere della Sera (1992) 'La Caporetto del latte italiano', 24 May.
Corriere della Sera (1992) 'Ma per vincere a Bruxelles occorre riguadagnare credibilità', 5 July.
Costa Pinto, A. and Teixera, N.S., eds. (2002) *Southern Europe and the Making of the European Union, 1945–1980s*, New York: Columbia University Press.
Cotta, M. (1996) 'La crisi del governo di partito all'italiana', in M. Cotta and P. Isernia, eds. *Il gigante dai piedi d'argilla. La crisi del regime partitocratico in Italia*, Bologna, Italy: Il Mulino.
Cotta, M. and Isernia, P., eds. (1996) *Il gigante dai piedi d'argilla. La crisi del regime partitocratico in Italia*, Bologna, Italy: Il Mulino.
Cotta, M. and Verzichelli, L. (2007) *Political Institutions in Italy*, Oxford: Oxford University Press.
Cowles, M.G., Caporaso, J. and Risse, T., eds. (2001) *Transforming Europe: Europeanization and Domestic Change*, Ithaca, NY: Cornell University Press.
Cram, L. (1996) 'Theories of Integration', in J. Richardson, ed. *Policy-making in the European Union*, London: Routledge.
D'Antone, L. (1995) 'L' "interesse straordinario per il Mezzogiorno" (1943–1960)', *Meridiana*, 24: 17–64.
Daneo, C. (1980) *Breve storia dell'agricoltura italiana 1860–1970*, Milano, Italy: Mondadori.
Daugbjerg, C. (2003) 'Policy Feedback and Paradigm Shift in Agricultural Policy: The Effects of the MacSharry Reform on Future Reform', *Journal of European Public Policy*, 10(3): 421–437.
Daugbjerg, C. (2009) 'Sequencing in Public Policy: The Evolution of the CAP over a Decade', *Journal of European Public Policy*, 16(3): 395–411.
Della Sala, V. (2008) 'Italy and Macroeconomic Policy', in S. Fabbrini and S. Piattoni, *Italy in the European Union*, Lanham, MD: Rowman and Littlefield.
Denzin, N.K. and Lincoln, Y.S. (2005) *The Sage Handbook of Qualitative Research*, London and Thousand Oaks, CA: Sage.
Diamanti, I. (1993) *La Lega. Geografia, storia e sociologia di un nuovo soggetto politico*, Rome, Italy: Donzelli.
Duina, F. and Blithe, F. (1999) 'Nation-states and Common Markets: The Institutional Conditions for Acceptance', *Review of International Political Economy*, 6(4): 494: 530.
Dyson, K. (2007) 'Economic Policy', in P. Graziano and M.P. Vink, eds. *Europeanization: New Research Agendas*, Basingstoke: Palgrave Macmillan.
Dyson, K. and Featherstone, K. (1996) 'Italy and EMU as *"Vincolo esterno"*: Empowering the Technocrats, Transforming the State', *Southern European Society and Politics*, 1(2): 272–299.
ECPRD – European Centre for Parliamentary Research and Documentation (2002) *European Affairs Committees: The Influence of National Parliaments on European Politics*, Brussels.
Eising, R. (2007) 'Interest Groups and Social Movements', in P. Graziano and M.P. Vink, eds. *Europeanization: New Research Agendas*, Basingstoke: Palgrave Macmillan.
Exadaktylos, T. and Radaelli, C. (2009) 'Research Design in Europeanization Studies: The Case of Europeanization', *Journal of Common Market Studies*, 47(3): 507–530.
Fabiani, G. (1986) *L'agricoltura italiana tra sviluppo e crisi (1945–1985)*, Bologna, Italy: Il Mulino.

166 Bibliography

Fabbrini, S. (2000) *Tra pressioni e veti*, Roma-Bari, Italy: Laterza.

Fabbrini, S. and Brunazzo, M. (2003) 'Federalizing Italy: The Convergent Effects of Europeanization and Domestic Mobilization', *Regional & Federal Studies*, 13(1): 100–120.

Fabbrini, S. and Piattoni, S., eds. (2008) *Italy in the European Union*, Lanham, MD: Rowman and Littlefield.

Fabbrini, S., Di Palma, G. and Freddi, G., eds. (2000) *Condannata al successo? L'Italia nell'Europa integrata degli anni Novanta*, Bologna, Italy: Il Mulino.

Falkner, G. (1999) 'European Social Policy', in B. Kohler-Koch and R. Eising, eds. *The Transformation of Governance in the European Union*, London and New York: Routledge.

Falkner, G. (2000) 'The Council of the Social Partners? EC Social Policy between Diplomacy and Collective Bargaining', *Journal of European Public Policy*, 7(5): 705–724.

Falkner, G. (2001) 'The Europeanization of Austria: Misfit, Adaptation and Controversies', *European Integration Online Papers*, 5(13).

Falkner, G. (2007) 'Social Policy', in P. Graziano and M.P. Vink, eds. *Europeanization: New Research Agendas*, Basingstoke: Palgrave Macmillan.

Falkner, G. and Treib, O. (2008) 'Three Worlds of Compliance or Four? The EU-15 Compared to New Member States', *Journal of Common Market Studies*, 46(2): 293–313.

Falkner, G., Hartlapp, M. and Treib, O. (2007) 'Worlds of Compliance: Why Leading Approaches to European Union Implementation are Only "Sometimes-true Theories"', *European Journal of Political Research*, 46(3): 395–416.

Falkner, G., Treib, O., Hartlapp, M. and Leiber, S. (2005) *Complying with Europe: EU Harmonisation and Soft Law in the Member States*, Cambridge: Cambridge University Press.

Fanfani, R. (1998) *Lo sviluppo della politica agricola comunitaria*, Rome, Italy: La Nuova Italia Scientifica.

Fargion, V. (2002) *Decoupling Passive and Active Labour Market Policies: The Italian Case in Comparative Perspective*, working paper prepared for the Cost A13 Unemployment Working Group Meeting, 1–2 November, Malta.

Featherstone, K. (2003) 'Introduction: In the Name of "Europe"', in K. Featherstone and C. Radaelli, *The Politics of Europeanization*, Oxford: Oxford University Press.

Featherstone, K. and Kazamias, G., eds. (2001) *Europeanization and the Southern Periphery*, London and Portland, OR: Frank Cass.

Featherstone, K. and Radaelli, C. (2003) *The Politics of Europeanization*, Oxford: Oxford University Press.

Felice, E. (2007) *Divari regionali e intervento pubblico. Per una rilettura dello sviluppo in Italia*, Bologna, Italy: Il Mulino.

Feltrin, P. (1991) 'Partiti e sindacati: simbiosi o dominio?', in L. Morlino, ed. *Costruire la democrazia. Gruppi e partiti in Italia*, Bologna, Italy: Il Mulino.

Ferrera, M. (2005) *The Boundaries of Welfare*, Oxford: Oxford University Press.

Ferrera, M. and Gualmini, E. (2004) *Rescued by Europe? Social and Labour Market Reforms in Italy from Maastricht to Berlusconi*, Amsterdam: Amsterdam University Press.

Ferrera, M. and Sacchi, S. (2005) 'The OMC and National Institutional Capabilities: The Italian Case', in J. Zeitlin and P. Pochet, with L. Magnusson, eds. *The Open Method of Coordination in Action: The European Employment and Social Inclusion Strategies*, Brussels: P.I.E. Peter Lang.

Ferrera, M., Gualmini, E., Graziano, P. and Alti, T. (2000) 'Labour Market Governance

in the Italian Regions: The Experience of the 1990s', *Quaderni di ricerca*, POLEIS, 27.
Financial Times (2012) 'The EU Rests on Monti's Shoulders', 27 January.
Flockhart, T. (2010) 'Europeanization or Eu-ization? The Transfer of European Norms across Time and Space', *Journal of Common Market Studies*, 48(4): 787–810.
FORMEZ (2001) *I nuovi servizi per l'impiego*, Rome, Italy: Donzelli.
Freeman, G.P. and Ögelmann, N. (1998) 'Homeland Citizenship Policies and the Status of Third Country Nationals in the European Union', *Journal of Ethnic and Migration Studies*, 24(4): 769–788.
Friedmann, H. and McMichael, P. (1989) 'Agriculture and the State System: The rise and decline of national agricultures, 1870 to present', *Sociologia Ruralis*, 29(2): 93–117.
Geroldi, G. (2005) 'Il sistema degli ammortizzatori sociali in Italia: aspetti critici e ipotesi di riforma', in P. Onofri and S. Giannini, eds. *Per lo sviluppo. Fisco e welfare*, Bologna, Italy: Il Mulino.
Ginsborg, P. (1989) *Storia dell'Italia dal dopoguerra ad oggi*, Torino, Italy: Einaudi.
Giuliani M. (1996) *Italy and the European Union: Internal Dynamism and External Stagnation?*, Milan, Italy: Quaderni del Centro studi e ricerche di politica comparata, Poleis, Università Bocconi.
Giuliani, M. (2006) *La politica europea*, Bologna, Italy: Il Mulino.
Goetschy, J. (1999) 'The European Employment Strategy: Genesis and Development', *European Journal of Industrial Relations*, 5(2): 117–137.
Goetschy, J. (2001) 'The European Employment Strategy from Amsterdam to Stockholm: Has It Reached its Cruising Speed?', *Industrial Relations Journal*, 32(5): 401–418.
Goetz, K. and Hix, S., eds. (2000) *Europeanised Politics? European Integration and National Political Systems*, London: Frank Cass.
Grabbe, H. (2001) 'How Does Europeanization affect CEE Governance? Conditionality, Diffusion and Diversity', *Journal of European Public Policy*, 8(6): 1013–1031.
Grant, W. (1997) *The Common Agricultural Policy*, Basingstoke: Macmillan.
Graziani, A. (2000) *Lo sviluppo dell'economia italiana*, Torino, Italy: Bollati Boringhieri.
Graziano, L. (1980) *Clientelismo e sistema politico: il caso dell'Italia*, Milano, Italy: Franco Angeli.
Graziano, P. (2003) 'Europeanization or Globalization? A Framework for Empirical Research (with Some Evidence from the Italian Case)', *Global Social Policy*, 3(2): 173–194.
Graziano, P. (2004) *Europeizzazione e politiche pubbliche italiane. Coesione e lavoro a confronto*, Bologna, Italy: Il Mulino.
Graziano, P. (2007) 'Adapting to the European Employment Strategy? Continuity and Change in Recent Italian Employment Policy', *International Journal of Comparative Labour Law and Industrial Relations*, 23 (4): 543–565.
Graziano, P. (2010) 'From Local Partnerships to Regional Spaces for Politics? Europeanization and EU Cohesion Policy in Southern Italy', *Regional & Federal Studies*, 20(3): 315–333.
Graziano, P. (2011) 'Europeanization and Domestic Employment Policy Change: Conceptual and Methodological Background', *Governance: An International Journal of Policy, Administration, and Institutions*, 24(3): 583–605.
Graziano, P. and Vink, M.P., eds. (2007) *Europeanization: New Research Agendas*, Basingstoke: Palgrave Macmillan.
Graziano, P.R., Jacquot, S. and Palier, B., eds. (2011a) 'Letting Europe In: The Domestic Usages of Europe in (Re)conciliation Policies', *European Journal of Social Security*, Special Issue, 13(1–2): 312–326.

Graziano, P.R., Jacquot, S. and Palier, B., eds. (2011b) *The EU and the Domestic Politics of Welfare State Reforms*, Basingstoke: Palgrave Macmillan.

Groete, J. (1996) 'Cohesion in Italy: A View on Non-economic Disparities', in L. Hooghe, ed. *Cohesion Policy and European Integration*, Oxford: Oxford University Press.

Grote, J. and Lang, J. (2003) 'Europeanization and Organizational Change in National Trade Associations: An Organizational Ecology Perspective', in K. Featherstone and C. Radaelli, eds. *The Politics of Europeanization*, Oxford: Oxford University Press.

Gualini, E. (2003) 'Challenge to Multi-level Governance: Contradictions and Conflicts in the Europeanization of Italian Regional Policy', *Journal of European Public Policy*, 10(4): 616–636.

Gualmini, E. (1998) *La politica del lavoro italiana*, Bologna, Italy: Il Mulino.

Gualmini, E. (2008) 'Restructuring Weberian Bureaucracy: Comparing Managerial Reforms in Europe and in the United States', *Public Administration*, 86(1): 75–94.

Guidi, M. (2012) *Press release*, 2 February.

Haas, E.B. (1958) *The Uniting of Europe: Political, Social and Economic Forces, 1950–1957*, Stanford, CA: Stanford University Press.

Hall, P.A. 1993. 'Policy Paradigm, Social Learning and the State: The Case of Economic Policy-making in Britain' *Comparative Politics*, 25(3): 275–296.

Hall, P.A. and Taylor, R.C.R. (1996) 'Political Science and the Three New Institutionalisms', *Political Studies*, 44(5): 936–957.

Hank, K. and Soetendorp, B., eds. (1998) *Adapting to European Integration: Small States and the European Union*, London and New York: Longman.

Harmsen, R. (1999) 'The Europeanization of Public Administration: A Comparative Study of France and the Netherlands', *Governance*, 12(11): 81–113.

Haverland, M. (2005) 'Does the EU Cause Domestic Developments? The Problem of Case Selection', *European Integration Online Papers*, 9(2).

Heidenreich, M. and Bischoff, G. (2008) 'The Open Method of Co-ordination: A Way to the Europeanization of Social and Employment Policies?' *Journal of Common Market Studies*, 46(3): 497–532.

Heidenreich, M. and Zeitlin, J. (2009) 'The Open Method of Coordination: A Pathway to the Gradual Transformation of National Employment and Welfare Regimes?', in M. Heidenreich and J. Zeitlin, eds. *Changing European Employment and Welfare Regimes: The Influence of the Open Method of Coordination on National Reforms*, London: Routledge.

Héritier, A., Kerwer, D., Knill, C., Lehmkuhl, D., Teutsch, M. and Douillet, A.-C. (2001) *Differential Europe: The European Union Impact on National Policymaking*, Boulder, CO: Rowman and Littlefield.

Hoffmann, S. (1966) 'Obstinate or Obsolete? The Fate of the Nation-state and the Case of Western Europe', *Daedalus*, 95(3): 862–915.

Hoffmann, S. (1982) 'Reflections on the Nation-state in Western Europe Today', *Journal of Common Market Studies*, 20(1): 21–38.

Holzacker, R.L. (2002) 'National Parliamentary Scrutiny over EU Issues: Comparing the Goals and Methods of Governing and Opposition Parties', *European Union Politics*, 3(4): 459–479.

Hooghe, L., ed. (1996) *Cohesion Policy and European Integration*, Oxford: Oxford University Press.

Hooghe, L. and Keating, M. (1994) 'The Politics of European Union Regional Policy', *Journal of European Public Policy*, 1(3): 367–393.

Hooghe, L. and Marks, G. (2001) *Multi-level Governance and European Integration*, Lanham, MD: Rowman and Littlefield.

Hooghe, L. and Marks, G. (2009) 'A Postfunctionalist Theory of European Integration', *British Journal of Political Science*, 39(1): 1–23.

Howlett, M., Ramesh, M. and Perl, A. (2009) *Studying Public Policy: Policy Cycles and Policy Subsystems*, Toronto: Oxford University Press.

Ichino, P. (1982) *Il collocamento impossibile*, Bari, Italy: De Donato.

INEA-Istituto Nazionale di Economia Agraria (2008) *Italian Agriculture 2008*, Rome.

ISFOL (2002) *Rapporto di valutazione sull'impatto della strategia per l'occupazione*, Rome.

Jessoula, M. (2009) *La politica pensionistica*, Bologna, Italy: Il Mulino.

Jessoula, M., Graziano, P.R. and Madama, I. (2010) '"Selective" Flexicurity in Segmented Labour Markets: The Emergence of Mid-siders in the Italian Case', *Journal of Social Policy*, 39(4): 561–583.

Jupille, J. and Caporaso, J. (1999) 'Institutionalism and the European Union: Beyond International Relations and Comparative Politics', *Annual Review of Political Science*, 2: 429–444.

Kaeding, M. (2006) 'Determinants of Transposition Delay in the European Union', *Journal of Public Policy*, 26(3): 229–253.

Kassim, H. (2005) 'Member State Institutions and the European Union: Impact and Interaction', in S. Bulmer and C. Lequesne, eds. *Member States and the European Union*, Oxford: Oxford University Press.

Kassim, H. (2007) '"Mission Impossible", but Mission Accomplished: The Kinnock Reforms and the European Commission', *Journal of European Public Policy*, 15(5): 648–668.

Kassim, H., Menon, A., Peters, B.G. and Wright, V., eds. (2000) *The National Coordination of EU Policy: The National Level*, Oxford: Oxford University Press.

Kassim, H., Menon, A., Peters, B.G. and Wright, V., eds. (2001) *The National Coordination of EU Policy: The EU Level*, Oxford: Oxford University Press.

Kay, A. (2000) 'Towards a Theory of the Common Agricultural Policy', *European Integration Online Papers*, 4(9).

Kenner, J. (1999) 'The EC Employment Title and the "Third Way": Making Soft Law Work?', *International Journal of Comparative Labour Law and Industrial Relations*, 15(2): 34–60.

King, G., Keohane, R.O. and Verba, S. (1995) 'Designing Social Inquiry: Scientific Inference in Qualitative Research', *American Political Science Review*, 89(2): 475–481.

Knill, C. and Lehmkuhl, D. (1999) 'How Europe Matters: Different Mechanisms of Europeanization', *European Integration Online Papers*, 3(7).

Knill, C. and Lenschow, A. (1998) 'The Impact of British and German Administrations on the Implementation of EU environmental Policy', *Journal of European Public Policy*, 5(4): 595–614.

Kritzinger, S. (2003) 'The Influence of the Nation-state on Individual Support for the European Union', *European Union Politics*, 4(2): 219–241.

Kunhle, S., ed. 2000. *The Survival of the Welfare State*, London: Routledge.

Kvist, J. and Saari, J., ed. 2007. *The Europeanisation of Social Protection*, Bristol: Policy Press.

Ladrech, R. (1994) 'Europeanization of Domestic Politics and Institutions: The Case of France', *Journal of Common Market Studies*, 32(1): 69–88.

Ladrech, R. (2002) 'Europeanization and Political Parties: Towards a Framework for Analysis', *Party Politics*, 8(4): 389–403.

Bibliography

Ladrech, R. (2005) 'The Europeanisation of Interest Groups and Political Parties', in S. Bulmer and C. Lequesne, eds. *Member States and the European Union*, Oxford: Oxford University Press.

Laffan, B. (2007) 'Core Executives', in P. Graziano and M.P. Vink, eds. *Europeanization: New Research Agendas*, Basingstoke: Palgrave Macmillan.

Lanaro, S. (1992) *Storia dell'Italia repubblicana*, Venice, Italy: Marsilio.

Lanza, O. (1991) 'L'agricoltura, la Coldiretti e la DC', in L. Morlino, ed. *Costruire la democrazia. Gruppi e partiti in Italia*, Bologna, Italy: Il Mulino.

La Spina, A. (2003) *La politica per il Mezzogiorno*, Bologna, Italy: Il Mulino.

Lavenex, S. (2001) *The Europeanization of Refugee Policies: Between Human Rights and Internal Security*, Aldershot: Ashgate.

Lenschow, A. (1999) 'The Greening of the EU: The Common Agricultural Policy and the Structural Funds', *Environment and Planning C: Government and Policy*, 17(1): 91–108.

Leonardi, R. and Nanetti, R.Y. (2001) 'L'innovazione dei QCS: il processo interattivo tra Stato, Regioni ed Unione Europea', *Le istituzioni del federalismo*, 22(2): 325–359.

Lindberg, L. (1963) *The Political Dynamics of European Integration*, Stanford, CA: Stanford University Press.

Lizzi, R. (1997) 'Licenza di mungere. L'esemplare storia delle quote latte', *Il Mulino*, 2: 351–370.

Lizzi, R. (2002) *La politica agricola*, Bologna, Italy: Il Mulino.

Lizzi, R. (2008) 'Italy and Agricultural Policy', in S. Fabbrini and S. Piattoni, *Italy in the European Union*, Lanham, MD: Rowman and Littlefield.

Lönnroth, J. (2000) *The European Employment Strategy, a Model for Open Coordination and the Role of the Social Partners*, presentation at the SALTSA Conference on Legal Dimensions of the European Strategy, 9–10 October, Brussels.

López-Santana, M. (2009) 'Soft Europeanization? The Differential Influence of the European Employment Strategy in Belgium, Spain, and Sweden', in M. Heidenreich and J. Zeitlin, eds. *Changing European Employment and Welfare Regimes: The Influence of the Open Method of Coordination on National Reforms*, London: Routledge.

Lowi, T. (1972) 'Four Systems of Policy, Politics and Choice', *Public Administration Review*, 32(2): 298–310.

Mair, P. (2000) 'The Limited Impact of Europe on National Party Systems', *West European Politics*, 23(4): 27–51.

Mair, P. (2007) 'Political Parties and Party Systems', in P. Graziano and M.P. Vink, eds. *Europeanization: New Research Agendas*, Basingstoke: Palgrave Macmillan.

Mailand, M. (2008) 'The Uneven Impact of the European Employment Strategy on Members States' Employment Policies: A Comparative Analysis', *Journal of European Social Policy*, 18 (4): 353–365.

Mania, R. and Sateriale, G. 2002. *Relazioni pericolose. Sindacati e politica dopo la concertazione*, Bologna, Italy: Il Mulino.

Manzella, G.P. and Mendez, C. (2009) *The Turning Points of EU Cohesion policy*, working paper prepared for the 'An Agenda for the Reform of Cohesion Policy' report.

Marcolini, E. (2007) 'La coesistenza tra colture tradizionali e transgeniche rilievi normativi e giurisprudenziali. Il caso della Regione Marche', *Agriregionieuropa*, 3(9).

Marini, S. (2012) 'Conclusioni', in F. De Filippis, ed. *La nuova PAC 2014–2020. Un'analisi delle proposte della Commissione*, Rome: Tellus.

Marks, G. (1992) 'Structural Policy in the European Community', in A.M. Sbragia, ed. *Europolitics: Institutions and Policymaking in the "New" European Community*, Washington, DC: Brookings Institution.

Marks, G., Hooghe, L. and Blank, K. (1996) 'European Integration from the 1980s: State-centric vs. Multi-level Governance', *Journal of Common Market Studies*, 34(3): 341–378.
Martin, C. and Palier, B., eds. (2008) *Reforming the Bismarckian Welfare Systems*, Oxford: Blackwell.
Mastenbroek, E. (2005) 'EU Compliance: Still a Black Hole?', *Journal of European Public Policy*, 12(6): 1103–1120.
Mastenbroek, E. and Kaeding, M. (2006) 'Europeanization Beyond the Goodness of Fit: Domestic Politics in the Forefront', *Comparative European Politics*, 4(4): 331–354.
Mattina, L. (1991) 'La Confindustria oltre la simbiosi', in L. Morlino, ed. *Costruire la democrazia. Gruppi e partiti nel consolidamente democratico in Italia*, Bologna, Italy: Il Mulino.
Maurer, A. (2002) *National Parliaments in the European Architecture: Elements for Establishing a Best Practice Mechanism*, working document 8, working group IV 'Role on National Parliaments', Secretariat of the European Convention.
MacSharry, R. (1998) 'Interview, Historical Archives of the European Union', http://www.eui.eu/Research/HistoricalArchivesOfEU/Index.aspx
Meeting of Finance Minister and Central Bank Governors (2011) *Press release*, 15 April, Washington, DC.
Meetings of Heads of State of Government (1972) *Conclusion of the Preparatory Work – The First Summit Conference of the Enlarged Community*, Paris.
Mény, Y. (1992) 'Should the Community Regional Policy be Scrapped?', *Common Market Law Review*, 19(3): 373–388.
Mény, Y., Muller, P. and Quermonne, J.-L., eds. (1996) *Adjusting to Europe: Impact of the European Union on National Institutions and Policies*, London: Routledge.
Merlo, A.M. and Sciotto, A. 2006. *La rivoluzione precaria*, Rome, Italy: Ediesse.
Milio, S. (2007) 'Can Administrative Capacity Explain Differences in Regional Performances? Evidence from Structural Funds Implementation in Southern Italy', *Regional Studies*, 41(4): 429–444.
Milio, S. (2008) 'How Political Stability Shapes Administrative Performance: The Italian Case', *West European Politics*, 31(5): 915–936.
Milward, A.S. (1994) *The European Rescue of the Nation-state*, London: Routledge.
Ministero del Lavoro e delle Politiche Sociali (2001) *Libro Bianco Sul Mercato Del Lavoro*, Rome, Italy.
Ministero del Lavoro e delle Politiche Sociali (2003) *Rapporto di monitoraggio sulle politiche occupazionali e del lavoro*, Rome, Italy.
Ministero del Lavoro e delle Politiche Sociali (2011) *Rapporto sulla Coesione Sociale*, Vol. I–II, Rome, Italy.
Ministero del Lavoro e delle Politiche Sociali (2012) *Rapporto sulla coesione sociale. Anno 2011*, Rome, Italy.
Ministero del Lavoro, della Salute e delle Politiche Sociali (2008) *Rapporto di monitoraggio sulle politiche occupazionali e del lavoro*, Rome, Italy.
Ministero delle Politiche Agricole Alimentari e Forestali (2011) *Indirizzi generali sull'attività amministrativa e sulla gestione per il 2011*, Rome, Italy.
Ministero del Tesoro, Bilancio e Programmazione Economica (2001) *Terzo rapporto sullo sviluppo territorial 1999–2000*, Rome, Italy.
Ministero per le politiche europee (2010) *The Case for a Better European Economic Governance*, Rome, Italy.
Montpetit, E. (2000) 'Europeanization and Domestic Politics: Europe and the Development of a French Environmental Policy for the Agricultural Sector', *Journal of European Public Policy*, 7(4): 576–592.

172 Bibliography

Morlino, L., ed. (1991a) *Costruire la democrazia. Gruppi e partiti in Italia*, Bologna, Italy: Il Mulino.

Morlino, L. (1991b) 'La Confagricoltura tra attesa e compromesso', in L. Morlino, ed. *Costruire la democrazia. Gruppi e partiti in Italia*, Bologna, Italy: Il Mulino.

Morlino, L. (1999) *Europeanization and Representation in Two Europes*, paper delivered at the conference on 'À la récherche de l'Europe méridionale', Pole Universitaire Européen de Montpellier et du Languedoc-Roussillon, CNRS, and CEPEL, 27–29 May, Montpellier.

Mortara, V. (1992) 'L'apparato ministeriale: il nucleo centrale della pubblica amministrazione', in G. Freddi, G., ed. *Scienza dell'amministrazione e politiche pubbliche*, Rome, Italy: La Nuova Italia Scientifica.

Moravcsik, A. (1993) 'Preferences and Power in the European Community: A Liberal Intergovernmentalist Approach', *Journal of Common Market Studies*, 3(1–4): 473–524.

Moravcsik, A. (1998) *The Choice for Europe: Social Purpose and State Power from Messina to Maastricht*, Ithaca, NY: Cornell University Press.

Mosher, J.S. and Trubek, D.M. (2003) 'Alternative Approaches to Governance in the EU: EU Social Policy and the European Employment Strategy', *Journal of Common Market Studies*, 41(1): 63–88.

Nannicini, T. (2006) Il decollo del lavoro interinale in Italia, unpublished paper.

Nomisma (1994) *Rapporto 1994 sull'agricoltura italiana*, Bologna, Italy: Il Mulino.

Nyikos, S. A. (2007) 'Courts', in P. Graziano and M.P. Vink, eds. *Europeanization: New Research Agendas*, Basingstoke: Palgrave Macmillan.

OECD (2006) *Employment Outlook 2006*, Paris.

Olivi, B. (2000) *L'Europa difficile. Storia politica dell'integrazione europea 1948–2000*, Bologna, Italy: Il Mulino.

Olsen, J.P. (1996) 'Europeanization and Nation-state Dynamics', in S. Gustavsson and L. Lewin, eds. *The Future of the Nation-state*, London: Routledge.

Olsen, J.P. (2002) 'The Many Faces of Europeanisation', *Journal of Common Market Studies*, 40(5): 921–952.

Ongaro, E. (2009) *Public Management Reform and Modernization: Trajectories of Administrative Change in Italy, France, Greece, Portugal and Spain*, Cheltenham: Edward Elgar.

Pasquier, R. (2005) 'Cognitive Europeanization and the Territorial Effects of Multi-level Policy Transfer: The Case of Local Development in French and Spanish Regions', *Regional and Federal Studies*, 15(3): 295–310.

Patterson, L.A. (2000) 'Biotechnology Policy', in H. Wallace and W. Wallace, eds. *Policy-making in the European Union*, Oxford: Oxford University Press.

Pavan Woolfe, L. (1998) *Il Fondo Sociale Europeo nello sviluppo italiano*, Rome, Italy: SEAM.

Piana, D. (2009) 'The Power Knocks at the Courts' Back Door: Two Waves of Postcommunist Judicial Reforms', *Comparative Political Studies*, 42(6): 816–840.

Piattoni, S. (2009) *The Theory of Multi-level Governance*, Oxford: Oxford University Press.

Piattoni, S. and Giuliani, M. (2001) 'Italy: Both Leader and Laggard', in E.E. Zeff and E.B. Pirro, eds. *The European Union and the Member States: Co-operation, Co-ordination and Compromise*, Boulder, CO: Lynne Rienner.

Piermattei, M. (2009) *Dal vincolo esterno all'europeizzazione? Le culture politiche italiane e l'integrazione europea nella rincorsa alla moneta unica*, Tesi di dottorato, Università degli Studi della Tuscia.

Pierson, P., ed. (2001) *The New Politics of the Welfare State*, Oxford: Oxford University Press.
Poggi, G. (1978) *La vicenda dello stato moderno*, Bologna, Italy: Il Mulino.
Politi, G. (2012) *Press release*, 28 February.
Porte, C. de la and Nanz, P. (2004) 'The OMC: A Deliberative Democratic Mode of Governance? The Cases of Employment and Pensions', *Journal of European Public Policy*, 11(2): 267–288.
Predieri, A., ed. (1996) *Fondi strutturali e coesione economica e sociale nell'Unione europea*, Milan, Italy: Giuffré.
Puchala, D.J. (1972) 'Of Blind Men, Elephants and International Integration', *Journal of Common Market Studies*, 10(3): 267–285.
Putnam, R.D. (1978) 'Interdependence and the Italian Communists', *International Organization*, 32(2): 301–349.
Putnam, R.D. (1988) 'Diplomacy and Domestic Politics: The Logic of Two-level Games', *International Organization*, 42(3): 427–460.
Quaglia, L. and Radaelli, C.M. (2007) 'Italian Politics and the European Union: A Tale of Two Research Designs', *West European Politics*, 30(4): 924–943.
Radaelli, C.M. (2000) 'Whither Europeanization? Concept Stretching and Substantive Change', *European Integration Online Papers*, 4(8).
Radaelli, C.M. (2003a) 'The Europeanization of Public Policy', in K. Featherstone and C. Radaelli, eds. *The Politics of Europeanization*, Oxford: Oxford University Press.
Radaelli, C.M. (2003b) 'The Open Method of Co-ordination: A New Governance Architecture for the European Union?', Research report, Stockholm: Swedish Institute for European Policy Studies.
Radaelli, C.M. (2004) 'Europeanization: Solution or Problem?', *European Integration Online Papers*, 8(4).
Ramerà, F. (1995) 'L'Europa come strumento di *nation-building*: storia e storici dell'Italia repubblicana, *Passato e presente*, 36: 19–32.
Ramos, F. (2002) 'Judicial Cooperation in the European Courts: Testing Three Models of Judicial Behaviour', *Global Judicial Frontiers*, 2(1): 1535–1653.
Raveaud, G. (2007) 'The European Employment Strategy: Towards More and Better Jobs?', *Journal of Common Market Studies*, 45(2): 411–434.
Regalia, I. (1984) 'Le politiche del lavoro', in U. Ascoli, ed. *Welfare state all'italiana*, Roma-Bari: Laterza.
Regini, M. (2000) 'Between Deregulation and Social Pacts: The Responses of European Economies to Globalization', *Politics & Society*, 28(1): 5–33.
Rey, J. (1968) *Discours de M. Jean Rey, Président de la Commission des Communautés Européennes, devant le Parlement Européen*, Strasbourg, France.
Reyneri, E. (1987) 'Il mercato del lavoro italiano tra controllo statale e regolazione sociale', in P. Lange and M. Regini, eds. *Stato e regolazione sociale*, Bologna, Italy: Il Mulino.
Reyneri, E. (1990) 'Le politiche del lavoro', in B. Dente, ed. *Le politiche pubbliche in Italia*, Bologna, Italy: Il Mulino.
Revelli, M. (1989) *Lavorare in Fiat*, Milano, Italy: Garzanti.
Rieger, E. (2000) 'The Common Agricultural Policy', in H. Wallace and W. Wallace, eds. *Policy-making in the European Union*, Oxford: Oxford University Press.
Risse-Kappen, T. (1996) 'Exploring the Nature of the Beast: International Relations Theory and Comparative Policy Analysis meet the European Union', *Journal of Common Market Studies*, 34(1): 53–80.

Risse, T., Cowles, M.G. and Caporaso, J. (2001) 'Europeanization and Domestic Change: Introduction', in M. Green Cowles, J. Caporaso and T. Risse, eds. *Europeanization and Domestic Change*, Ithaca, NY: Cornell University Press, 1–20.

Roederer-Rynning, C. (2002) 'Farm Conflict in France and the Europeanisation of Agricultural Policy', *West European Politics*, 25(3): 107–126.

Roederer-Rynning, C. (2007) 'Agricultural Policy', in P. Graziano and M.P. Vink, eds. *Europeanization: New Research Agendas*, Basingstoke: Palgrave Macmillan.

Romagnoli, U. (1995) *Il lavoro in Italia*, Bologna, Italy: Il Mulino.

Rometsch, D. and Wessels, W., eds. (1996) *The European Union and Member States: Towards Institutional Fusion?*, Manchester: Manchester University Press.

Rosamond, B. (2000) *Theories of European Integration*, Basingstoke: Macmillan and New York: St. Martin's Press.

Ross, G. (1995) *Jacques Delors and European Integration*, Oxford: Oxford University Press.

Sacchi, S. (2008) 'Italy and Social Policy', in S. Fabbrini and S. Piattoni, eds. *Italy in the European Union*, Lanham, MD: Rowman and Littlefield.

Sandholtz, W. and Stone Sweet, A. (1998) *European Integration and Supranational Governance*, Oxford: Oxford University Press.

Sartori, G. (1970) 'Concept Misformation in Comparative Politics', *American Political Science Review*, 64(4): 1033–1053.

Sbragia, A.M. (2001) 'Italy Pays for Europe: Political Leadership, Political Choice, and Institutional Adaptation', in M. Cowles, J. Caporaso and T. Risse, eds. *Transforming Europe: Europeanization and Domestic Change*, Ithaca, NY: Cornell University Press, 79–96.

Scharpf, F.W. (1997) *Games Real Actors Could Play: The Tools of Actor-centered Institutionalism*, Boulder, CO: Westview Press.

Scharpf, F.W. (2000) 'Notes Toward a Theory of Multi-level Governing in Europe', *MPIfG Discussion Paper*, 00/5.

Scharpf, F.W. and Schmidt, V.A., eds. (2000) *Welfare and Work in the Open Economy*, Oxford: Oxford University Press.

Schmidt, V.A. (2008) 'Discursive Institutionalism: The Explanatory Power of Ideas and Discourse', *Annual Review of Political Science*, 11: 303–326.

Schmidt, V.A. (2010) 'Taking Ideas and Discourse Seriously: Explaining Change through Discursive Institutionalism as the Fourth "New Institutionalism"', *European Political Science Review*, 2(1): 1–25.

Schmitter, P. (2004) 'Neo-neo-functionalism?', in A. Wiener and T. Diez, eds. *European Integration Theory*, Oxford: Oxford University Press, 45–74.

Serra Caracciolo, F. (2006) 'La politica agraria nella comunità economica europea', in AA.VV. – Esposto, A., ed. *Democrazia e contadini in Italia nel XX secolo. Il ruolo dei contadini nella formazione dell'Italia contemporanea*, Rome, Italy: Robin Edizioni.

Settembri, P. (2011) 'I gruppi di interesse agricoli in Italia. Ridefinizione e differenziazione dopo le riforme della PAC degli anni '90 e 2000', *Rivista Italiana di Politiche Pubbliche*, 2: 243–274.

Solima, R. (1996) 'I Principi della normative comunitaria sui fondi strutturali con particolare riferimento al FESR nel Mezzogiorno', in A. Predieri, ed. *Fondi strutturali e coesione economica e sociale nell'Unione europea*, Milan, Italy: Giuffré.

Stone Sweet, A. (2004) *The Judicial Construction of Europe*, Oxford: Oxford University Press.

Sverdrup, U. (2007) 'Implementation', in P. Graziano and M.P. Vink, eds. *Europeanization: New Research Agendas*, Basingstoke: Palgrave Macmillan.

Tallberg, J. (2007) *Bargaining in the European Council*, paper presented at the Tenth Biennial EUSA Conference, 17–19 May, Montreal.
Thomson, R. (2009) 'Same Effects in Different Worlds: The Transposition of EU Directives', *Journal of European Public Policy*, 16(1): 1–18.
Tondl, G. (1998) 'EU Regional Policy in the Southern Periphery: Lessons for the Future', in *Southern European Society and Politics*, 3(1): 93–129.
Toshkov, D. (2007) 'In Search of the Worlds of Compliance: Culture and Transposition Performance in the European Union', *Journal of European Public Policy*, 14(6): 933–954.
Trampusch, C. (2009) 'Europeanization and Institutional Change in Vocational Education and Training in Austria and Germany', *Governance*, 22(3): 369–395.
Treu, T. (2001) *Le politiche del lavoro*, Bologna, Italy: Il Mulino.
Varsori, A. (1998) *L'Italia nelle relazioni internazionali dal 1943 al 1992*, Roma-Bari: Laterza.
Varsori, A. (2011) *Italy's European Policy*, UNISCI Discussion Papers, 25.
Vink, M.P. (2001) 'The Limited Europeanization of Domestic Citizenship Policy: Evidence from the Netherlands', *Journal of Common Market Studies*, 39(5): 875–896.
Vink, M.P. and Graziano, P. (2007) 'Challenges of a New Research Agenda', in P. Graziano and M.P. Vink, eds. *Europeanization: New Research Agendas?*, Basingstoke: Palgrave Macmillan, 3–20.
Wallace, H. (1983) 'Distributional Politics: Dividing up the Community Cake', in H. Wallace, W. Wallace and C. Webb, eds. *Policy-making in the European Communities*, Chichester: Wiley.
Watt, A. (2004) 'Reform of the European Employment Strategy after Five Years: A Change of Course or Merely of Presentation?', *European Journal of Industrial Relations*, 10(2): 117–137.
Webb, C. (1979) 'Eurocommunism and the European Communities', *Journal of Common Market Studies*, 17(3): 236-258.
Webber, D. (1998) *The Hard Core: The Franco–German Relationship and Agricultural Crisis Politics in the European Union*, European University Institute, RSC Working Paper, 98.
Woll, C. and Jacquot, S. (2010) 'Using Europe: Strategic Action in Multi-level Politics', *Comparative European Politics*, 8(1): 110–126.
Wong, R. (2007) 'Foreign Policy', in M.P. Graziano and M.P. Vink, eds. *Europeanization: New Research Agendas?*, Basingstoke: Palgrave Macmillan.
Zamagni, V. (1990) *Dalla periferia al centro. La seconda rinascita economica dell'Italia, 1861–1980*, Bologna, Italy: Il Mulino.
Zeff, E.E. and Pirro, E.B., eds. (2001) *The European Union and the Member States: Co-operation, Co-ordination and Compromise*, Boulder, CO: Lynne Rienner.
Zeitlin, J. (2009) 'The Open Method of Coordination and Reform of National Social and Employment Policies: Influences, Mechanisms, Effects' in M. Heidenreich and J. Zeitlin, eds. *Changing European Employment and Welfare Regimes: The Influence of the Open Method of Coordination on National Reforms*, London: Routledge.
Zeitlin, J. and Pochet, P., with Magnusson, L., eds. (2005) *The Open Method of Coordination in Action: The European Employment and Social Inclusion Strategies*, Brussels: P.I.E. Peter Lang.
Zoppi, S. (2003) *Il Mezzogiorno di De Gasperi e Sturzo*, Soveria Mannelli (CS), Italy: Rubbettino.

Index

Page numbers in *italics* denote tables, those in **bold** denote figures.

A Regional Policy for the Community 79
accession negotiations 81
accountability, European Commission to European Parliament 22–3
actors, institutional and social 19
adaptability, in employment 107
adaptation: differential 140; patterns of 5
adaptive pressure 76, 92, 148–9
adaptive processes 8, 11, 12, 23
additionality principle 84
administration, adaptive processes 23
Agency for Agricultural Support (AIMA) 63
Agency for the Development of the South (Agenzia per lo sviluppo del Mezzogiorno) 90
Agenda 2000 41–2, 58–9, 73
agenda setting: domestic systemic 149–50; systemic and policy-based 28–9, 51; systemic and policy-based, power concentration *29*; systemic and policy-based, power fragmentation *29*
agenda setting capacities *52*
Agenzia per le erogazioni in agricoltura (AGEA) 74
aggregated debt 149–50
agrarian consortia, reform of 68
agricultural and forest document 69
agricultural associations 63
agricultural policy: domestic adaptation 133–5; external challenges 58; goodness of fit 132; imposition mechanism 72, 76; institutional effects 72, 75; Italy *see* Italy, agricultural policy; policy adjustment *60*; policy adjustment, continuity and transformation 132–3; policy transformation 147, 148, 150; revision 142–4; structure 1992–2010 58–61
agricultural sectors: balance of payments 64; competitiveness 54; price support 54; production capacities 54
agriculture: domestic and European resources 67; government support 53; importance of 38; move away from 64; price-setting 55; prices 58; public support for 61; regionalization 64; set-aside scheme 58
Agriculture 80 56
Ambler, J.S. 20
Amsterdam Treaty 106–7
Anderssen, S.S. 3, 4
Andreotti, Giulio 30–1, 33–4
autonomy, of government officials 67

balance of payments, agricultural sectors 64
Balme, R. 20
band of four 42
Barbier, J.-C. 121
bargaining dynamics, European Council 32–3
Barnier, M. 44
benchmarking 126, *127*
beneficiaries of 'active' and 'passive' policies *123*
Berlusconi governments 31–2, 124, 137
Berlusconi, Silvio 31
best practice analysis 127
Beyers, J. 21
Biagi reform 122, 138
bicameral commission 89
Blithe, F. 153
Borras, S. 21

Brunazzo, M. 46, 145
Bulmer, S. 3, 10, 11
Burch, M. 11
Bureau, J.-C. 38, 41–2, 54, 58–9
bureaucratic functioning 20, 22–3
bureaucrats: agricultural policy 74; employment policy 118, 125; Italian in Europe 27; regional cohesion policy 88–9, 98
Bursens, P. 21

Cabina di Regia 47
Caporaso, J. 1, 4, 6, 10
Carli, Guido 31
Cassa integrazione guadagni ordinaria e straordinaria (CIGO) 110, 117, 118, 124
Cassa integrazione guadagni straordinaria (CIGS) 111, 117, 118, 124
Cassa per il Mezzogiorno 62, 63, 86–7, 88, 89–91
Catania, M. 143
causality 10
centre-periphery relationships 20, 21; *see also* power balance
Christian Democrats, attitude to Europe 35
Ciampi, Carlo Azeglio 48
Cini, M. 83, 84–5
citizens: attitudes to Europe 37–8; positive evaluation of membership to the EU 37
Clasen, J. 109
Clegg, D. 109
clientelism 62
clout 20
co-funding 84
coalitions 19
cognitive Europeanization 11
Cohesion Fund 84, 85
Cole, A. 20
collective dismissal 117
Common Agricultural Policy 23–4, 38–44; adaptation to 63–8; Agenda 2000 41–2, 58–9; agricultural self-sufficiency and support 53–8; allocation of powers 56; creation of 39; dairy quotas reform 57; and domestic policy 133–4; impact assessment 142–3; longer-term perspective 43–4; as multi-targeted 59; organization, objectives and principles 54; policy adjustment 60–1; price-setting 55; redefinition 142–4; redistribution mechanisms 60; reform 40–1; reform 1992–2010 58–61; residual implementation 134–5; selective funding 64; stabilizing reforms 57; *see also* EU agricultural policy
Community Charter of Fundamental Social Rights of Workers 105
compliance 149
concentration principle 84
concertation 73, 97, 125, 134, 137, 138, 144
conformity option 89, 90
contratti di formazione e lavoro 115
convergence 9, 83
coordination mechanism 15; employment policy 126, 127
Coordination Room (*Cabina di Regia*) 93
Cowles, M.G. 6, 19
Craxi, Bettino 30, 33, 115
creative appropriation 19

dairy quotas reform 57
De Gasperi, Alcide 30, 88
De Michelis, Gianni 31, 116, 119
decentralization, employment services and training 121
decision-making: power of executive 20–1; role of government 67
delegation, EU policy implementation responsibilities 96
Della Sala, V. 31
Delors, Jacques 105
Delors White Paper 106
deregulation, employment protection 116
diffusion phase, mediating factors 19
Dipartimento delle Politiche di Sviluppo e Coesione (DPS) 93, 95–6
Dipartimento delle Politiche di Sviluppo e di Coesione 47
direct transfers 74
direction mechanism 14; employment policy 126, 127
discursive institutionalism 11
dismissal 112, 138–9; benefits for workers 117
distribution policies 23
division of labour, in policy decisions 28–9
domestic adaptation 13–14; agricultural policy 133–5; differential patterns 132–3; effects of Europeanization 148–50; employment policy 136–9, 140–1; and goodness of fit 153–4; overview 131; policy adaptation 149; policy misfit 132, 133, 134, 147, 148, 150; policy taking 149; politics of 131–9; recent developments 141; regional cohesion policy 135–6; and strength of EU rules 148

domestic employment regulation reform 49
domestic executive-legislature relationships 20–1
domestic executive, role of 30
domestic funds allocation 82
domestic funds, and EU funds 84
domestic politics approach 3, 5–6
domestic preferences, negotiation for 51
domestic public administration, challenge to 22–3
domestic shift 4–5
Drake, H. 20
Duina, F. 153

early retirement 113
electoral manifestos, attitudes to Europe 36
Eliassen, K.A. 3, 4
elites, non-state 2
employability 107
Employment Committee 50
employment contracts 115
employment guidelines 107
employment opportunities 109, 112
employment policy 24, 48–51, *128*; 1960–1970 102–3; 1971–1991 103–5; 1991–1997 105–6; assessment and reform 140; deregulation of protection 138; differential adaptation 140; domestic adaptation 136–9; domestic employment regulation reform 49; European Employment Strategy (EES) 48–9; evaluation report 50; goodness of fit 132; Italy *see* Italy, employment policy; mid-term review (2001–2003) 49–50; overview 102; policy adjustment and transformation 133, 139, 140, 147, 148, 150; pressure for reform 103; procedural adjustments 108; surveillance of 107; targets 107
employment protection 116, 123, 124
employment protection legislation index, 1990–2008 **122**
employment services and training 110, 121, 124
Employment Title 106
employment trends, and social cohesion 124
empty chair crisis 55–6
enhanced protection 111–14
enlargement 80–1, 82–3, 85
entrepreneurship 107, 116, 118
environmental associations, increased influence 74

equal opportunities 107
EU agricultural policy: change over time 75; *see also* Common Agricultural Policy
EU decision making, parliamentary involvement *52*
EU multi-level system 18–19
EU powers, expansion of 6
EU structural funds expenditure 92, **94**
Eurobarometer data 37
'Europe 2020: A Strategy for Smart, Sustainable and Inclusive Growth' 140, 141
Europe, as political issue 34–5
European Agricultural Guarantee and Guidance Fund (FEOGA) 55
European Agricultural Orientation and Guarantee Fund – Orientation section (FEOGA-O) 45–6
European Centre for Parliamentary Research and Documentation (ECPRD) 36
European Commission: capacity to legislate 106; employment policy revision 140; enlarged role 82, 83; influence 40; management of ESF 103–4; programming principle 83; regional cohesion policy 146
European Council, bargaining dynamics 32–3
European Court of Justice 126–7, 129
European Employment Strategy (EES) 48–9, 105–9, 119–25, 126, 129
European food regime 53
European integration theory 10
European Investment Bank (EIB), aims and purpose 77–8
European Monetary System (EMS) 30, 35
European political organization, academic interest 1
European Regional Development Fund (ERDF) 44, 45, 81, 85
European Social Dialogue 105
European Social Fund (ESF) 45, 78, 85, 102–4, 106, 112–13, 118, 124, 126
European Studies: American and European approaches 1–3; emergence and consolidation 1–3; Europeanization turn 3–7
European Union (EU): 1988 reform 83–4; financial execution by member state *94*; knowledge about 37; and national politics 5–6; policy revision 140; as species of integration 12

Europeanization: agenda setting 30–4; analysis of policy change 152; conceptualization 151; as construction and diffusion 9–10; construction phase 13; defining 7–9; diffusion phase 13–14; domestic support 148; formulation and adoption phase 34; literature 6; mechanisms 13–15; methodology 10; operationalization 151–2; research design 10; research focus 5; theoretical challenge 10–12; theoretical relevance 12; use of term 4; what it is not 9
Europeanization analysis, as framework of study 10
Europeanization and national public policies **15**
Europeanization and policy change **14**
Europeanization mechanisms 14–15; political-institutional effects 70–5, 95–9, 126–9
Europeanization turn 3–7
Europeification 3
eurosupport 37–8
Exadaktylos, T. 10, 13, 17, 151
executive, increased centrality 73
executive–legislature relationship *see* power balance
executive power concentration model 29, 51
executive power fragmentation model 29, 51
executives, decision-making power 20–1
expertise 33–4

Fabbrini, S. 26, 34
Falkner, G. 102, 103, 104, 106, 153
Fanfani, Armintore 33
Fanfani, R. 43
Fargion, V. 117, 121
farm size 56–7
farms, multifunctionality 75
Federconsorzi 62, 63, 68
FEOGA-Guarantee 55, 75
FEOGA-Guidance 55, 64, 75, 85
Ferrera, M. 138
FIAT 113
financial instruments 16, 62, 70, 78, 85, 87–8, 90
'Financing of Economic Development of Southern Italy' 86
first order policy change 16
first pillar 59
fiscal policy 115
fit/misfit hypothesis 17, 18–19; *see also* goodness of fit hypothesis

flexibility, in employment 108–9, 115–16, 122–3, 125, 126
flexicurity 125
Flockhart, T. 9
food regime 53
formal institutions 19
formulation and adoption phase 34
Forza Italia, attitude to Europe 35–6
freedom of movement, of workers 102
French–German bilateralism 39, 40
funding: allocation 84–5, 86–7, 91, 97; complementarity 84; EU funds 92; management 97; parliamentary powers 88; political control 87; regional cohesion policy 81, 83

GATT trade liberalization package 57–8
GATT Uruguay Round 40
general social assistance (SA) 109
general strike 139
genetically modified organisms (GMOs) 70
Ginsborg, P. 61
Giuliani, M. 35–6
global economic crisis 124
Goetschy, J. 104, 105, 107
goodness of fit 92–3, 153–4; agricultural policy 67; limitation of misfit 147; operationalization *17*, 17; and policy change 75–6; and policy-shaping capacities 132
goodness of fit hypothesis 12, 18–19, 51; *see also* fit/misfit hypothesis
government: role in agricultural policy 62; role in employment policy 119; role in regional cohesion policy 88
Graziano, L. 8–9, 13, 19
Green Plans 63–4
Green Tables 73–4
Gronchi, Giovanni 33
Growth and Stability Pact reform 149
'Growth, competitiveness, employment' White Paper 106
Gualmina, E. 138

Haas, E.B. 1–2, 8
Hall, Peter 11, 16–17, 152
harmonization 9
Haverland, M. 10
historical institutionalism 11
historical neo-institutional perspective 24
Hoffman, S. 2
hypotheses 132
hypothesis development 18–23

implementation studies 5
imposition mechanism 14; agricultural policy 72, 76; employment policy 126–7; regional cohesion policy 95–6
in-depth process-tracing 24–5
income policy 115
income protection 109, 118, 123, 124, 137–8
industrial relations 104, 111, 115, 139; FIAT 113; *see also* trades unions
ineffectiveness, Italy in Europe 26–7
Institute for Labour and Training (ISFOL) 50
institutional approaches 10–11
institutional effects 23; agricultural policy 72, 75, 95; dimensions 96–7; regional cohesion policy 95–6
institutional sources of power 33
Integrated Mediterranean Programmes (IMP) 82
integration: and domestic affairs 7; EU as type of 12; as focus of interest 3
integration studies 6
integration theory 2–3
interest groups 21–2; agricultural policy 143–4; employment policy 111, 130; increased influence 73–4; regional cohesion policy 88, 98–9; *see also* power balance
intergovernmentalism 2–3, 4
Interministerial Committee for Economic Programming (Comitato Interministeriale per la Programmazione Economica – CIPE) 68
International Relations, as framework for study of Europe 1–1
Intervento Straordinario 101
interviews 24–5
Ireland 80–1
issue-specific source of power 33
Italian Communist Party, attitude to Europe 35
Italian governments *156–7*
Italian Permanent Representation in Brussels (ITALRAP), weakening of 26
Italian policy-based EU agenda setting capacities *52*
Italian political system: and Europe 28; systemic change 31
Italy: in Europe 26–30; lack of voice 26; as weak actor 33
Italy, agricultural policy 61–70, *71*; adapting to CAP 63–8; adapting to CAP, 1992–2010 68–70; changing policy focus 69–70; continuity 67; convergence with EU 76; development 1944–1960 61–3; divergence from Europe 66; Europeanization and change 75–6; institutional perspective 72–4; main findings 75; objectives 61–2; policy misfit 68–70, 75–6; political-institutional effects of Europeanization mechanisms 70–5; public debate 63; role of government 62; structural reforms 63; substitution of EU policy 72
Italy, employment policy: 1945–1968 110–11; 1968–1983 111–14; 1983–1992 114–19; 1992–2010 119–25; beneficiaries of 'active' and 'passive' policies *123*; Berlusconi governments 124; controversy 127; decentralization 121; dismissal 112; early retirement 113; employment protection 116, 123; employment protection legislation index, 1990–2008 **122**; employment services and training 110; enhanced protection 111–14; Europeanization and change 129–30; income protection 109, 110, 118, 123; institutional features 111, 114, 118, 119, 125, 127; interest groups 111; job creation 115, 116; major changes 1990–2008 120; multi-tiered 121; objectives 122, 124; overview 109; passive and active employment policies expenditure *123*; policy change 121; policy misfit 129; policy structure analysis 110–11, 114; political-institutional effects of Europeanization mechanisms 126–9; power balance 111; principles and goals 117–18, 124–5; productive capacity 115; regional authorities 112–13; reorientation 125, 137; role of government 119; ten-year plan 116; training contract 112; unemployment benefit (UB) 110; vocational training 112–13, 124, 125, 126; young people 112, 118
Italy–EU executive interaction 30–4
Italy–EU party interaction 34–6
Italy, regional cohesion policy: 1965–1992 89–91; 1992–2010 91–5; bureaucracy 88–9; change and continuity 101; Europeanization and change 99–101; institutional change 92; institutional configuration 88, 90; institutional effects 95–6; overview 85–6; policy misfit 93, 95; political interference 89; power balance 90; reactions to proposed EU

revisions 146–7; shared goals 145; structure 87; trajectory 1950–1965 86–9

Job Centre I and II rulings 127
job creation 115, 116
job security 109
'Job(s) can be created. Enterprise and Work: Job Creation in Europe' 116
judicial construction 7
Jupille, J. 1, 10

Kaeding, M. 153, 154
Kassim, H. 20–1
Kritzinger, S. 37

La Spina, A. 101
Ladrech, R. 7, 8, 21–2
Laffan, B. 20
land concentration 61
Law 115/1968 111
Law 155/1981 113
Law 183/1976 89
Law 196/1997 120
Law 223/1991 117, 120, 126
Law 236/1993 120
Law 247/2007 120
Law 25/1955 110
Law 285/1977 112
Law 30/2003 120, 122
Law 388/2000 120
Law 410/1999 68
Law 44/1986 116
Law 451/1994 120
Law 488/1992 96
Law 56/1987 116
Law 57/2001 69
Law 64/1986 90, 96
Law 675/1977 112
Law 717/1965 89
Law 79/1983 115
Law 80/2005 120
Law 845/1978 112
Law 863/1984 115
Law Decree 276/2003 120
Lega Nord 32, 35–6, 91
Legislative Decree 185/2000 121
legitimacy 22
Leonardi, R. 91
liberalization, agricultural sectors 54
Lisbon 2020 126
Lisbon Special European Council 107
Lisbon Strategy 108–9, 140–1
Lisbon Summit 106
Lisbon Treaty 36

Lizzi, R. 38–9, 42, 43, 44, 61, 62, 63, 64, 65, 66, 67, 69, 73, 74, 134, 135
loyalty shift 2, 8
Luxembourg compromise 56
Luxembourg Jobs Summit 107

Maastricht criteria 137
Maastricht Treaty 3, 31
MacSharry, R. 40, 58
management by objectives 74
Mannino plan 66
Manzella, G.P. 78, 80, 81
Marcora plan 64–5
Marini, S. 143
market orientation 75
Mastenbroek, E. 153, 154
Matthews, A. 38, 41–2, 54, 58–9
mediating factors 12, 19
Mediterranean Integrated Programmes (MIP) 46
member states, uploading of preferences 13–14, 28
Mendez, C. 78, 80, 81
Mény, Y. 82
Ministero per le politiche europee 141
Ministry of Agriculture, reform 69
misfit/fit, national and European policy 17
mobility benefit 117
mobility lists 112
Monti government 150
Montpetit, E. 20, 21
Moravcsik, A. 2, 11
multi-functional goals 74
multi-level governance 4
multi-level governing theory 12
multi-level policy implementation process 23
Mura, M. 83, 84–5

Nanetti, R.Y. 91
National Action Plans for Employment 127
national agricultural plans 64–7
national Parliaments, influence 36
national politics, and EU 5–6
National Progress Report 127
national public policies, and Europeanization 15
negotiated programming initiatives 96
neofunctionalism 1–2, 4
non-compliance 68–9, 72
non-formalized pressure mechanism 15; employment policy 126; regional cohesion policy 95, 96

Index

non-state elites 2

oil shocks 113
Olive Tree coalition, attitude to Europe 35–6
Olsen, J.P. 4
One Hundred Ideas for Development (*Cento idee per lo sviluppo*) 97
ontological phase, European Studies 1
Open Method of Coordination (OMC) 106
orders of policy change 16
organizational logic 7–8
Osservatorio delle politiche regionali 47

Pandolfi plan 65
Paris Summit 80, 81
parliamentary involvement in EU decision-making *52*
Parliaments: budget allocation powers 88; weakening 20–1
part-time working 115–16, 122
partisan control, of funding 91
partnership mechanisms, regional cohesion policy 99
partnership principle 83
passive and active employment policies expenditure *123*
path dependency 11
Pavan Woolfe, L. 103, 104
peer review 127
personal authority 33–4; Ciampi 48
Piattoni, S. 26, 34, 46, 145
Pierson, P. 102, 105
policy adjustment 17, 60–1, 132–3
policy change: analysis 152; detection of 17; and Europeanization **14**; operationalizing 15–16; orders of 16; and policy shaping capacities 149
policy continuity 17, 132–3
policy, dimensions 16
policy direction, EU influence 76
policy interaction 38–52; Common Agricultural Policy 38–44; employment policy 48–51; evaluation 51–2; regional cohesion policy 44–8
policy-making process, as distinct from policy structure 16
policy misfit 18, 19, 29, 51; agricultural policy 68–70, 75–6; domestic adaptation 132, 133, 134, 147, 148, 150; employment policy 129; regional cohesion policy 93, 95; *see also* goodness of fit
policy objectives 16

policy paradigm 16
policy preferences: EES 49; regional cohesion policy 79; uploading 50
policy principles 16
policy procedures 16
policy research 5
policy-shaping capacities 13, 43, 140–8, 149
policy structure approach 16–17, 152–3
policy transformation 17, 76, 132–3
Politi, G. 143
political instability, effects of 30–4
political-institutional dimensions 20, 74, 96–7
political-institutional effects 20
political integration 1–2, 9
political parties: employment policy 111, 118; loss of power 22; regional cohesion policy 88; weakening of 73
political parties–interest groups dimension: agricultural policy 74; regional cohesion policy 96
political party–interest group power balance 20, 21–2, 63
politicians, Italian in Europe 27
politics, domestic focus 27
positive evaluation of membership to the EU 37
poverty 61, 62
power balance 129; centre–periphery 97, 114, 118, 125, 129; executive and legislative 62–3, 90, 97, 111, 114, 118, 125; interest groups 99, 111, 114, 129; parties and interest groups 20, 21, 22, 32–3, 125
power, individual sources 33–4, 43
power of the chair 33
power of veto 33
preference bargaining 150
preference formation: agricultural policy 144, 149; employment policy 137, 141, 149; and policy misfit 147; regional cohesion policy 135–6, 145, 149
price-setting, agriculture 55
price stabilization 63
Prodi governments 31, 73; agricultural reform 69; employment policy 137; role in Europe 31
Prodi, Romano 31–2
productive capacity 115
programming principles 83, 90
protectionism 61
public administration, challenge to domestic systems 22–3

Index

Quaglia, L. 9–10, 32
quota system 60

Radaelli, C.M. 3–4, 7, 8–10, 13, 17, 32, 151, 152
rational choice theory 11
Raveaud, G. 108
referendum 1992–1993 69
regional authorities, power of 90
regional cohesion policy 24, 44–8; 1958–1960 77–8; 1960–1975 79–81; 1975–1988 81–2; 1988 onwards 82–5; 1988 reform 45–6; 2000–2006 and 2006–2013 programming periods 46–7; and bureaucracy 98; capacity to implement 93; as challenge to domestic administration 92; domestic adaptation 135–6; domestic innovations and implementation 95; EU structural funds expenditure **94**; executive–legislature relationship 97; expenditure 94–5; expenditure capacity 97–8; funding 81; goals 83; goodness of fit 132; implementation 84–5; implementing authorities 95; imposition mechanism 95–6; institutional effects 95–7; interest groups 98–9; Italian and EU *100*; Italy *see* Italy, regional cohesion policy ; longer-term perspective 48; non-formalized pressure mechanism 95; partnership mechanisms 99; policy adaptation, taking and shaping 146–7; policy transformation 147, 148, 150; political-institutional effects of Europeanization mechanisms 95–9; power rebalancing 97; prioritization 80; programming principle 83; revision 144–7; standardized criteria 84; targeting 84; uploading capacity 51
regional development, lack of policy 79–80
regional employment observatories 116, 118
Regional Policy Directorate General 79
Regional Policy Observatory (*Osservatorio delle politiche regionali*) 93
regionalization, agricultural policy 70, 73
regulation 14; agricultural policy 70
Regulation 1787/1984 82
Reichert, M.S. 20
research strategy 15–19; analysis of policy change 152–3; case selection 23–4; conceptualization 151; hypotheses 132; hypothesis development 18–23; methods 24–5; operationalization 151–2; period covered 25; policy structure approach 16–17, 152–3; political-institutional dimensions 20–1
research, widening of scope 7
resource allocation 62, 70, 72
Rey, Jean 79
Risse-Kappen, T. 1
Risse, T. 8, 12, 153
Roederer-Rynning, C. 5, 55, 57
Rome Treaties 30

Sacchi, S. 49–50
sanctions 72
Scanio, Pecoraro 73
Scharpf, F.W. 13, 17
Schmidt, V.A. 11
Schmitter, P. 2
second order policy change 16
second pillar 59
seniority 33–4
service employment market 124
set-aside scheme 58
'Should the Community Regional Policy be Scrapped?' (*Mény) 82
Single European Act (SEA) 31, 82
single farm payment 59, 66
social action plan 104
social assistance (SA) 104, 109
social cohesion, and employment trends 124
social exclusion 123
Social Protocol 106
social useful jobs programme 121
Socially Useful Jobs (*Lavori socialmente utili*) (LSU) programme 121, 123
societal interest representation 21
sociological institutionalism 11
soft pressures 127
solidarity contract 116
Solima, R. 91
Southern Italy, development 86–7
sovereignty 84
special purpose institutions 145
specific unemployment assistance (UA) 109
spending powers 86
spillovers 2
structural funds: allocation negotiations 47; regional cohesion policy 81
supranational governance 4
systemic agenda setting capacities *35*

Tallberg, J. 32–3, 149

Tavolo Verde 73–4
tax relief 115
taxation 62
Taylor, R.C.R. 11
temporary working 122
territorial concentration 87
'The CAP towards 2020: Meeting the Food, Natural Resources and Territorial Challenges of the Future' 142–3
third order policy change 16
timing of policy change, EU influence 76
trades unions 111, 113, 115, 130, 139; *see also* industrial relations
Tremonti, Guilio 31
Treu reform 122, 127
triangulation 24–5

unemployment 103, 105, 107, 112, 113, 114–15, 124
unemployment assistance (UA) 109
unemployment benefit (UB) 110
unemployment insurance (UI) 109, 121
United Kingdom: Italian support for 33; regional development disparities 80

uploading capacity 13–14, 28, 31, 47, 50, 51, 147

validity, of research 7
Varsori, A. 27, 30, 31, 33
Vink, M.P. 8–9, 13, 19
vocational training 112–13, 124, 125, 126

wage indexation 115
Watt, A. 108
Webber, D. 39, 40, 53, 56, 57
White Book on the Italian Labour Market 138
wine sector 74
Woll, C. 20
workers: freedom of movement 102–3; hiring practice 115, 117
Workers' Statute 111, 138–9
working conditions 115
World Bank 86

young farmers programme 74
young people, employment policy 112, 118

Zeitlin, J. 18, 19